IMAGES
of America

MIDWEST SKIING
A GLANCE BACK

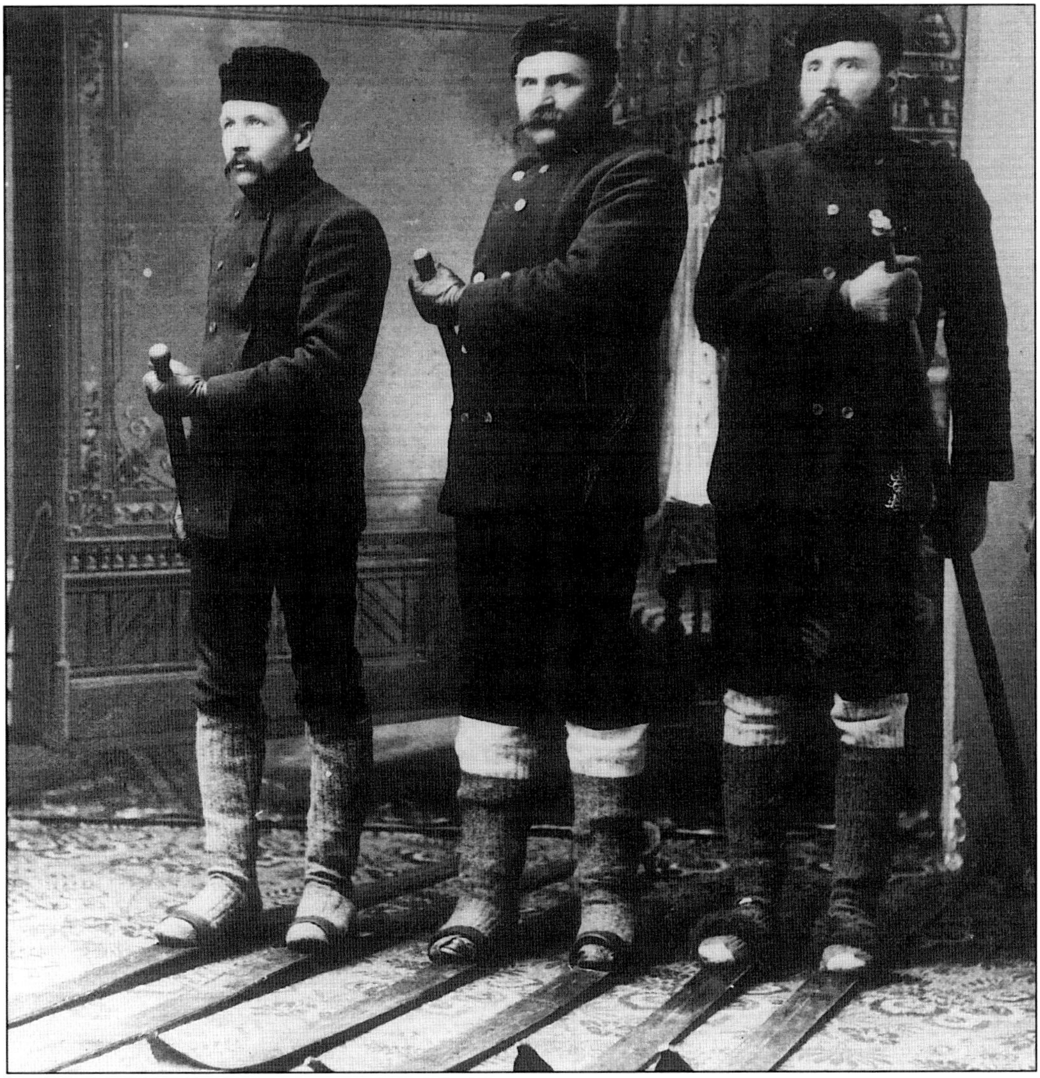

Pictured are members of the Norden Ski Club of Ishpeming, Michigan, sometime in the late 1800s. They are, from left to right: Sven Johnson, Haagen Asgaard, and Alec Tislov.

IMAGES
of America

MIDWEST SKIING
A GLANCE BACK

John Pontti and Kenneth Luostari

ARCADIA
PUBLISHING

ISBN 978-0-7385-0124-6

Published by Arcadia Publishing
Charleston, South Carolina

Printed in the United States of America

Library of Congress Catalog Card Number: 00-100287

For all general information contact Arcadia Publishing at:
Telephone 843-853-2070
Fax 843-853-0044
E-mail sales@arcadiapublishing.com
For customer service and orders:
Toll-Free 1-888-313-2665

Visit us on the Internet at www.arcadiapublishing.com

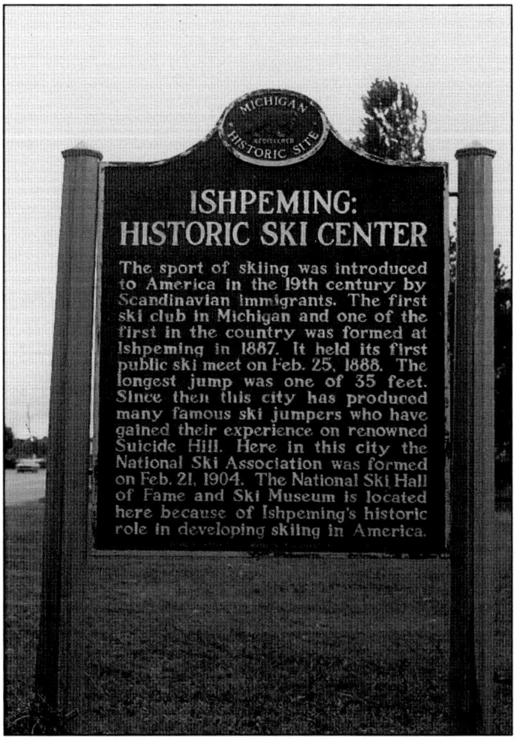

Pictured here is a State of Michigan historical marker proclaiming the City of Ishpeming as a Historic Ski Center. The sign was dedicated in January of 1958, by then Governor G. Mennen Williams, a devoted ski jumping enthusiast who attended several Ishpeming ski competitions.

Note: The date on this historical marker is incorrect. The formation of the National Ski Association actually happened on February 22, 1905.

Contents

ACKNOWLEDGMENTS

A dedicated seven-person committee, five of them members of the US National Ski Hall of Fame executive committee, and two hardworking volunteers, compiled this publication. Along with co-authors John Pontti and Kenneth Luostari, the group consisted of executive committee members Wesley Wentela, Knut Strom, and Burton Boyum, and volunteers Alice Johnson and Mary Morissette. Alice acted as secretary and proofreader of the book committee, while Mary brought the expertise needed to put the whole project in workable form, with her keen eye for significant photographs and layout skills that were most important to the project. Sherri Bockland, secretary at the museum, helped by finding information on the Internet. And thanks to Mary Beth Morissette, who helped her mother sharpen even the most faded images.

A vast majority of the images used in this ski history are from the archives of the US National Ski Hall of Fame and Museum in Ishpeming, Michigan. However, there were others who generously gave permission to use photographs from their personal collections, including Herbert Peterson and Lloyd Sundblad of Ishpeming, Jim Dehlin, Marquette Mountain Ski Area, US Olympic Education Center of Marquette, Michigan, Robert Keck of Oconomowoc, Wisconsin, and Stan Cohen of Missoula, Montana, who gave us "carte blanche" to use images from his book ***Downhill Skiing***. We would also be remiss if we did not acknowledge the help of Allen Adler of Barton, Vermont, Chairman of the United States Ski Association Historical Committee, for critiquing our efforts and smoothing out some of the "rough spots."

Lastly, our thanks to a trio of local "old-time" skiers, Ralph Bietila, Ken Oja, and Norman Juhola for identifying the names and faces in old photographs from the museum's archives. The book committee enjoyed revisiting skiing's past with these gracious gentlemen.

Introduction

As the glacial epoch ended, early man followed its icy retreat into the far northern areas where the climate included winter snow. Food gathering and transportation were essential, and deep snow made both arduous, at best. Man developed a rudimentary pair of "snowshoes" which enabled him to move about in the difficult winter season. The "snowshoes" were merely roughly formed boards with thongs of animal hide to fasten them to the feet. Not very sophisticated to be sure, but quite effective for man's purposes.

Over the next two hundred generations, these "snowshoes" were modified and improved to make them more efficient, eventually developing into what are known as "skis" today. In more recent times, skis were not needed solely to provide family food, but the hearty families living in the far northern areas still relied on them for transportation in the winter.

These folks were the sturdy Scandinavians who, as they migrated to other parts of the world, brought along their skis. These were the Norwegians, Finns and Swedes who came to America in the mid-1800s and settled in the northern parts of the Midwest and Far West. As the newcomers were being assimilated into American society in the northern regions, skiing developed into a sport in which both the new immigrants and native youngsters participated.

The early competitions were either cross-country running on skis, or jumping on hills created by the newcomers. The sport, as it developed in the Midwest, was mainly ski jumping. Parents of the young jumpers stood in awe of the "mad" immigrant lads, thinking this strange new activity would surely end in serious injury, at best. The townsfolk could hardly wait to try this new sport, and the young ladies "swooned" watching them "show their stuff."

Although competitive skiing was mainly a sport for the youth, the older members also used skis for transportation and recreation. They realized the healthy value of this new winter activity, forming social clubs and "get-togethers" where groups of men, women, and children traveled the countryside on their skis.

This is how it all began in the Midwest. The young immigrants and local lads banded together to form ski clubs in many of the towns and cities, and ski jumping competitions were held in many areas on a weekly basis during the winter months.

This pictorial history has been compiled to help the reader retrace the beginnings of the sport and to view the courageous competitors and promoters who were instrumental in developing skiing in the Midwest.

One

Roots Of Skiing

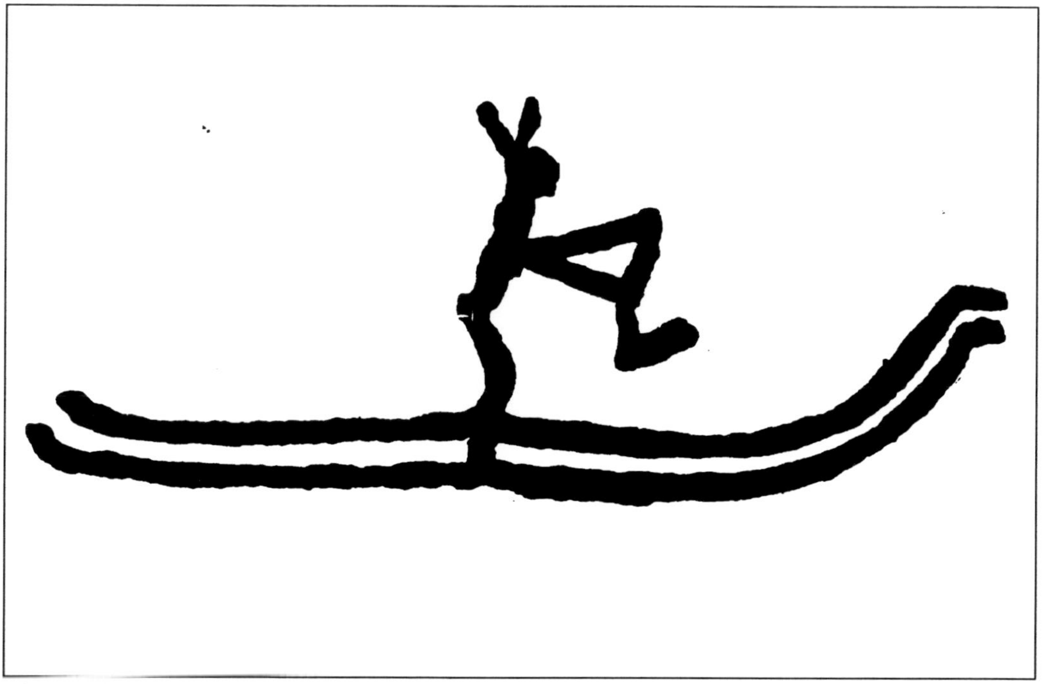

This Rodoy stone drawing (petroglyph), was found in a cave in northern Norway, and it is the earliest pictorial representation of skiing known to man. Two parts compose the word petroglyph – petro (rock) and glyph (symbol).

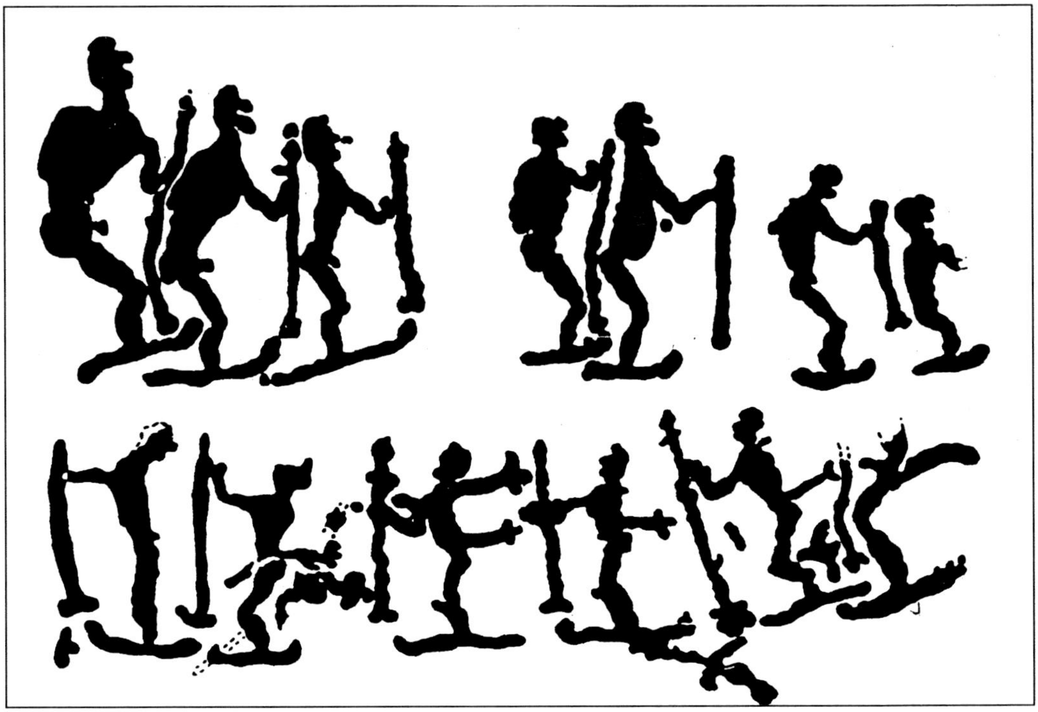

These Zalavrouga petroglyphs were found on the shore of the White Sea, and depict early man on skis. Note the short skis and single pole with a rudimentary "basket" on the end.

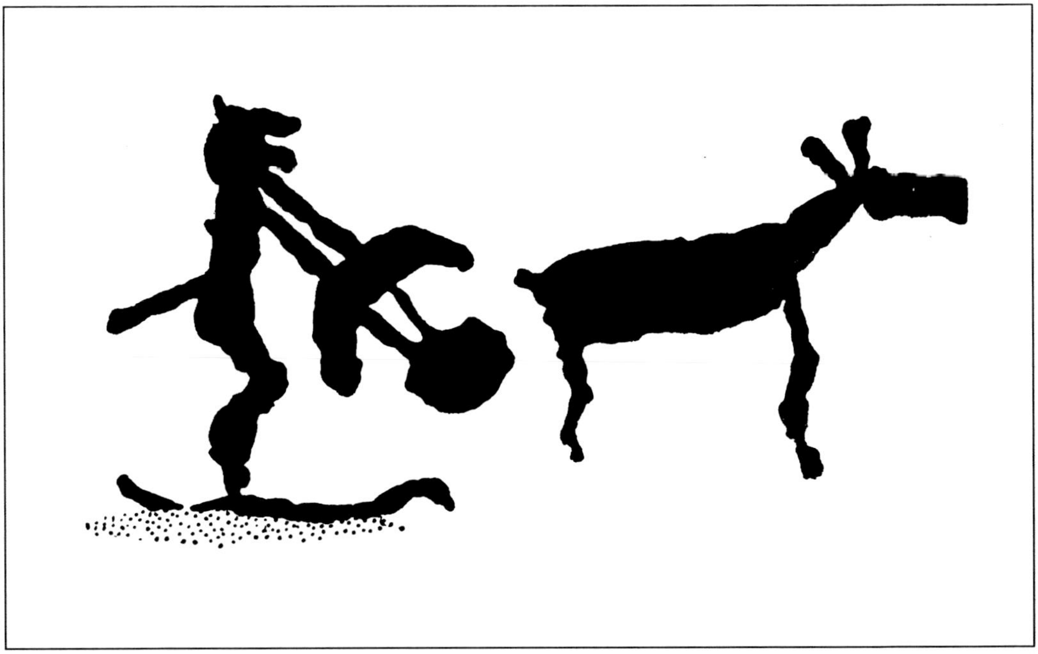

The Bessov-Ness petroglyph is from the island of Bessowy Sledki in the White Sea. It is dated to 1500 B.C. The skier wears a wolf's head, and is holding magic instruments, perhaps a sun and moon, which depict an imagined hunt.

The earliest ski type was the Southern, of which the 3500-year-old find at Riihimaki, Finland, is the oldest example (fig. 1). The long (159 cm) and broad (16.5 cm) ski with a plane underside and square back resembles more recent skis used widely in Eastern Europe from the Baltic states and Poland through Russia. (Bays 1980) A second ski type (fig. 2), succeeding the Southern ski chronologically and geographically as hunting nomads moved north, was the Scandic. The distinctive sidelists along the footrest of the Southern ski became inset from the edge in the Scandic skis. That is, the edges moved out from the sidelists as the ski itself broadened to provide support in the deeper snow of middle and northern Scandinavia, where the Scandic ski has been found.

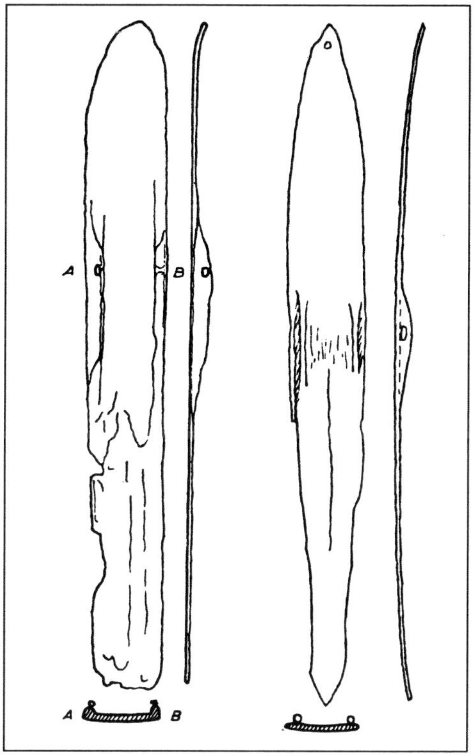

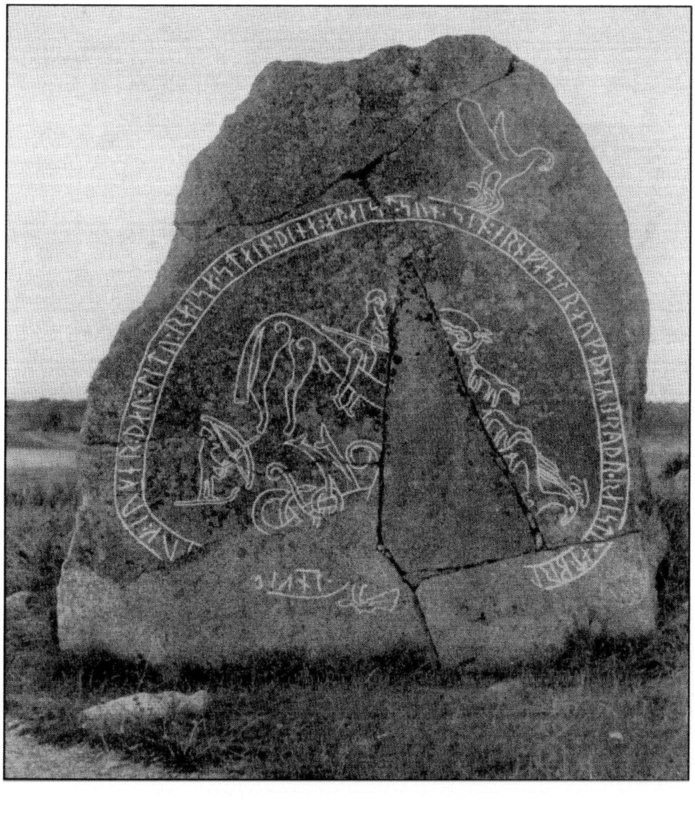

A ski-runner carrying a bow and a man on horseback hunting an elk, with falcons and hounds, are depicted in this rune-stone at Böksta, Uppland. The stone was erected about A.D. 1050.

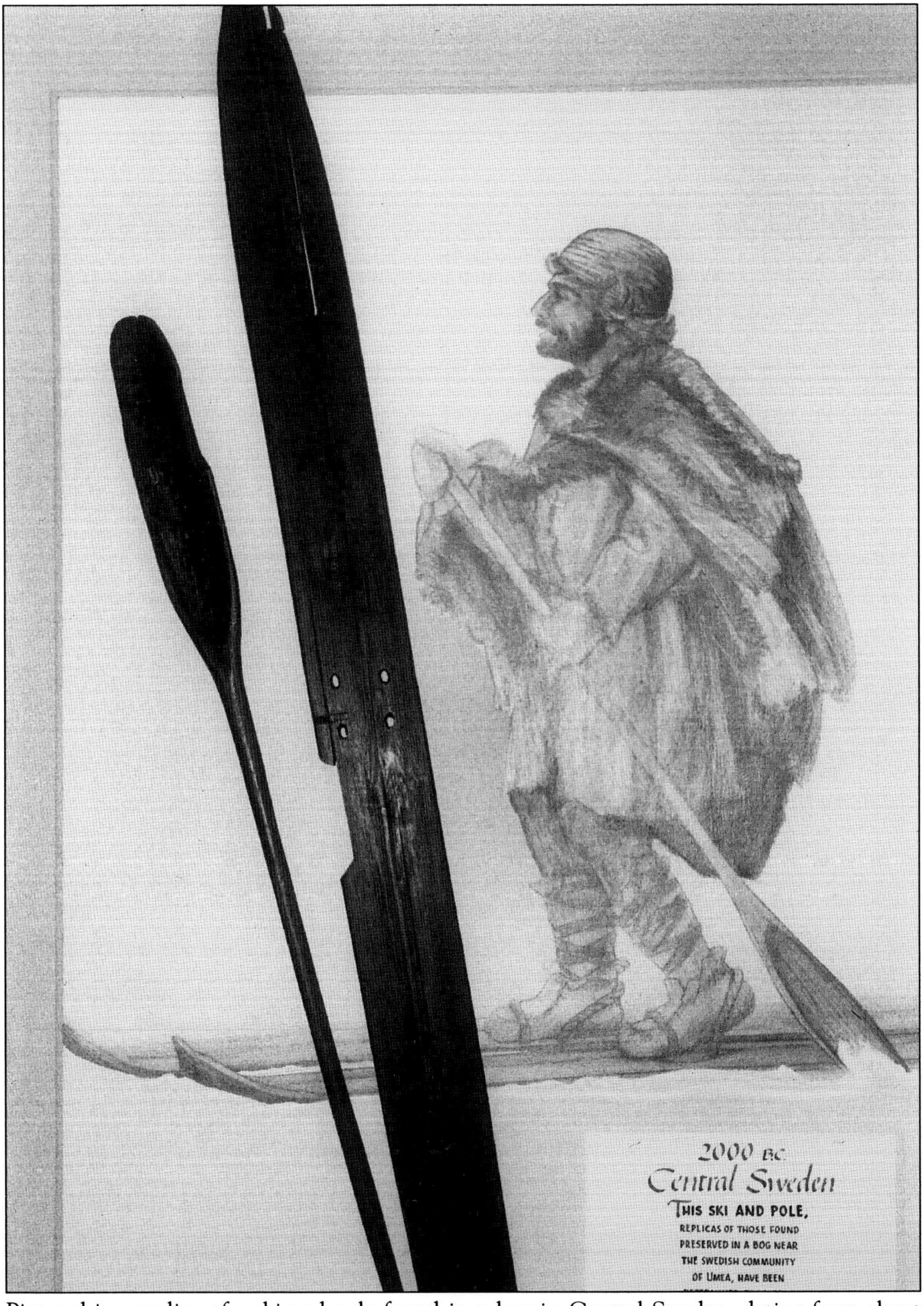

Pictured is a replica of a ski and pole found in a bog in Central Sweden, dating from about 2000 B.C. It was presented to the U.S. National Ski Museum at its dedication by Jakob Vaage, Norwegian National Historian.

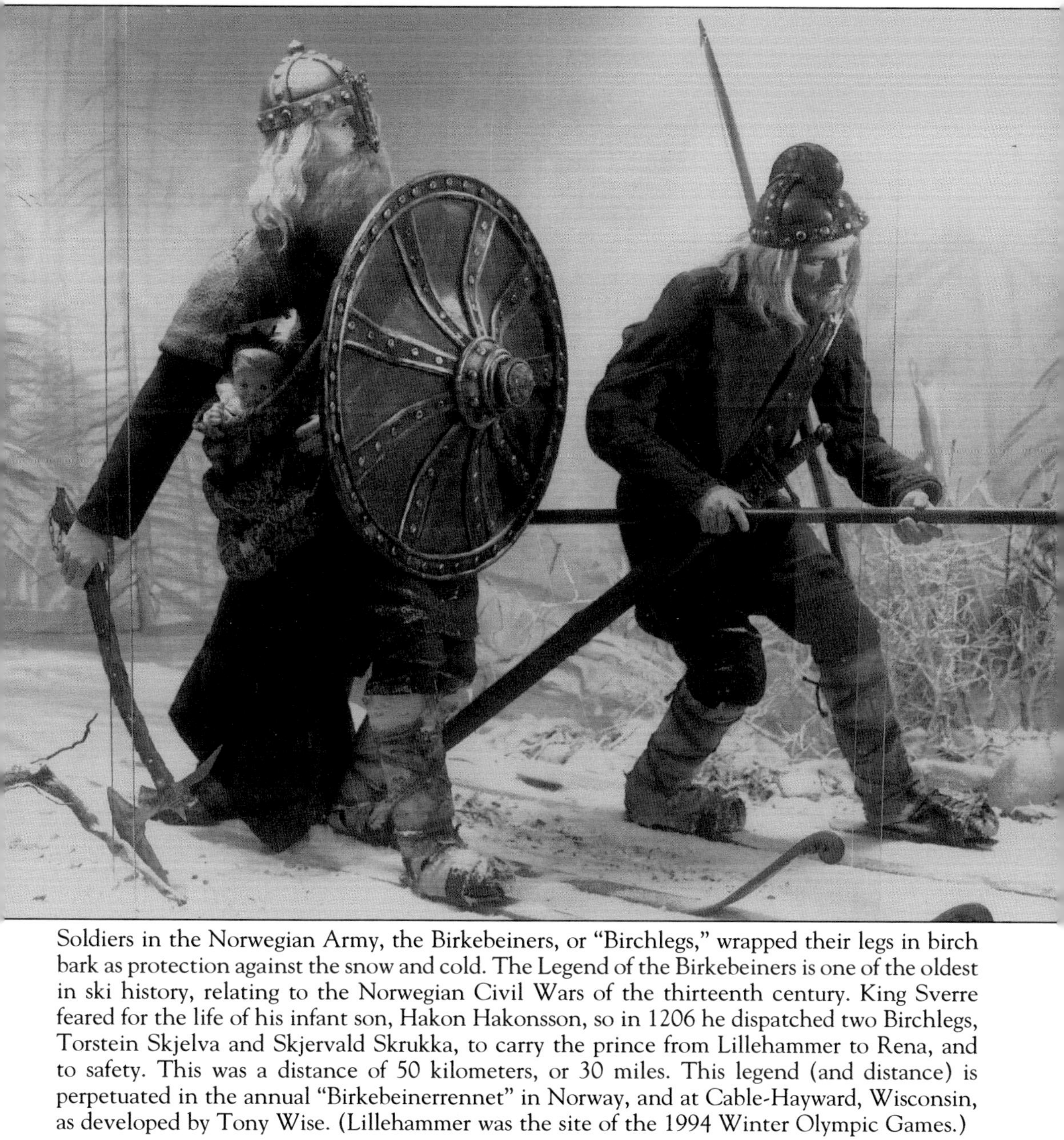

Soldiers in the Norwegian Army, the Birkebeiners, or "Birchlegs," wrapped their legs in birch bark as protection against the snow and cold. The Legend of the Birkebeiners is one of the oldest in ski history, relating to the Norwegian Civil Wars of the thirteenth century. King Sverre feared for the life of his infant son, Hakon Hakonsson, so in 1206 he dispatched two Birchlegs, Torstein Skjelva and Skjervald Skrukka, to carry the prince from Lillehammer to Rena, and to safety. This was a distance of 50 kilometers, or 30 miles. This legend (and distance) is perpetuated in the annual "Birkebeinerrennet" in Norway, and at Cable-Hayward, Wisconsin, as developed by Tony Wise. (Lillehammer was the site of the 1994 Winter Olympic Games.)

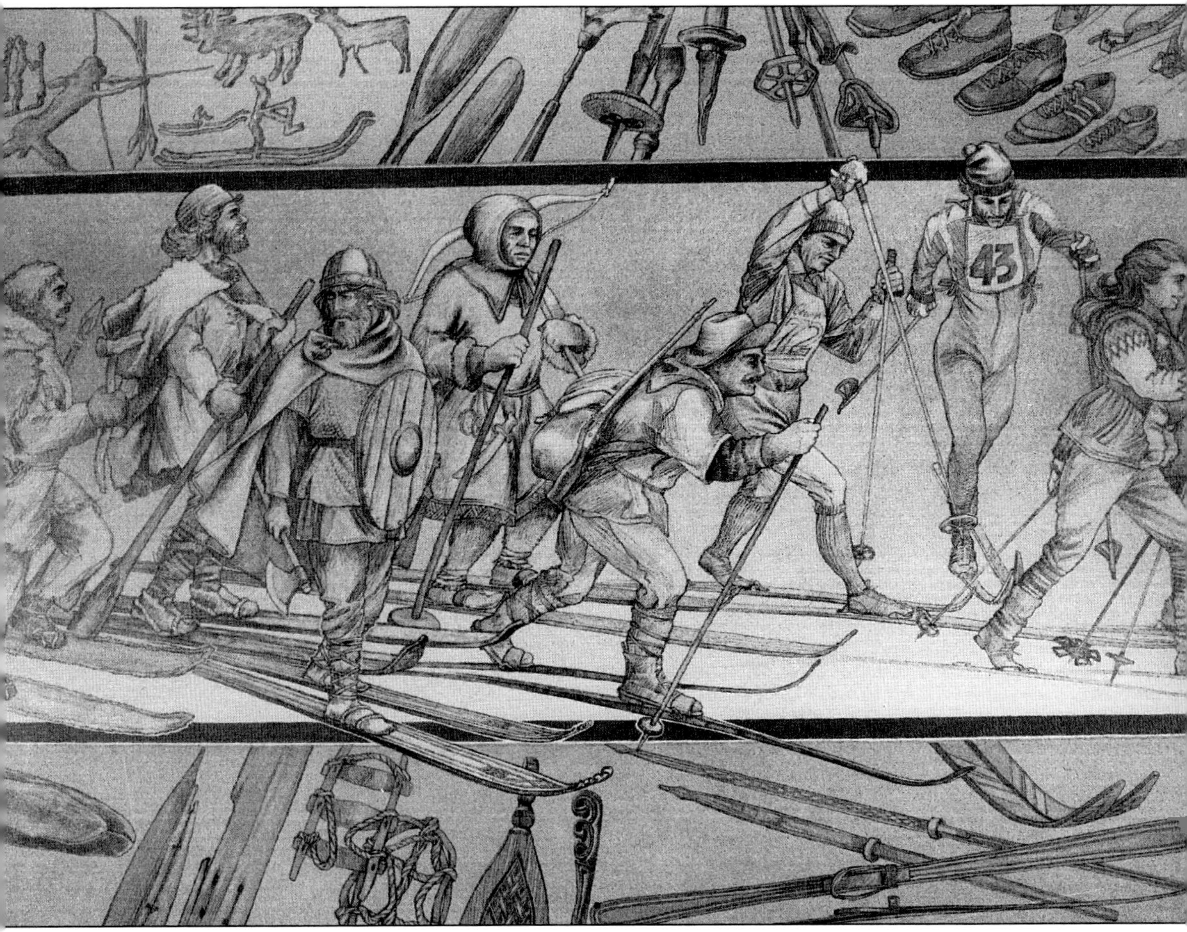

This original poster, commissioned by the U.S. National Ski Hall of Fame and Museum, depicts the evolution of skiing, and was painted by Roger Junak, a prominent Ishpeming artist.

Two

Skiing Invades North America

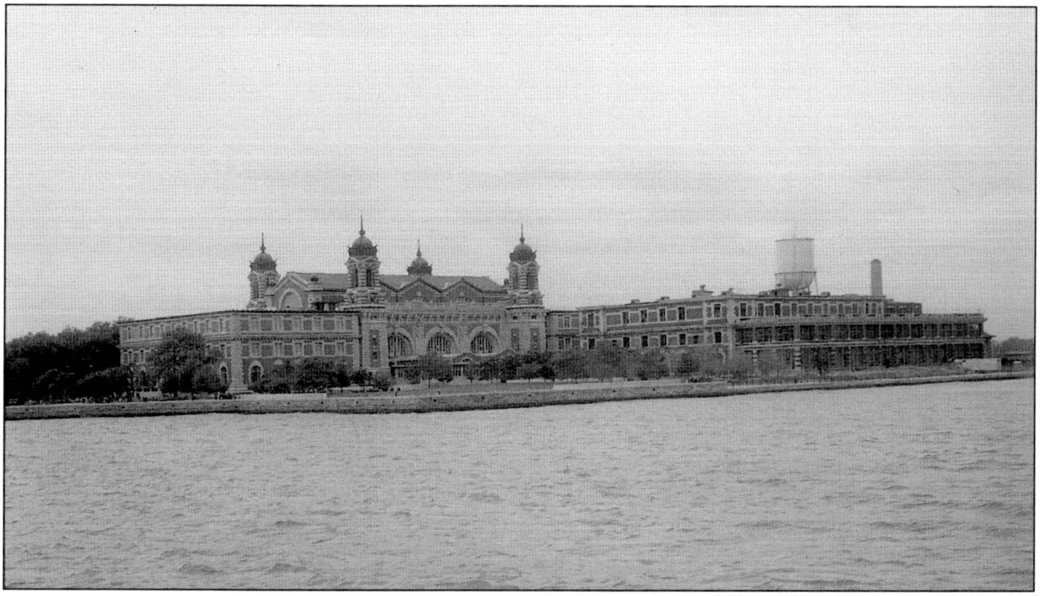

One of the first sights the European immigrants saw upon the arrival in their new country was Ellis Island in New York harbor. The original building was destroyed by fire on June 13, 1897.

Scandinavians arriving in the United States through Ellis Island:

	1871–1880	**1881–1890**	**1891–1900**	**1901–1910**
Norway	95,323	176,586	95,051	190,505
Sweden	101,169	324,285	200,524	219,249
Finland	1,942 (1872–73)	27,443 (1884–93)	35,527 (1894–1900)	133,065

(Allen, 1993)

After arriving, many Scandinavians moved to areas of snow and open forests where they could use their beloved "Skees."

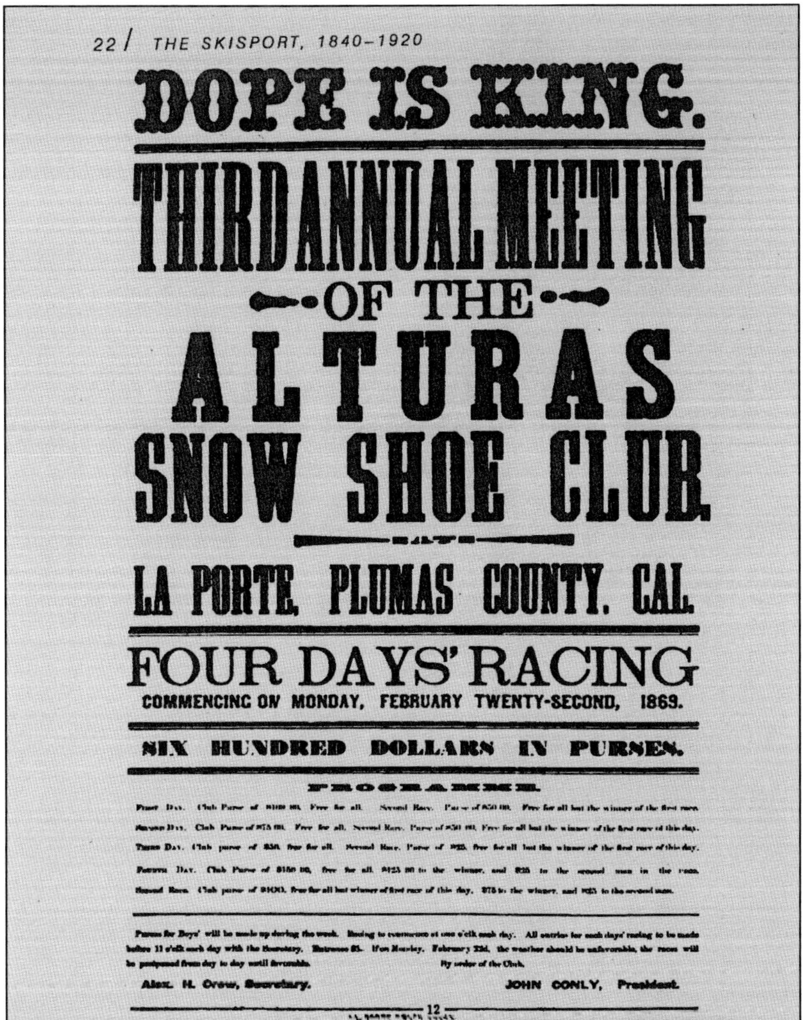

Broadside for the 1869 Alturas Snow Shoe Club meeting. John A. "Snowshoe" Thompson, who was roundly defeated, dismissed the La Porte meet as "nothing but dope racing." (Western Skisport Museum, Boreal Ridge, Calif.)

Some of the posters advertising the Sierra "snowshoe" races of the 1860s carried the bold-lettered proclamation that "DOPE IS KING." This was not a reference to some mind-altering substance (the racers preferred their courage in liquid form); rather, it described the importance of waxing in the early-day ski races. Dope was first introduced in Sierra and Plumas counties in California about 1854, as a way to increase speed and prevent snow from sticking to the skis. As the "snowshoe" racing craze grew, the dope and the "dopemen" who brewed and applied it became increasingly significant factors in competition, largely because the race courses demanded pure, straight-on speed to the exclusion of any turning technique. A common greeting among racers was, "What dope do you use?" rather than, "Hello," or "How's your family?" One of the original dopemen was Bill Clinch of Sawpit, who cooked up a concoction of spermaceti, burgundy pitch, Canada pitch, barbary tallow, camphor, castor oil, and other ingredients. The recipes for most dopes were well-guarded secrets, and they came with names like "Skedaddle," "Greased Lightning," "Slip Easy," "Catch'em Quick," "Breakneck," and "Slip Up." The finer brands were described as "double-distilled, extra-refined, chain-lightning dope." If these were half as fast as advertised, they were very quick indeed.

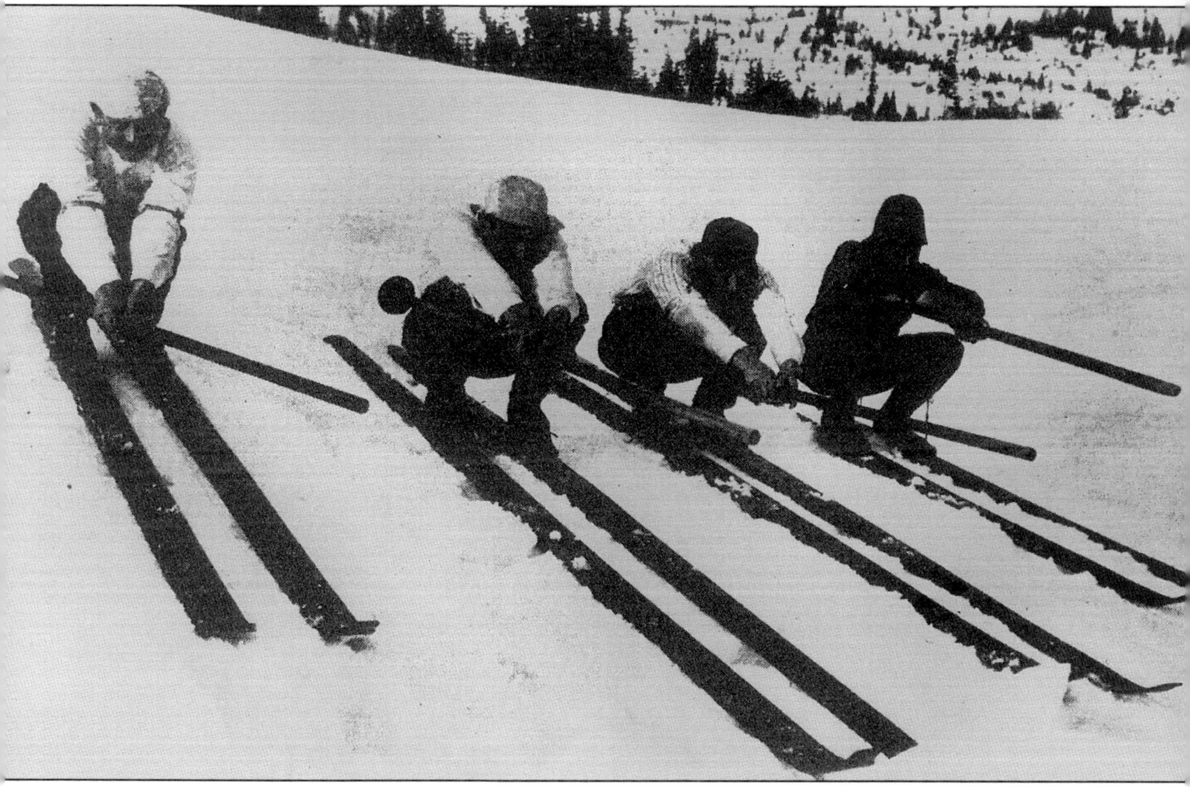

While a large number of Scandinavian immigrants settled in the Midwest, it was by no means the only area in which they settled. Many crossed the country to work in the mining camps in the high Sierras. They, of course, carried their regular skis with them. However, the great amount of snow and heavy loads of supplies they had to carry into camp made it necessary to use much longer skis, or "snowshoes," as they called them. The skis used in the Sierra-Nevadas were ten to fourteen feet long, also referred to as "Long Boards."

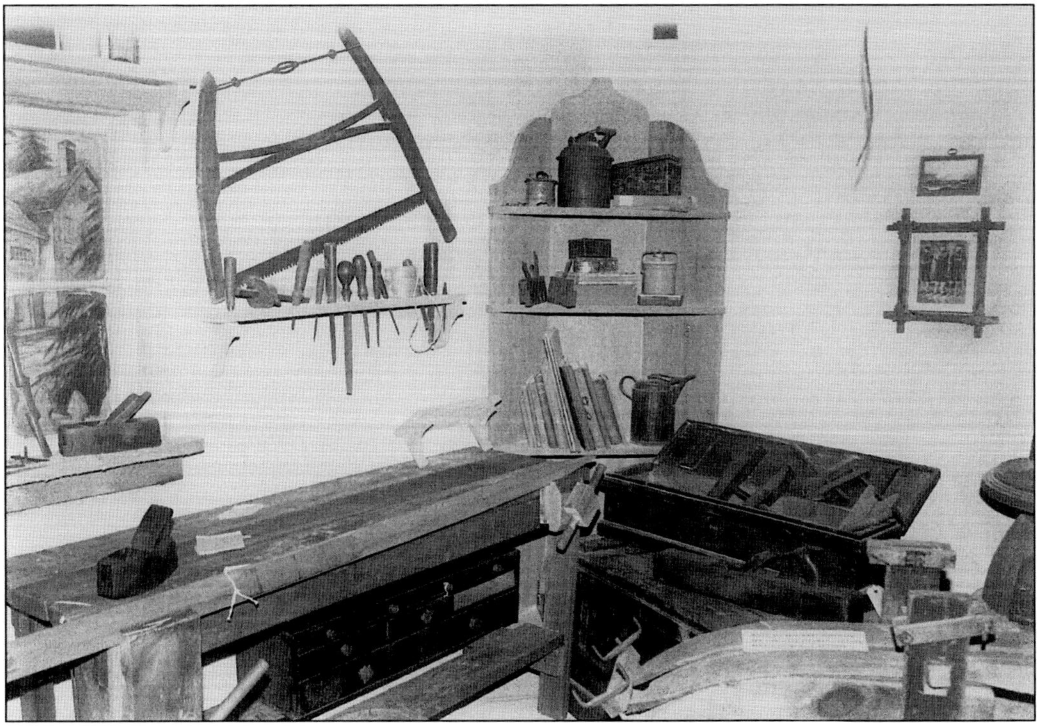

This reconstructed ski shop (c. 1910) is an exhibit in the U. S. National Ski Hall of Fame and Museum showing some of the original tools and artifacts of the early Scandinavian ski carpenters.

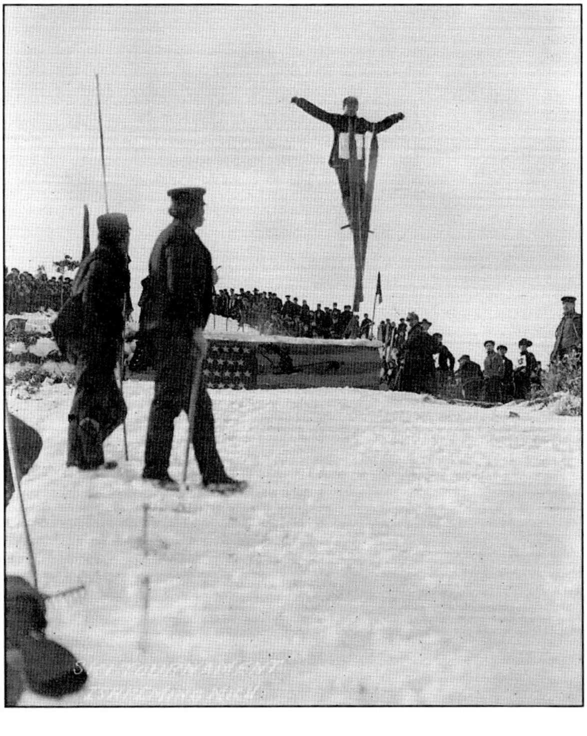

A ski jumping competition in 1905 at Brasswire Hill, which was located east of Ishpeming, Michigan.

In the mid-1800s, factory-made skis were nonexistent. Area carpenters and ski makers crafted skis in local shops from local wood. Hickory, ash, pine, birch, and maple were used for the skis, many of which were elaborately adorned with intricately carved engravings. (Roger Junak design)

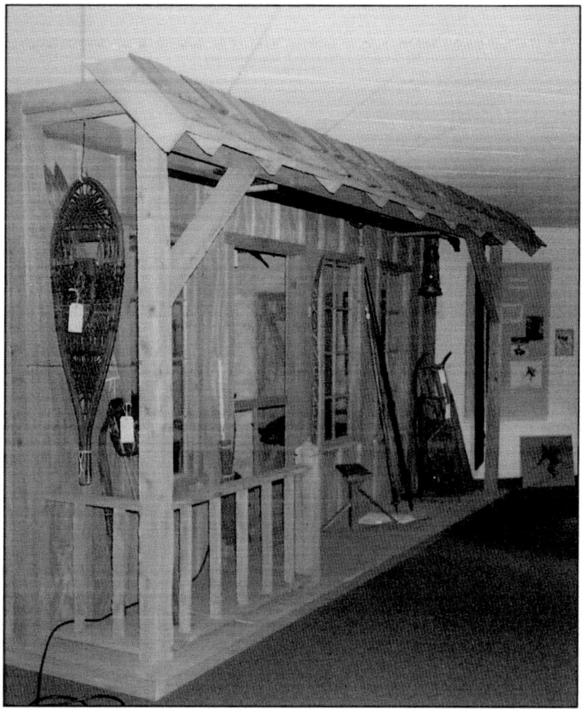

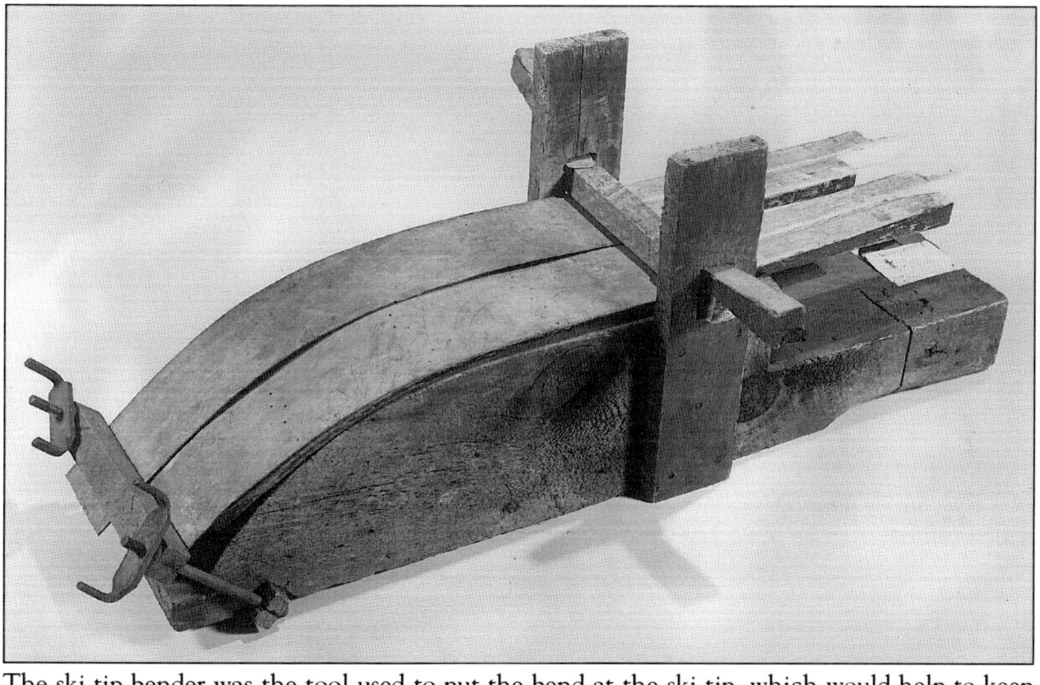

The ski tip bender was the tool used to put the bend at the ski tip, which would help to keep the ski flowing over and above the snow. The semi-finished ski was placed in a steam pipe or box. After the ski was steamed for several hours, the wood became pliable and the tips were clamped in the bender until dry. This resulted in a permanent bend of the tip. A ski tip bender is on display in the U.S. National Ski Hall of Fame and Museum.

SKIS AND SUPPLIES

Read the following unsolicited testimony of the true benefits derived from the use of a good equipment, such as I furnish my customers:

Portola, California, Jan. 18, 1911.

My Dear Mr. Holter:—

Your skis received in first-class condition; and same have proven entirely satisfactory in every respect. But for your skis, the train crew of a snowbound train, having been without food for 48 hours, might have been subjected to untold sufferings. There was no way of approaching the unfortunate men, but food was carried for miles over the mountains on your skis, the only pair fit for this use in the community, thus relieving the crew from further hardships. Since then the skis have received considerable notoriety, and they are now being used by the Government Mail Carrier every day, your skis being the only available mode of transportation at this time, after the most terrific snow storm in the history of the California Mountains.

Thanking you on behalf of everybody concerned and benefitted by Your skis, I am,

Yours very truly,

James A. Arkin.

I have made a specialty of outfits complete for Clubs for many years, and will be pleased to serve you. Second growth Hickory White Ash, White Oak, Birch and Pine Skis, Bamboo Skipoles, Bindings, and Skishoes, everything with my personal guarantee.

AKSEL H. HOLTER,
ASHLAND, WIS.

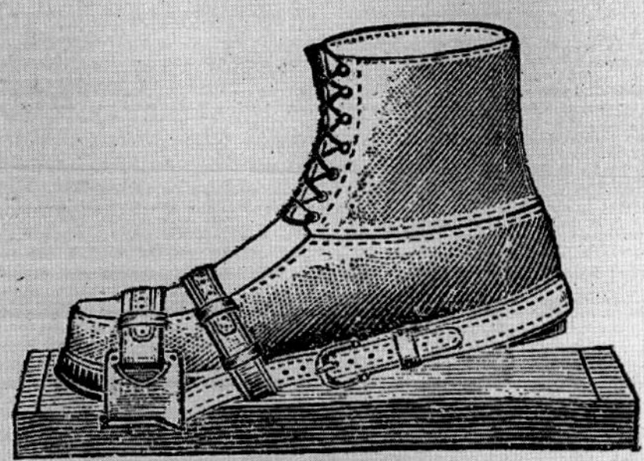

No better Shoes or Bindings made.

Skis and Supplies was written by Aksel H. Holter, the first secretary of the National Ski Association; he was also a pioneer in the ski supply business.

Three

Northern Michigan Ski Clubs

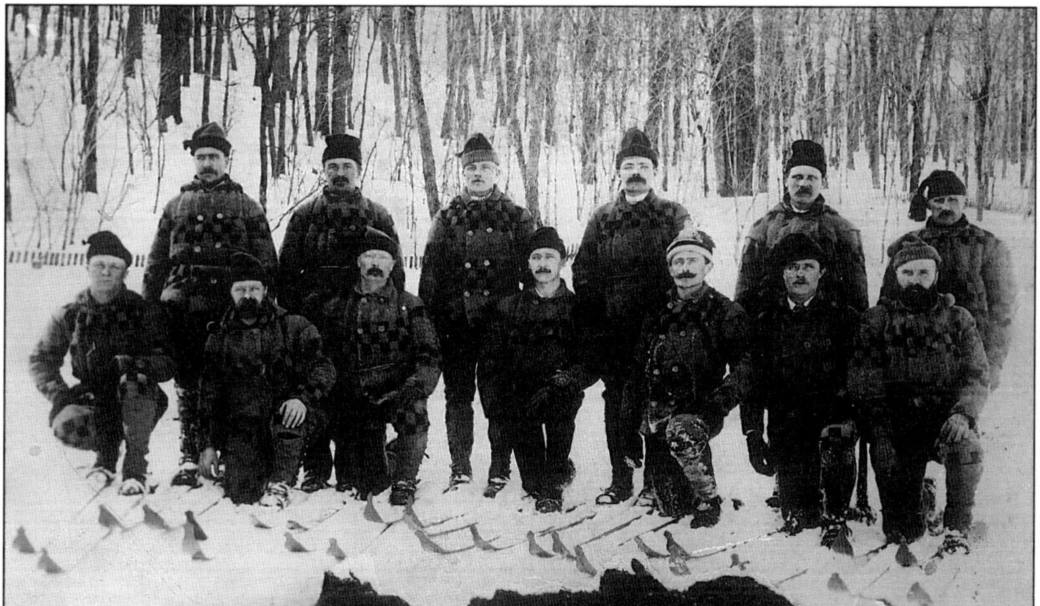

Pictured are the 1887 members of the Norden Ski Club of Ishpeming. They are, from left to right: (standing) Ole Bjornaas, Peter Saltness, Ole Engen, Henrik Sorlie, Lars Hoyseth, and Sivert Asgaard; (kneeling) Ole Sundlie, Ole Rye, Gust Olson, Iver Johnson, Ed Nelson, Martin Johnson, and Alex Tislov.

The Norden Ski Club of Ishpeming, Michigan, was one of the earliest ski clubs in the country. There were competitive events in jumping and cross-country, but the club was social as well, and often people just skied for the fun of it by taking group tours into the nearby forests, enjoying the solitude of the moment. The social aspect remained prevalent even after the club became the Ishpeming Ski Club. Groups of friends gathered their families and planned winter outings of ski tours and winter picnics on an almost weekly basis. The long winter hours passed in a healthy and enjoyable environment.

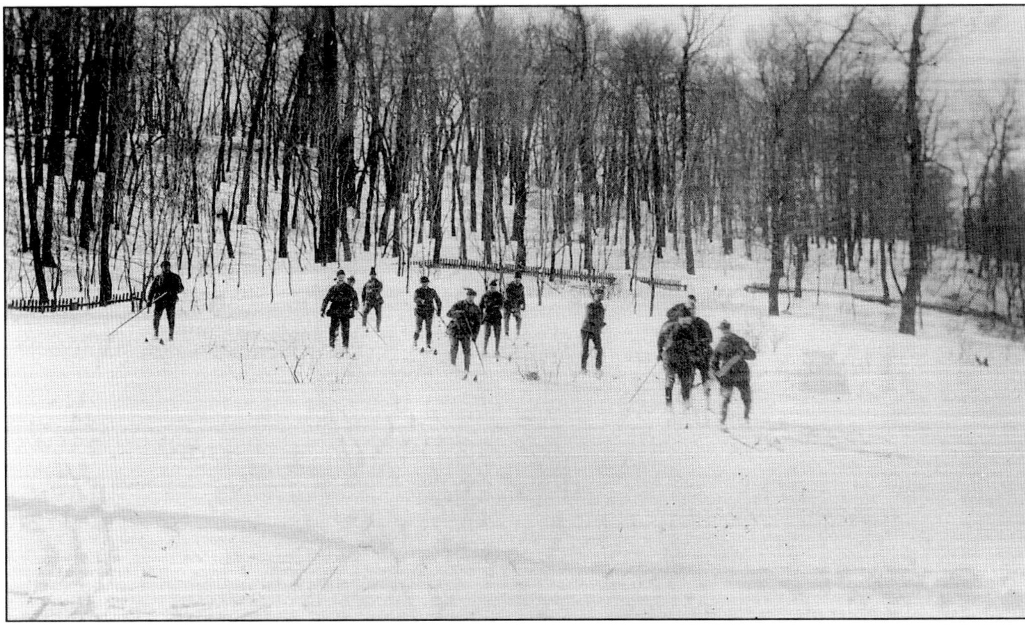

A Norden Ski Club Race in February of 1888, is pictured here. Note the early use of the single pole.

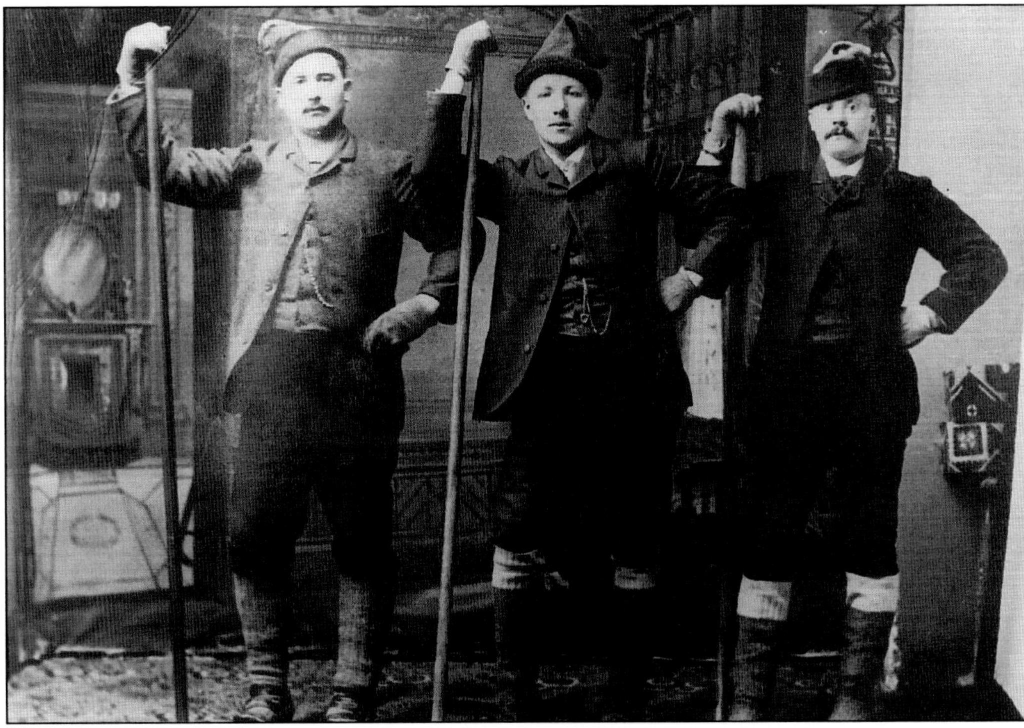

Pictured are three unidentified Norden Ski Club members, about 1887.

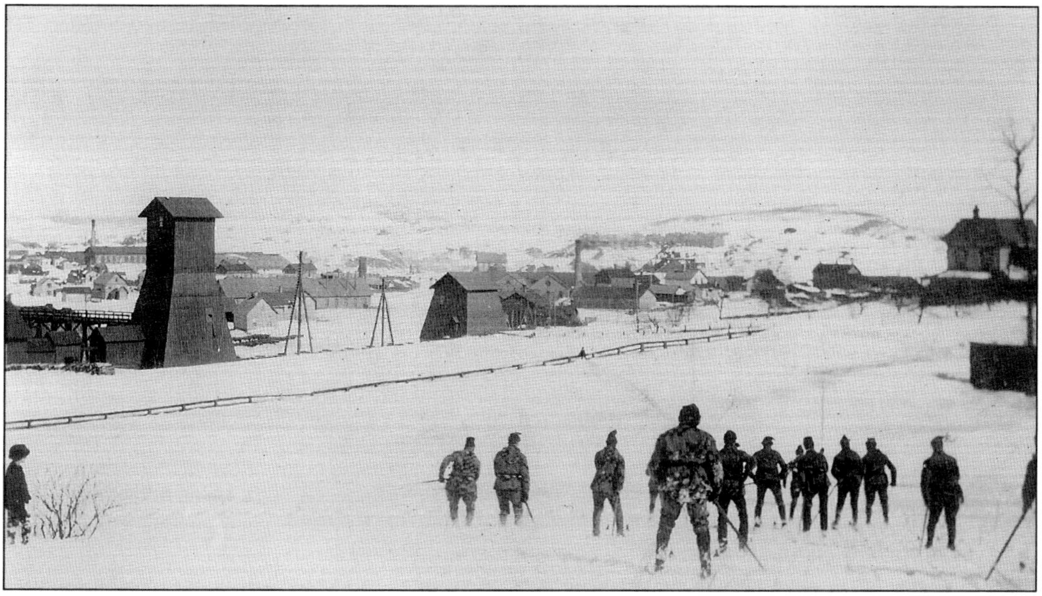

This photograph shows the Norden Ski Club on an outing near Ishpeming in 1887. The Norden Ski Club was the forerunner of the Ishpeming Ski Club, now in its 113th consecutive year of existence.

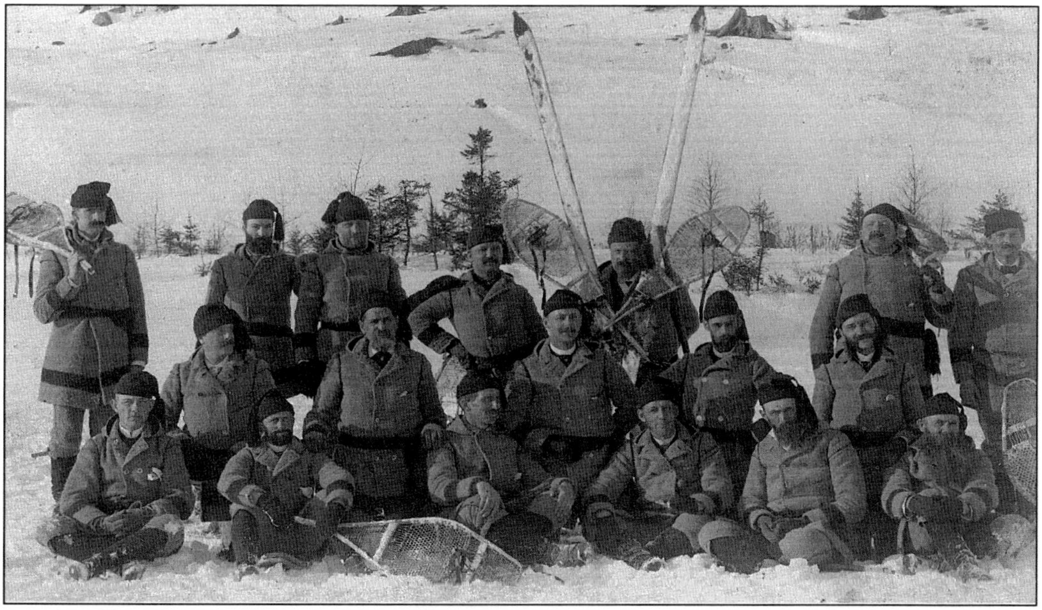

Norden Ski Club members pose for a photograph during a winter outing in the late 1880s. Note the snowshoes being used by some members.

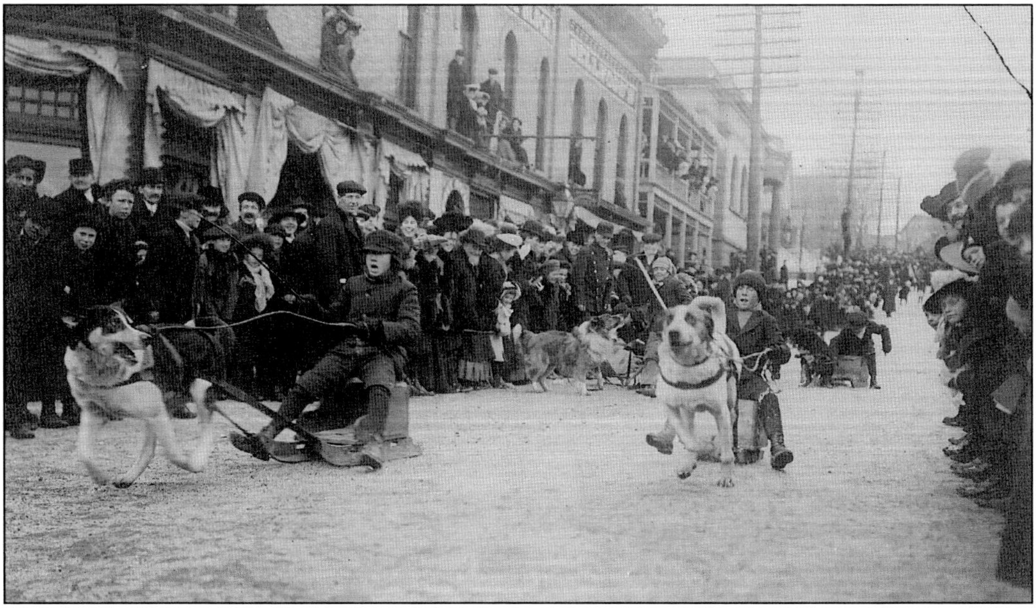

Dog racing was a popular event for the youngsters during the big ski tournament weekends. Loosely organized, the children brought their "mutts" to the downtown streets of Ishpeming, harnessed them to their "skimmers," and found out whose dog was best. This photo is from 1901.

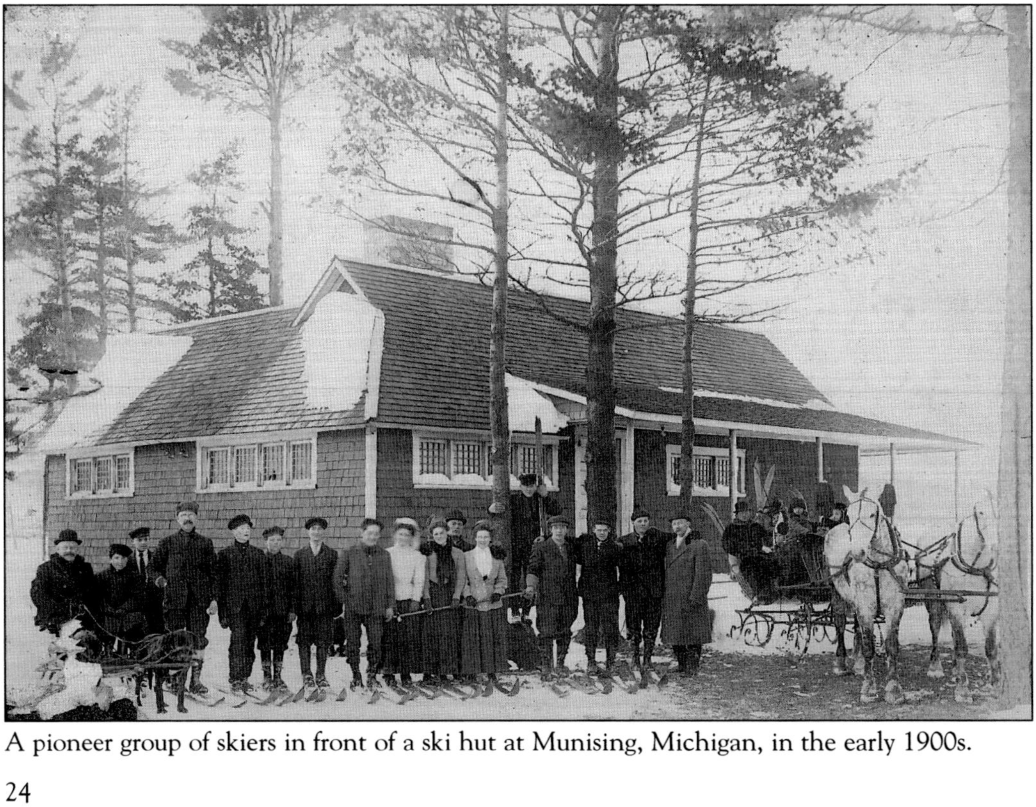

A pioneer group of skiers in front of a ski hut at Munising, Michigan, in the early 1900s.

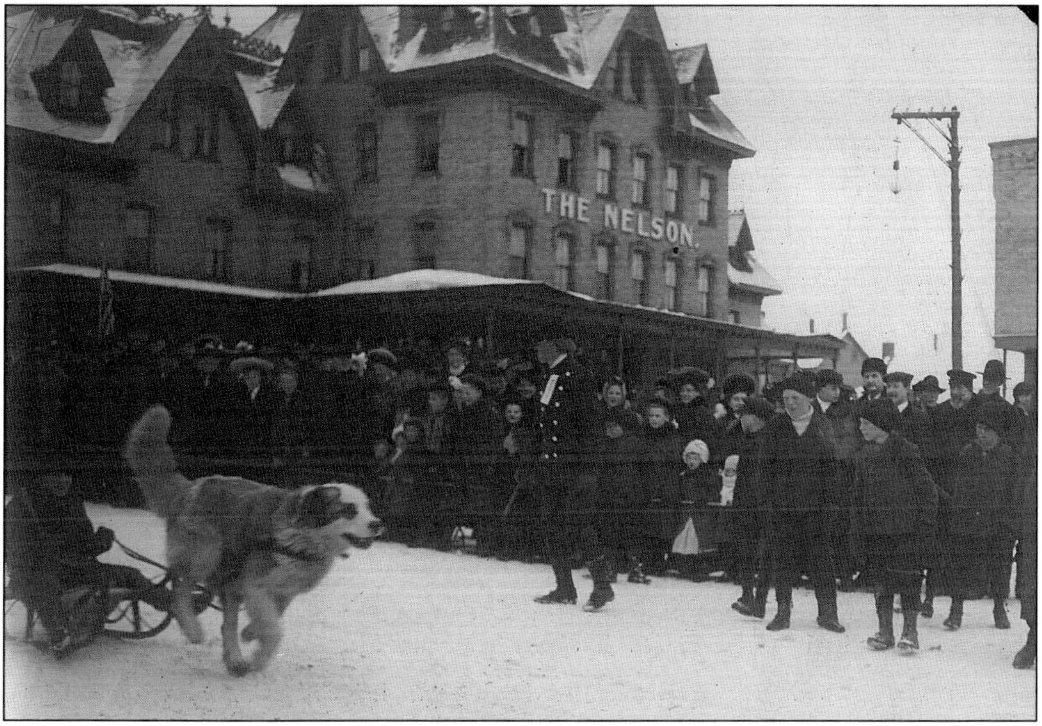

Dog races in front of The Nelson in Ishpeming, Michigan, when it was known as the best hotel in the Midwest. It boasted of hot and cold running water and had telephones.

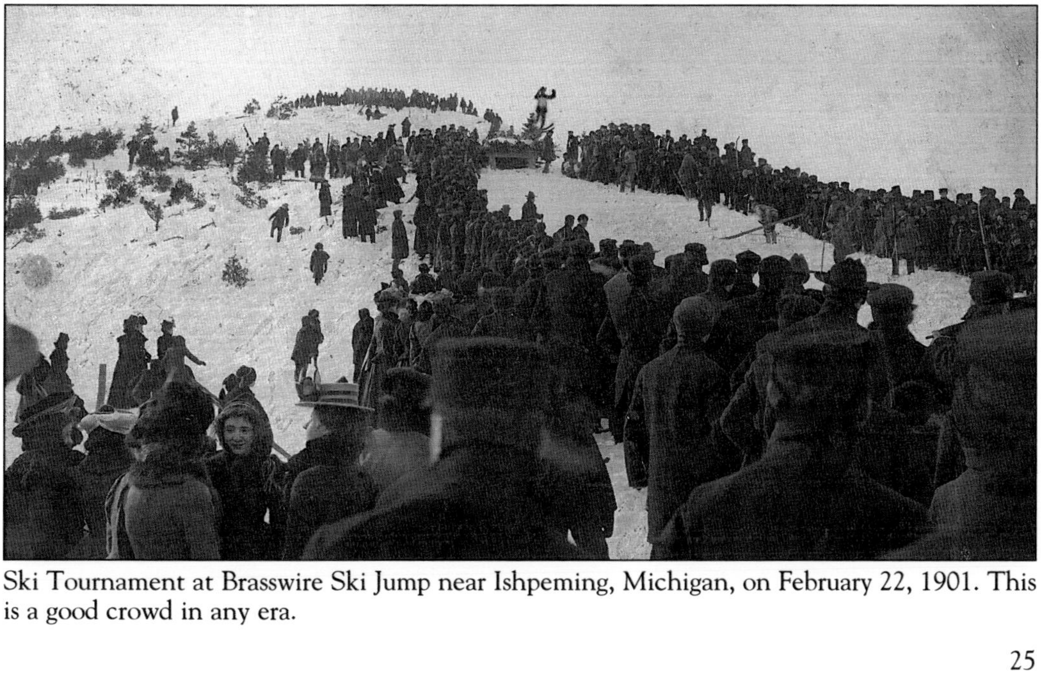

Ski Tournament at Brasswire Ski Jump near Ishpeming, Michigan, on February 22, 1901. This is a good crowd in any era.

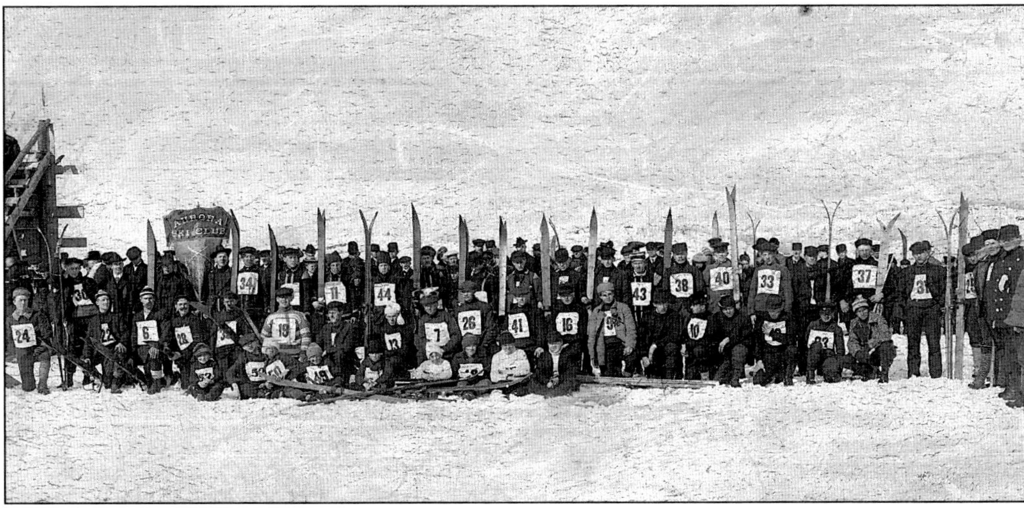

Pictured are entrants and officials at a ski tournament held in Ishpeming, Michigan, on February 22, 1904. In 1905, this meet was proclaimed the first National Ski Association Tournament.

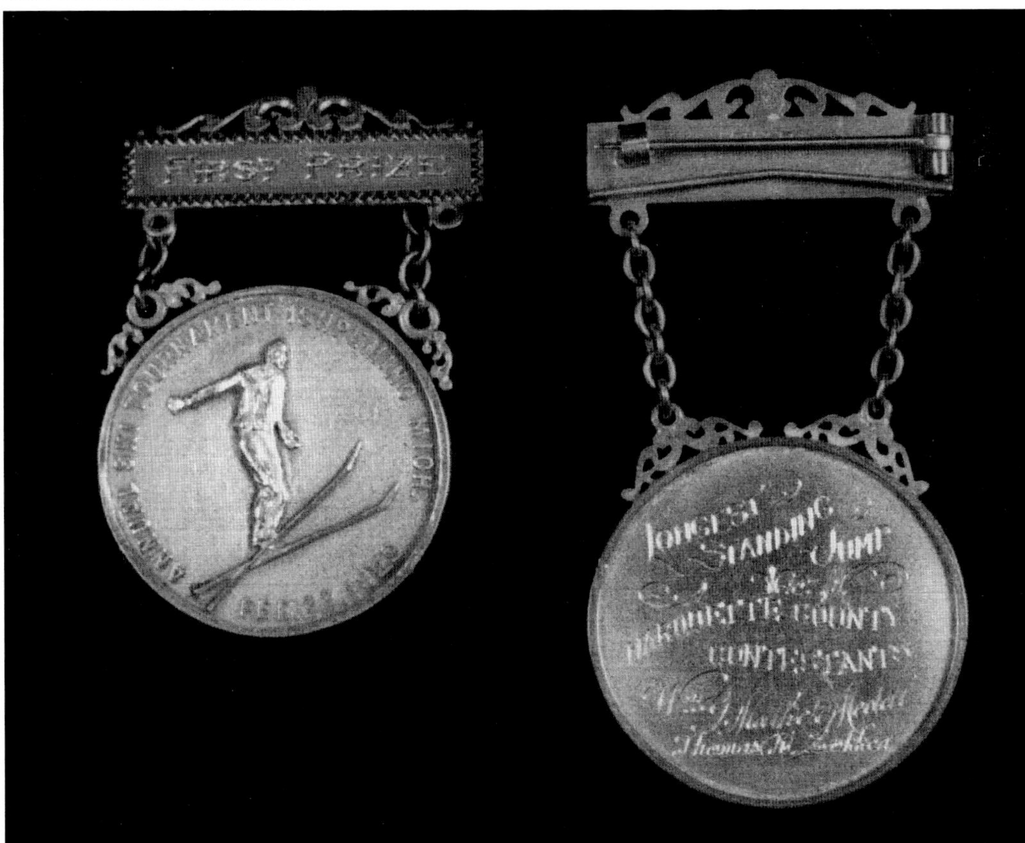

Pictured are the Mather Medals, donated by William G. Mather, president of Cleveland Cliffs Iron Company. They were presented to the tournament winners from 1905 to 1933, with gold medals awarded for first place, silver for second, and bronze for third.

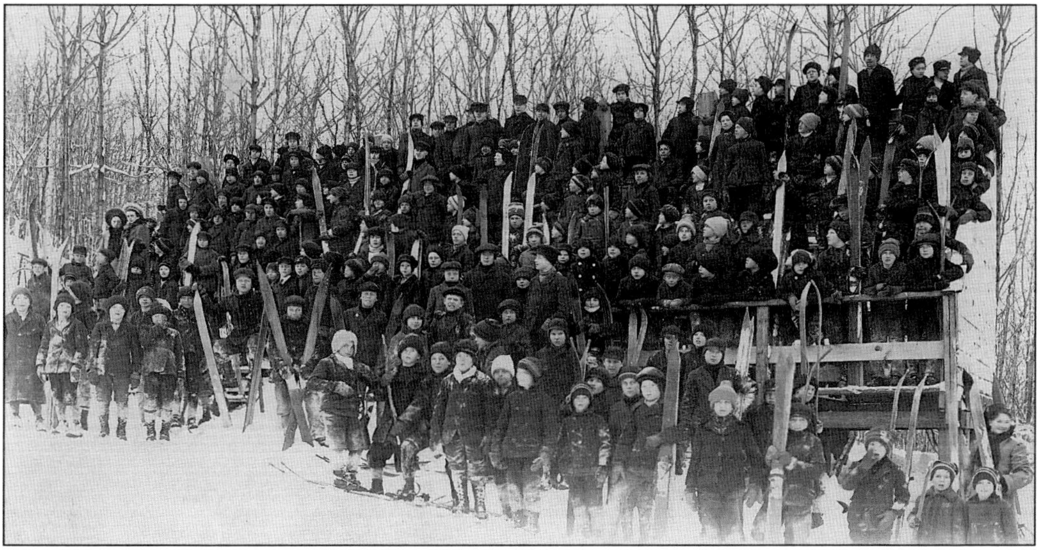

In 1906, a group of junior jumpers watch their heroes in action, each and every one waiting for the day he gets his chance to be a "star."

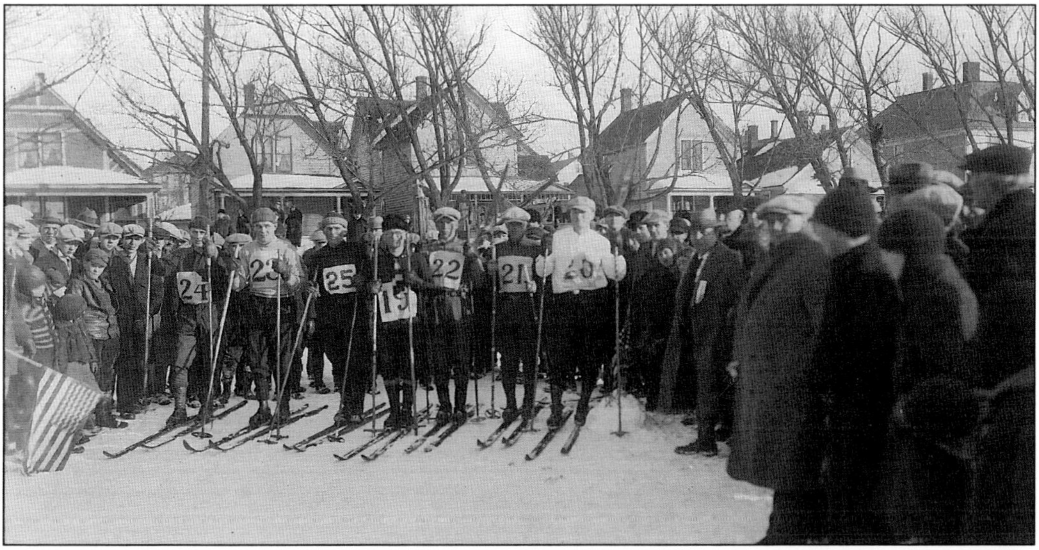

A Nordic cross-country skiing event about to begin in Ishpeming, in the 1920s is pictured above.

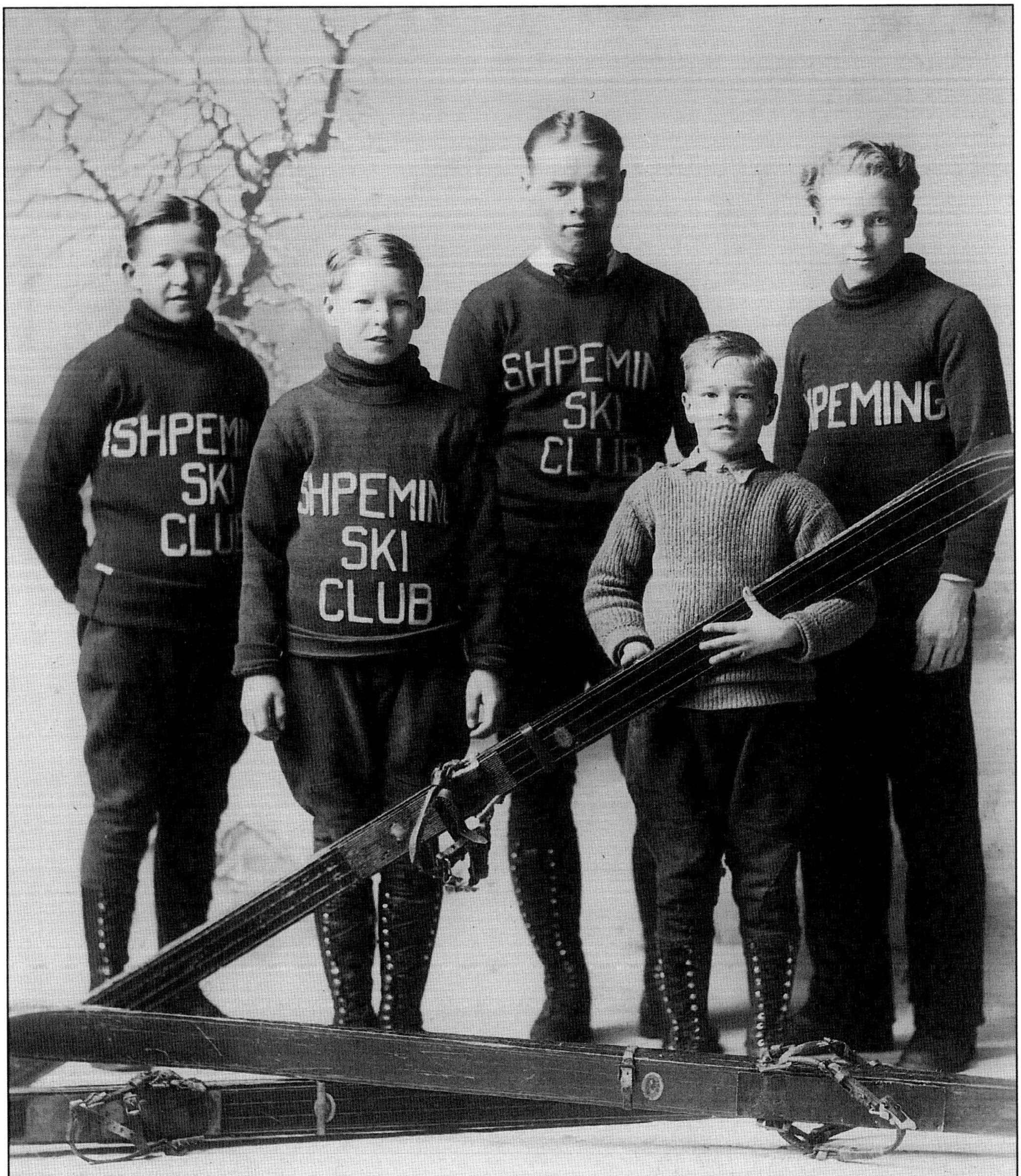

Pictured are the Ishpeming Ski Club boy skiers. They are, from left to right: Walt Bietila, Paul Bietila, George Hautamaki, Roy Bietila, and Ero Hecko.

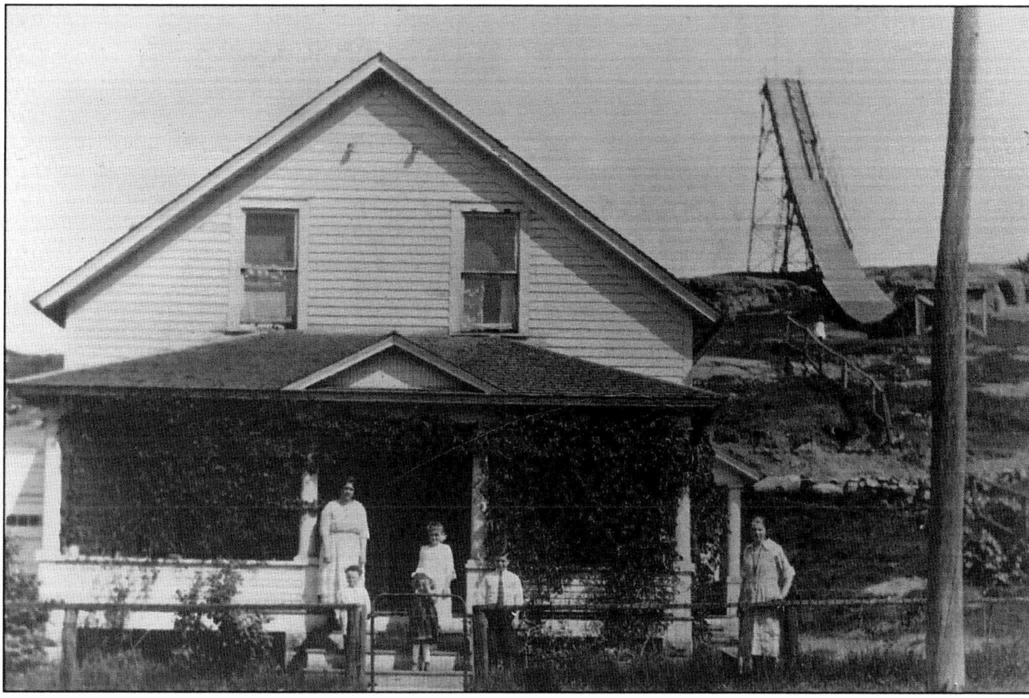

Shown here is a local ski slide built behind a home in Negaunee, Michigan, in the early 1930s. This was typical of the many hills skied on throughout the country. "Take-offs" were often constructed above the many good natural landing areas.

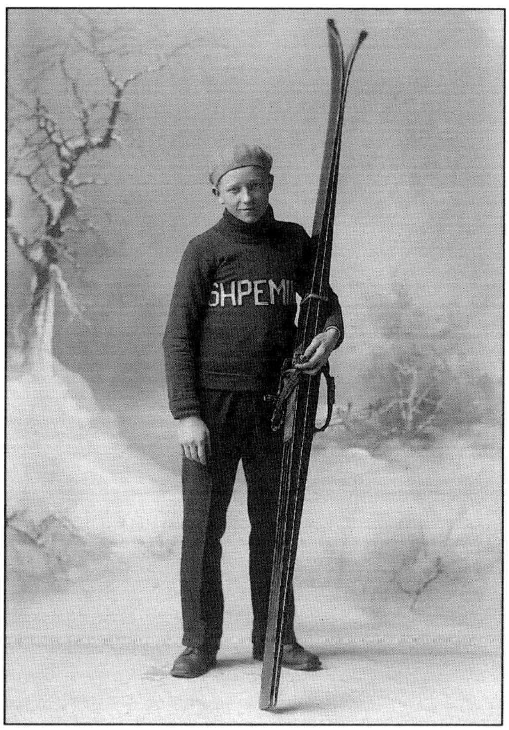

Ero Hecko, an excellent jumper, was a member of the Ishpeming Ski Club. Born on January 3, 1913, he was admitted to membership in the National Ski Association at the age of 10 after easily passing all the necessary tests. Ero was one of the finest boy jumpers and enjoyed a successful career as an amateur jumper.

Ski outfits were made by the H. W. Gossard Company, located in Ishpeming, Michigan.

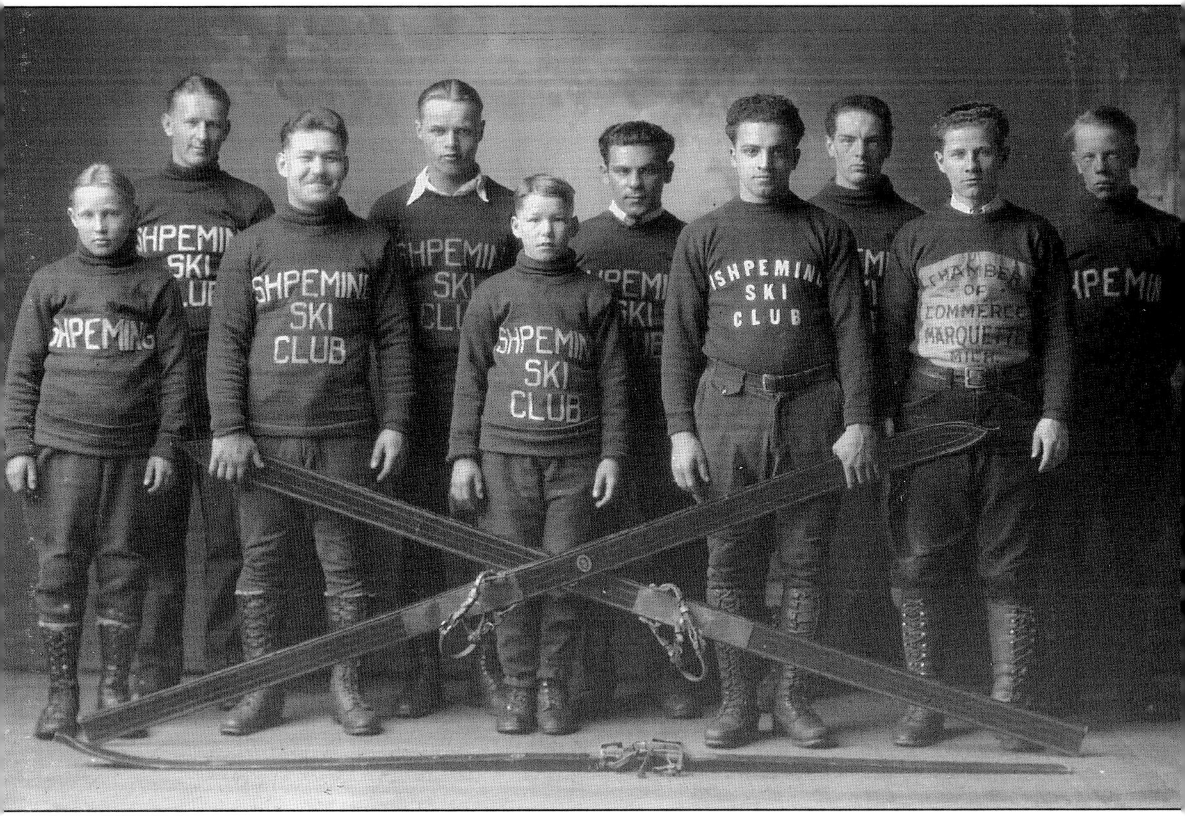

Pictured above are athletes of the Ishpeming Ski Club in the late 1920s. They are, from left to right: Elmer Saari, Bruno Saari, Anselm Bietila, George Hautamaki, Paul Bietila, Nick Donato, Bruno Tasson, Fran Tonkin, George Delbridge, and Earl Erkkila.

Four

Other Midwest Clubs

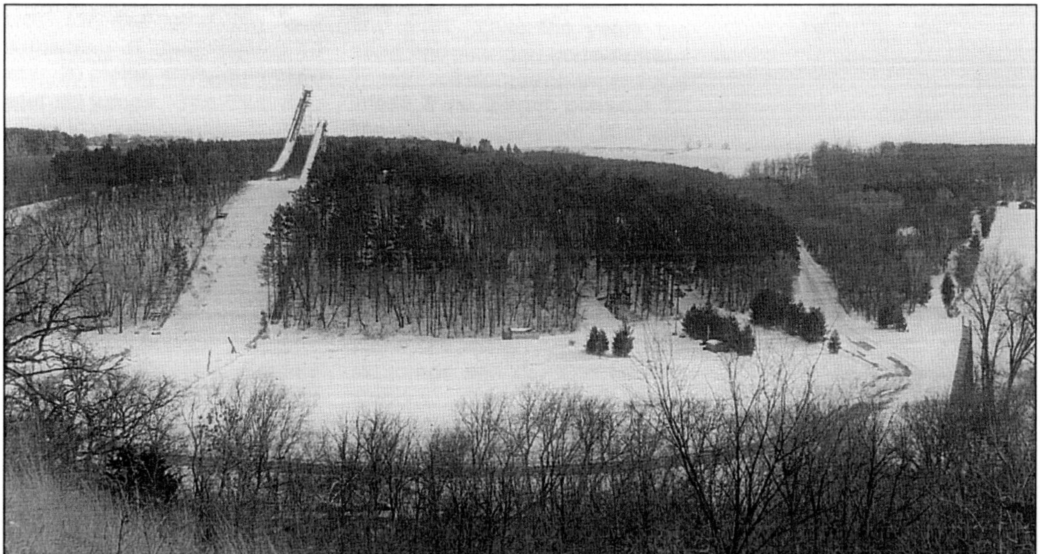

This is the Blackhawk Ski Club hill and scaffold in Madison, Wisconsin.

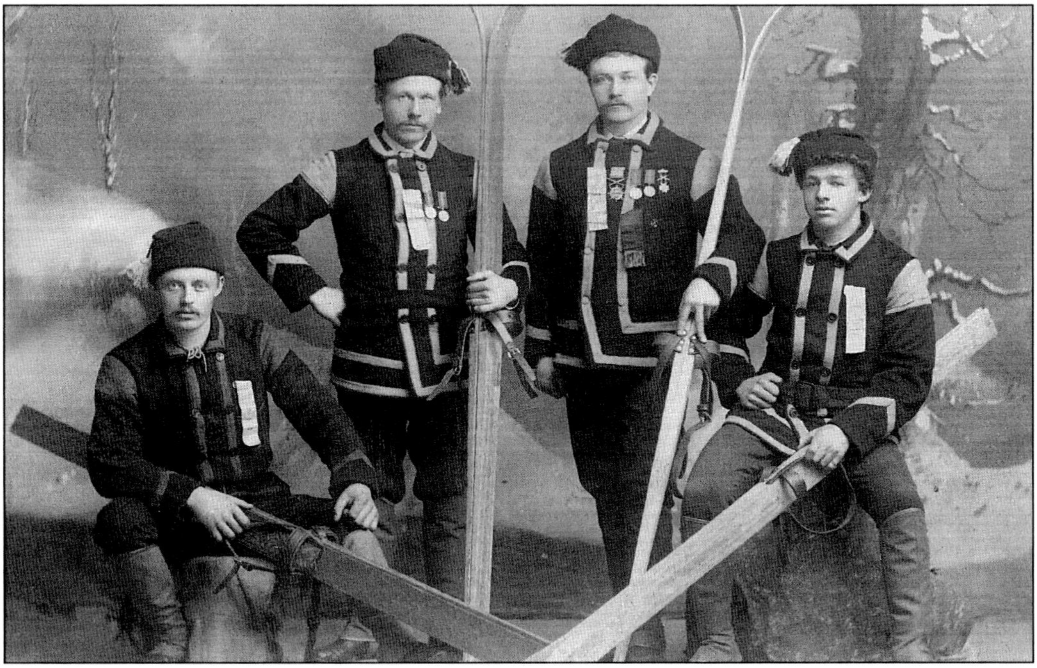

Both pictures on this page depict the Aurora Ski Club members of Red Wing, Minnesota, in 1891. Pictured above, from left to right: Paul Honningstad, Mikkel Hemmestvedt, Torjus Hemmestvedt, and Dr. B.L. Hjermstad.

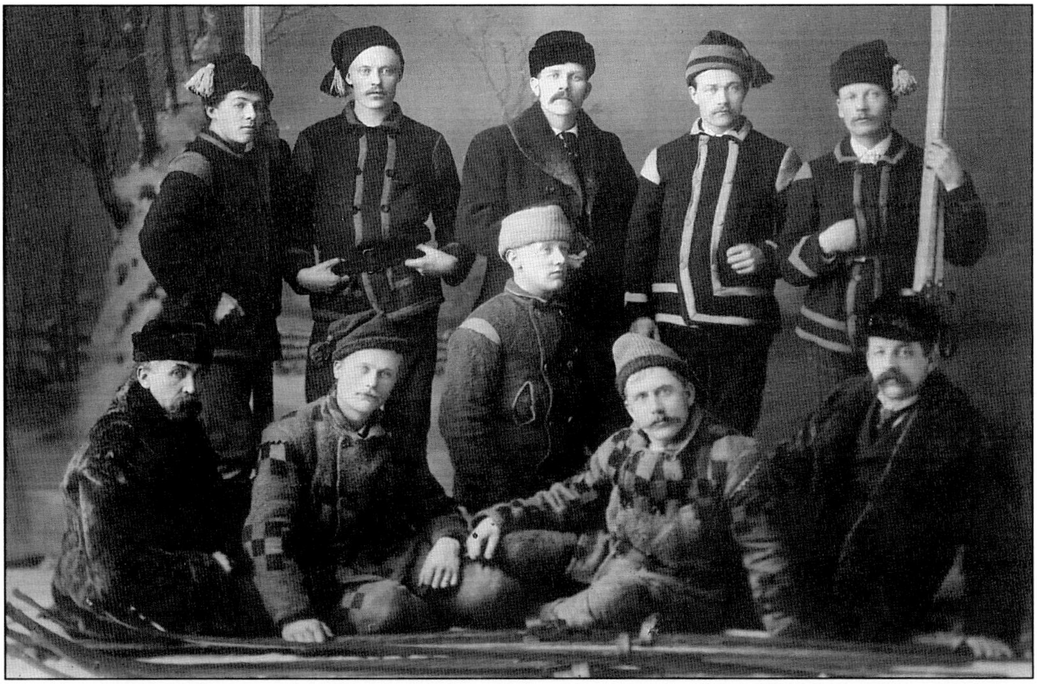

Pictured from left to right are (top) Dr. B.L. Hjermstad, Paul Honningstad, unknown, Mikkel Hemmesvedt, and Torjus Hemmesvedt; (bottom) Christ Boxrud, Erik Giswold, unknown, Lars Jamtars, and Nels Klifton (Ishpeming).

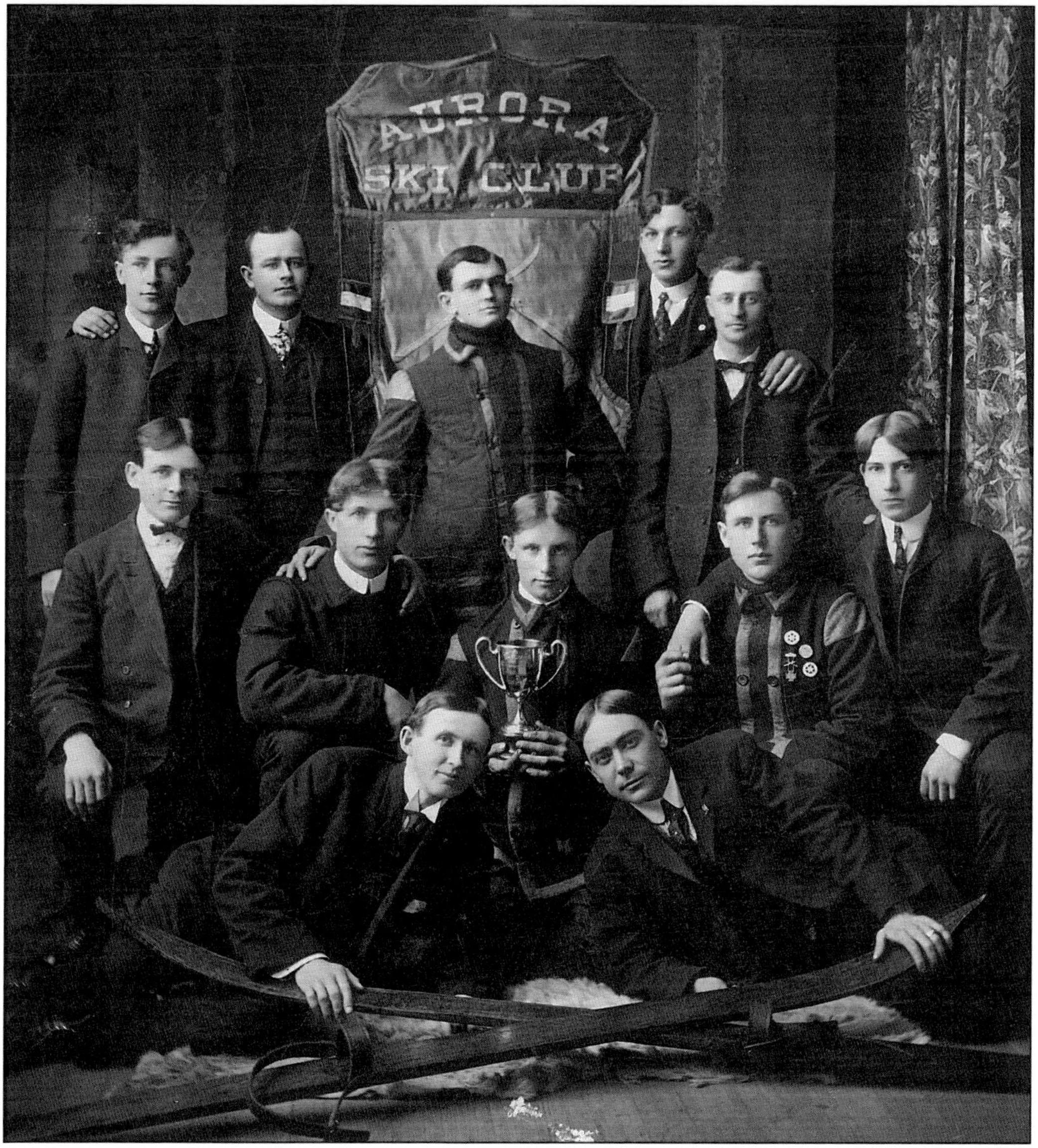

It is not likely the members of the Aurora Ski Club jumped in these clothes, which were donned for the studio photograph.

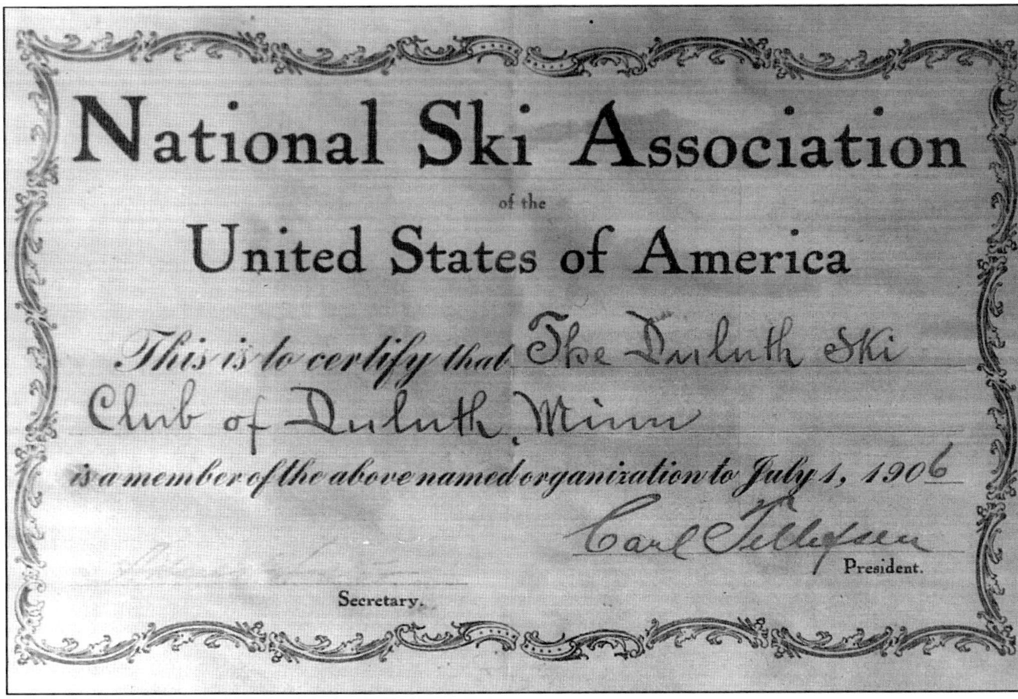

National Ski Association
of the
United States of America

This is to certify that The Duluth Ski Club of Duluth, Minn
is a member of the above named organization to July 1, 1906
Carl Tellefsen
President.

Secretary.

This certificate shows that the ski club of Duluth, Minnesota, became a member of the National Ski Association on July 1, 1906.

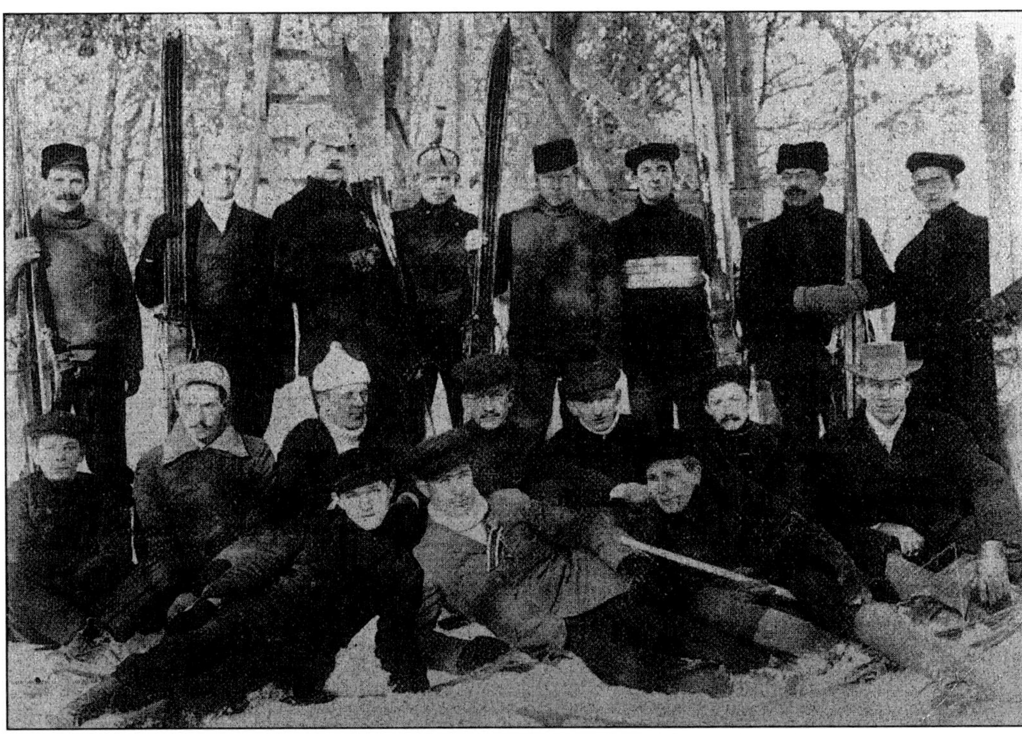

Pictured above is a group of St. Paul, Minnesota skiers from the early 1900s.

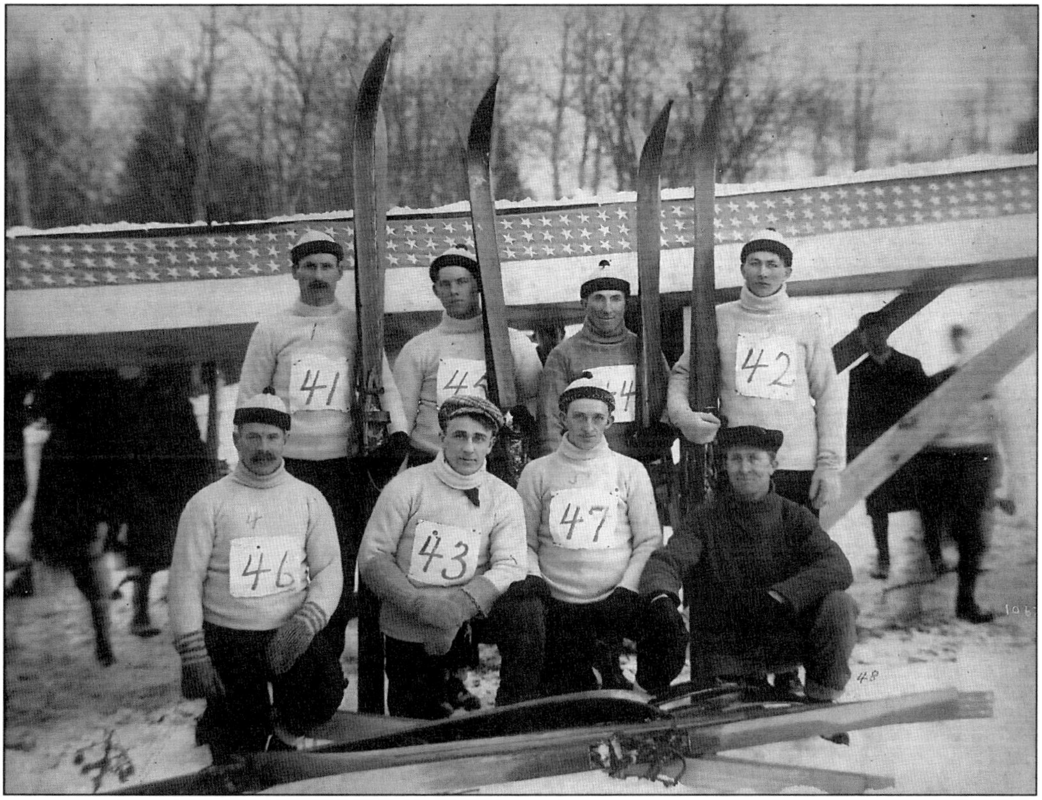

This is a group of lads skiing for the Duluth Ski Club in 1912. Identified by their numbers, they are: John Mangseth (41), Ole Feiring (45), unidentified (44), John Evenson (42), Gustave Bye (46), unidentified (43), and Olaf Larsen (47). Kneeling in the front row at the far right is Ole Mangseth.

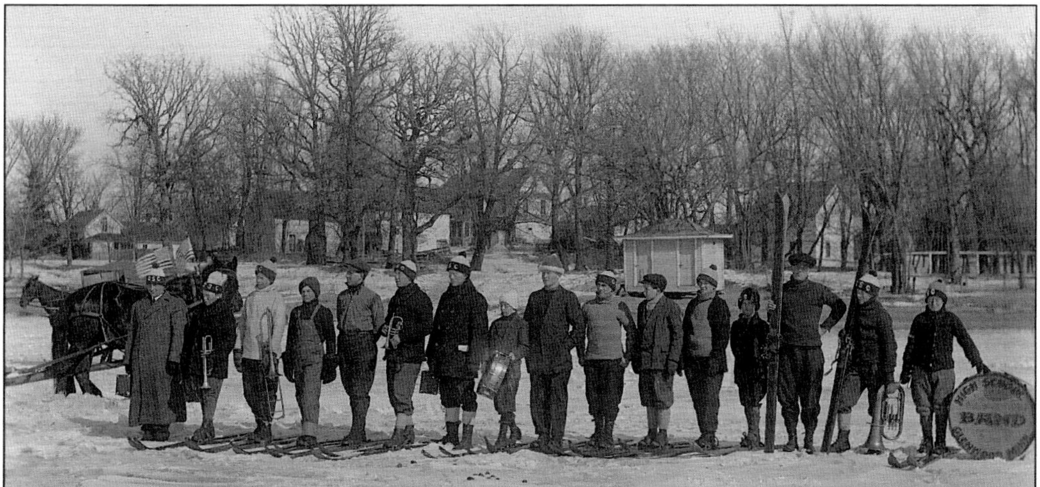

Pictured above is the Glenwood, Minnesota, Ski Band of 1913–1914. The band consisted of a group of Torguson's Junior Skiers of Glenwood. Incidentally, the three smallest boys had each jumped over 100 feet.

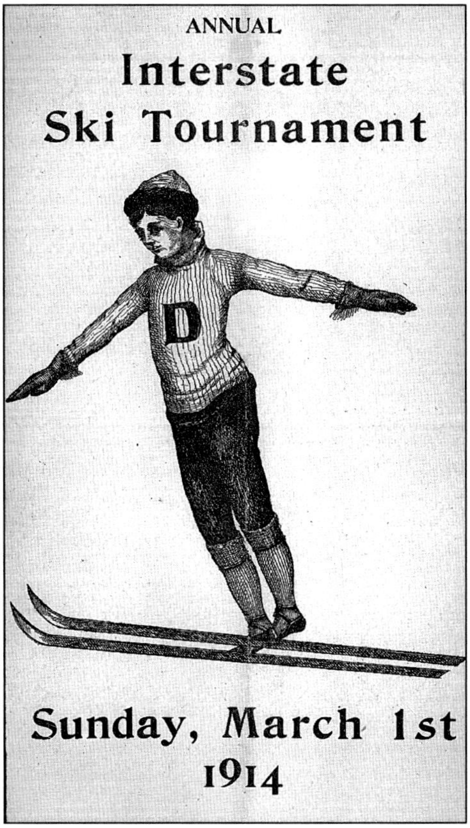

Pictured at left is a program from the Annual Interstate Ski Tournament in Duluth, Minnesota.

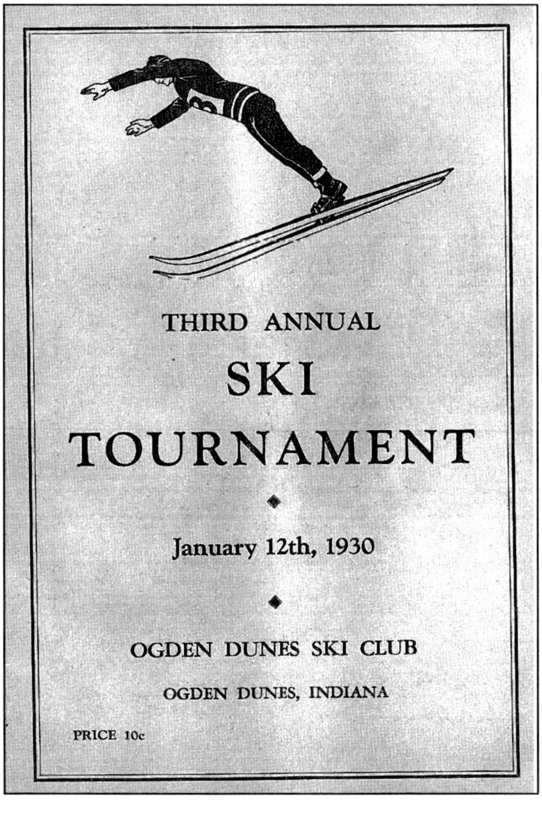

A program from the Third Annual Ski Tournament at the Ogden Dunes Ski Club in Ogden Dunes, Indiana, is pictured at right.

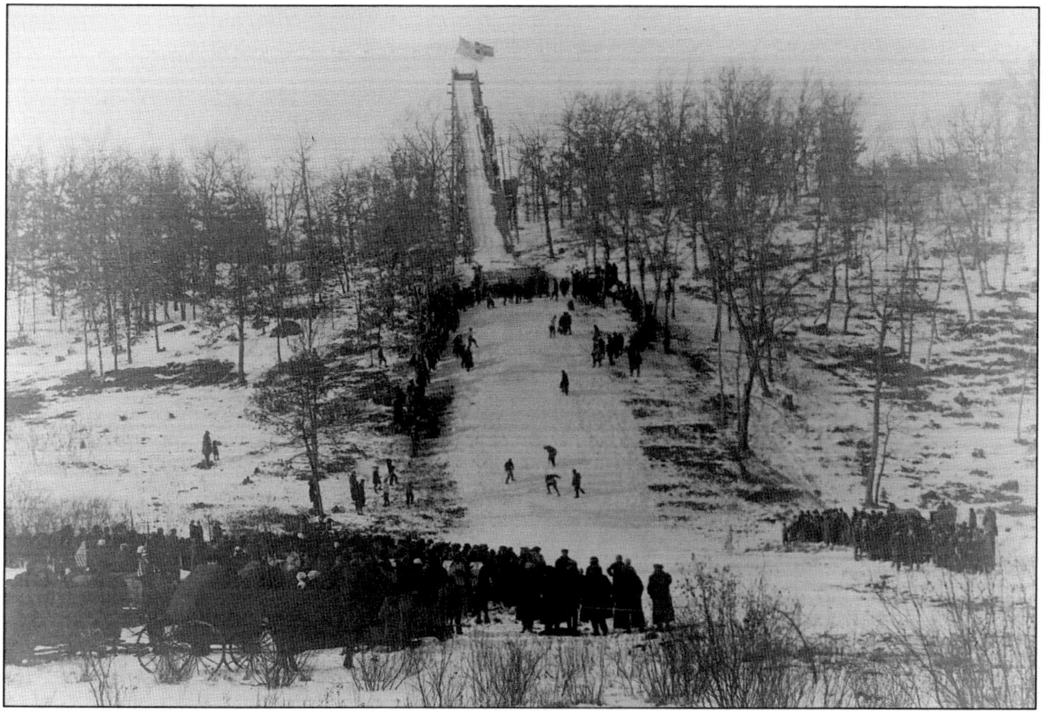

Pictured above is the Iola ski scaffold and hill in Iola, (Waupaca County), Wisconsin. This photo is from 1914. The Midwest ski jumps lacked the natural "take-off" areas that the mountain areas of North America possessed.

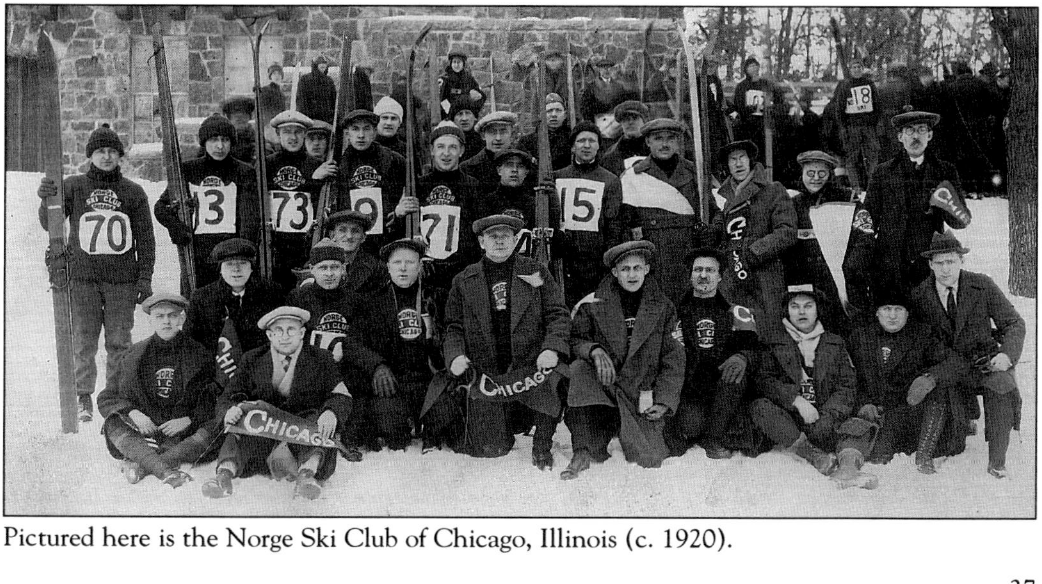

Pictured here is the Norge Ski Club of Chicago, Illinois (c. 1920).

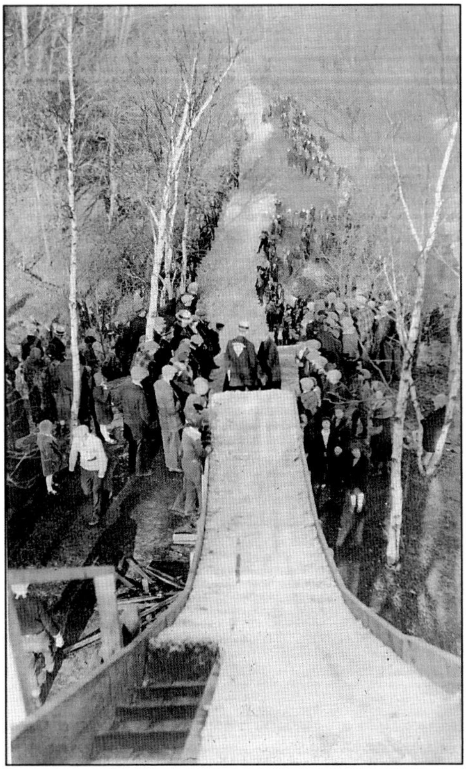

Pictured at left is the Boys' Slide Tournament at Lincoln Park (Duluth, Minnesota) on February 15, 1931.

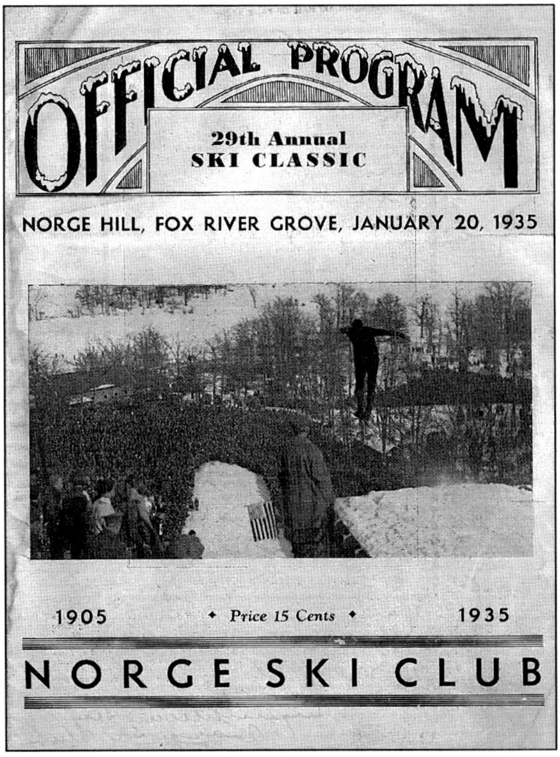

Shown at right is a Norge Ski Club program for its 29th Ski Classic in 1935.

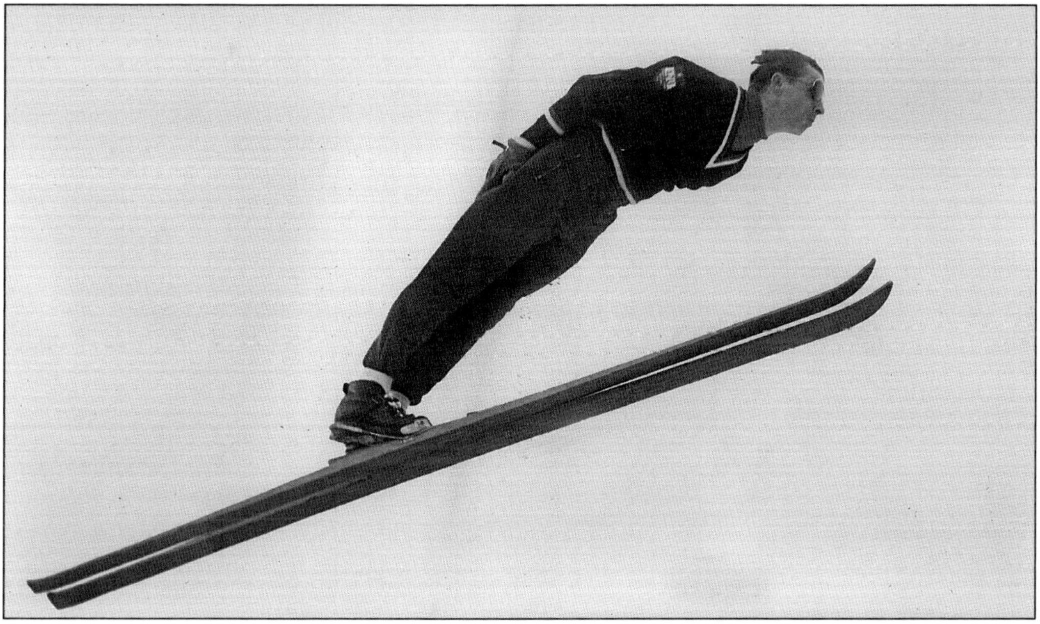

Willie Erickson of Iron Mountain, Michigan, is one of only three skiers in the Central Division to win jumping titles in three different classes: Class C in 1956, Class B in 1957, and Class A in 1959.

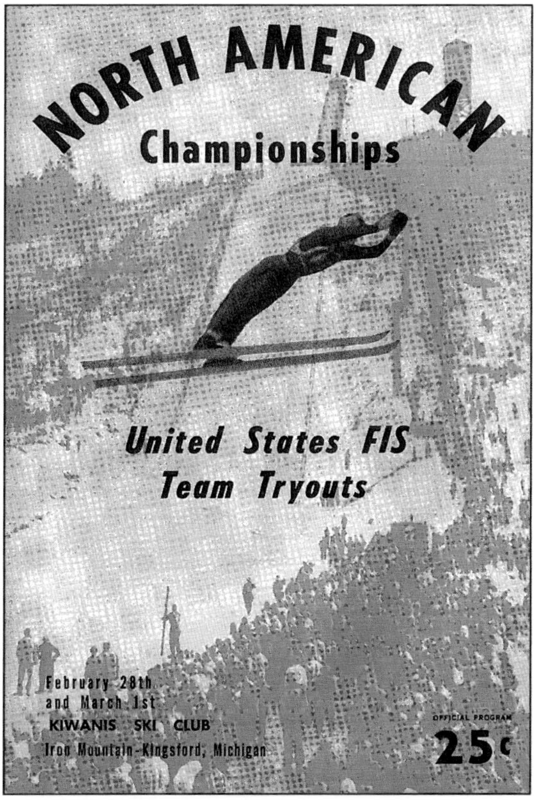

Pictured here is a program from the North American Championships in 1953. It was held at the Kiwanis Ski Club's Pine Mountain Hill, near Iron Mountain, Michigan. It is now listed as a 120-meter ski jump on the World Cup Circuit.

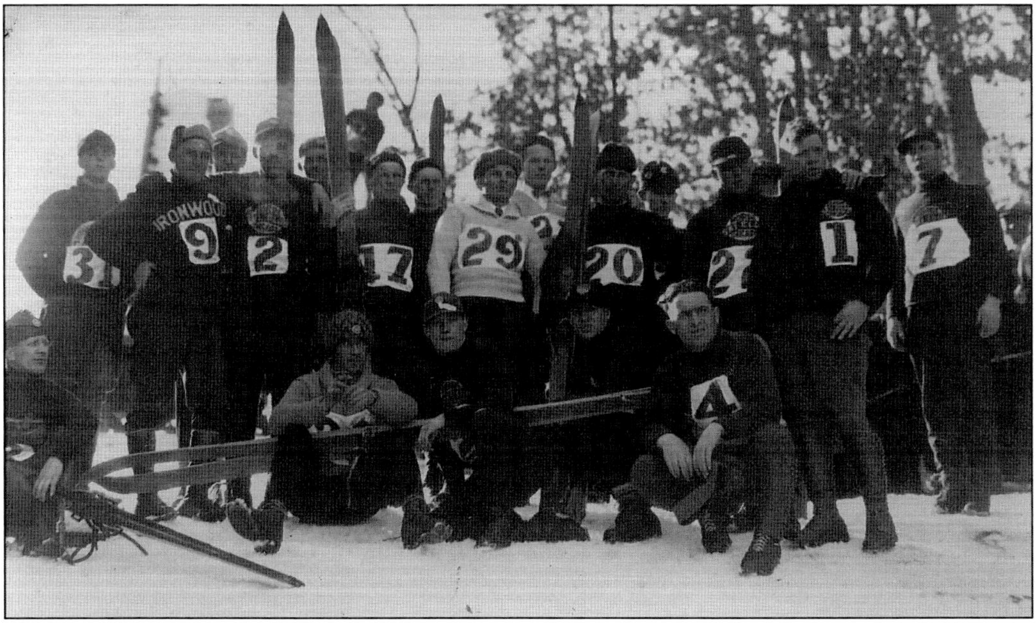

This is a group of Midwestern skiers posing for a photo.

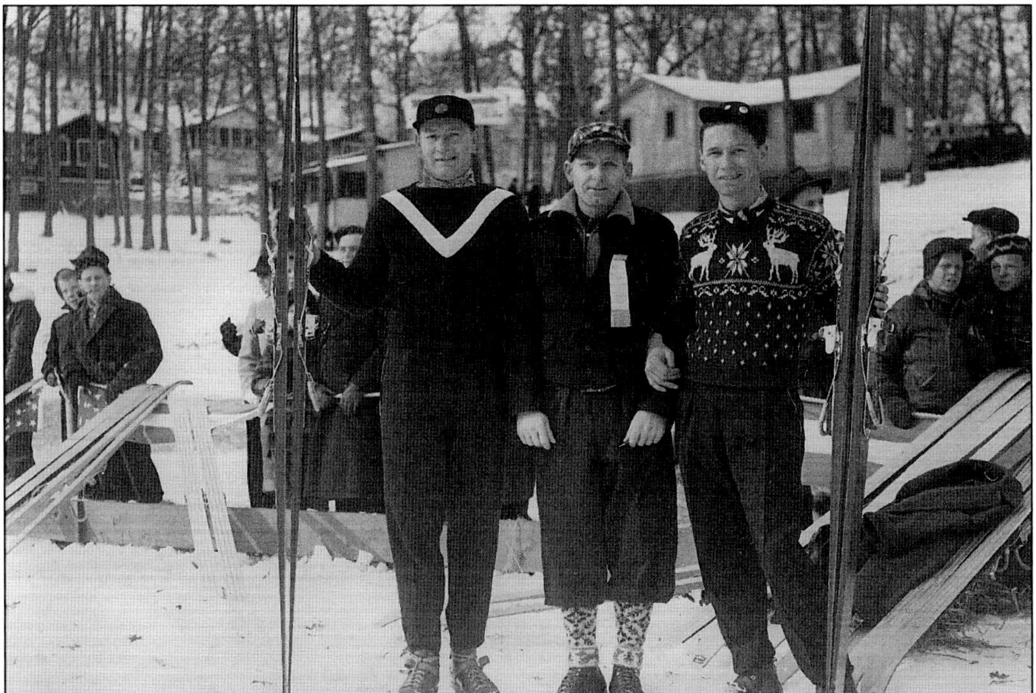

Pictured in 1946 at the Norge Ski Club in Chicago are three of the Midwest's finest. From left to right they are: Nick Heikkila of Ironwood, Michigan, Fred Bruun of Chicago, and Earl Minkin of Ironwood.

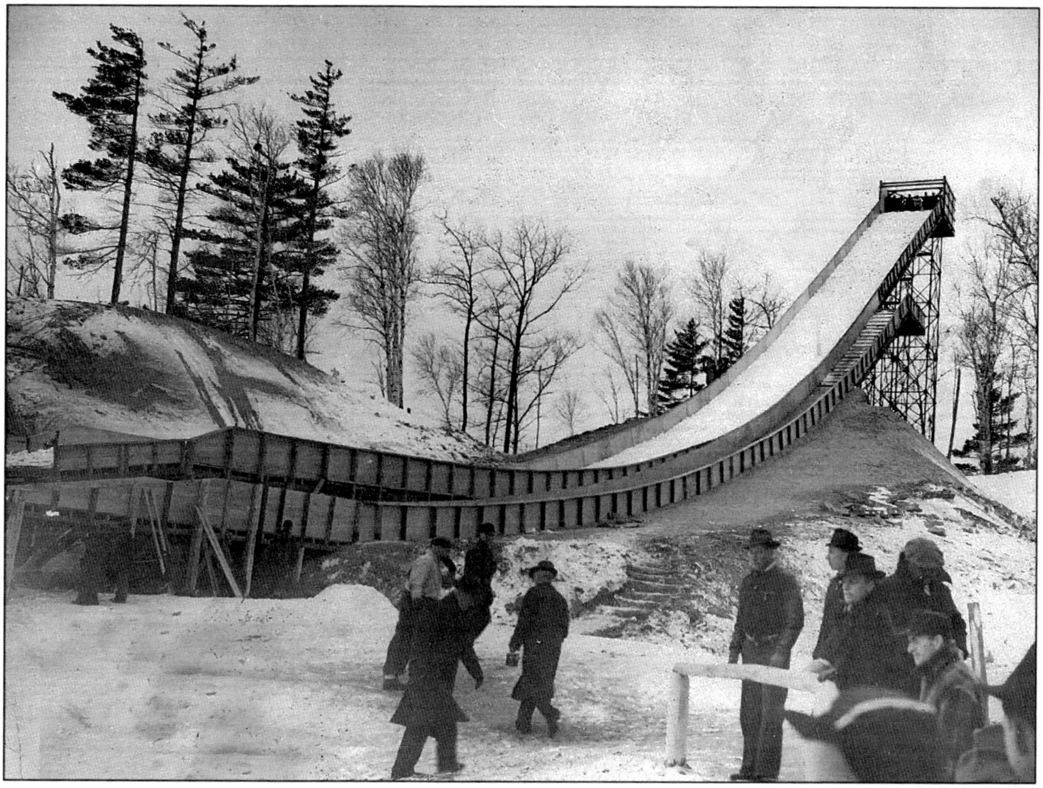

Pictured above and below is the dedication of Fond du Lac Ski Slide, Duluth, Minnesota (February 2, 1941).

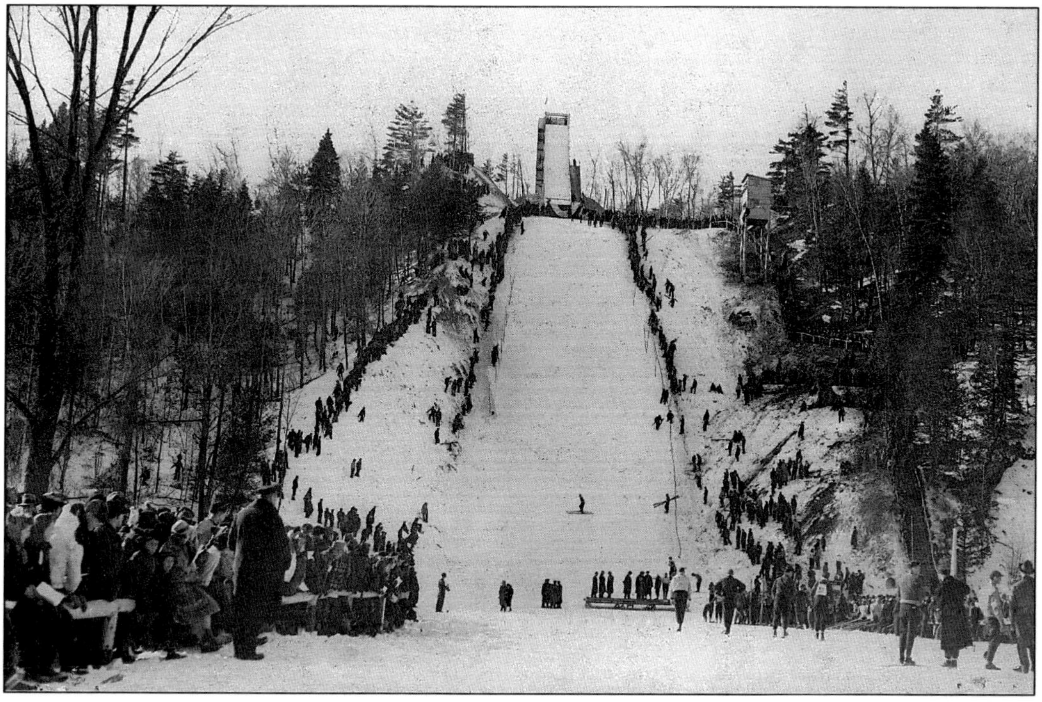

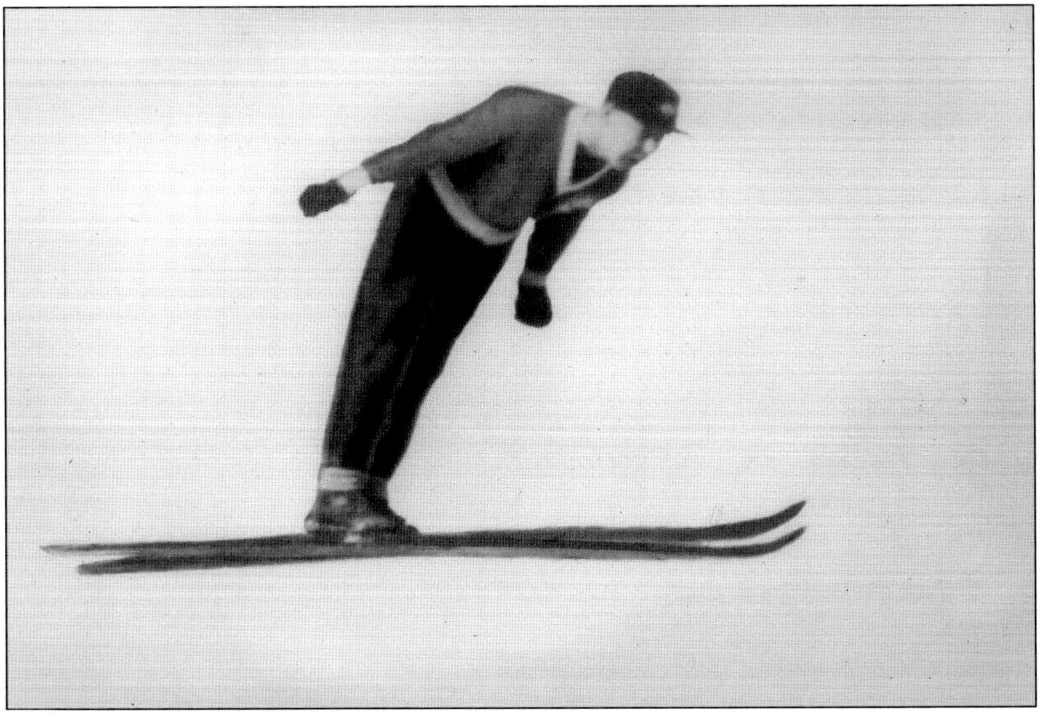

Paul Bietila, pictured above in 1938, was recognized as the outstanding American-born ski jumper at the time of his death. An award, established in 1940, is given in his memory each year to an American skier winning the normal hill competition. He was elected to the US National Ski Hall of Fame in 1970.

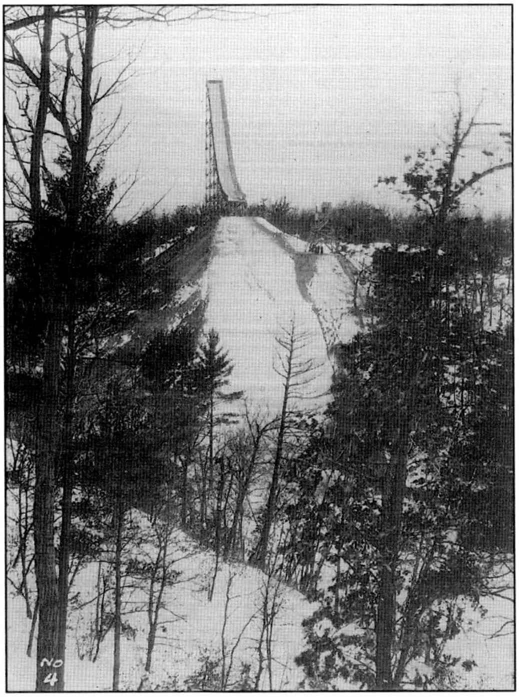

Pictured is the Battle Creek Ski Jump, one of the highest in the world at the time, located at the St. Paul (Minnesota) Winter Sports Carnival. On February 22, 1931, at the age of 12, Paul Bietila, one of six skiing brothers of Ishpeming, Michigan, set a new boy's record – a successful jump of 185 feet. In 1936, he won the intercollegiate ski championship at Lake Placid, New York. In the 1938 National Jumping Tournament, he placed behind Birger and Sigmund Ruud of Norway. On February 5, 1939, at age 20, he was injured practicing for the national ski jumping championships here at this jump. He sustained broken ribs and a broken jaw while making a 200-foot practice jump when he crashed into a steel post along the runway. He died of complications from pneumonia on February 26, 1939.

Five

THE SPORT ORGANIZES

FORMATION OF THE NATIONAL SKI ASSOCIATION

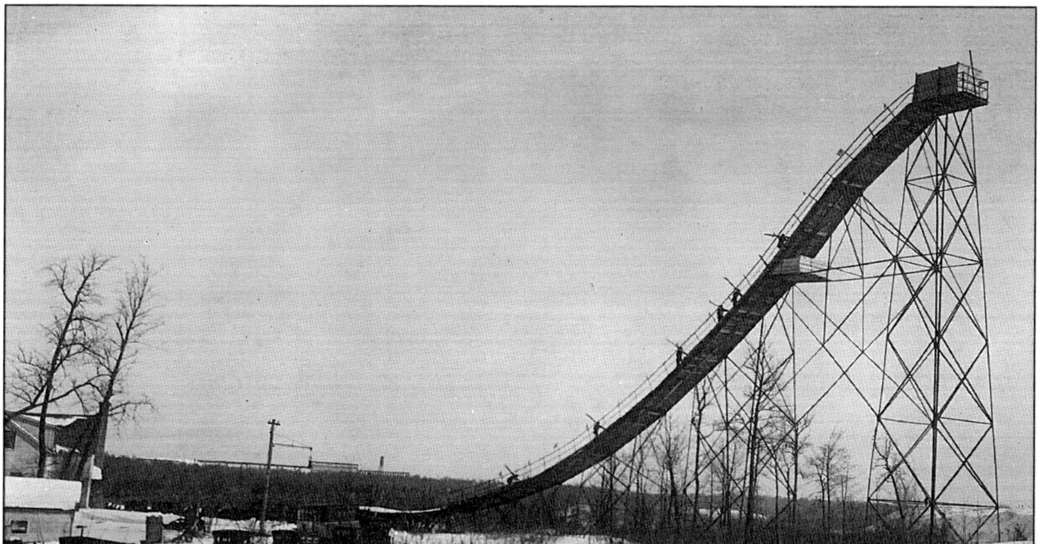

This is an early photo of a typical ski jumping hill with steel scaffold. Note the six skiers carrying their skis and climbing to the start of the scaffold.

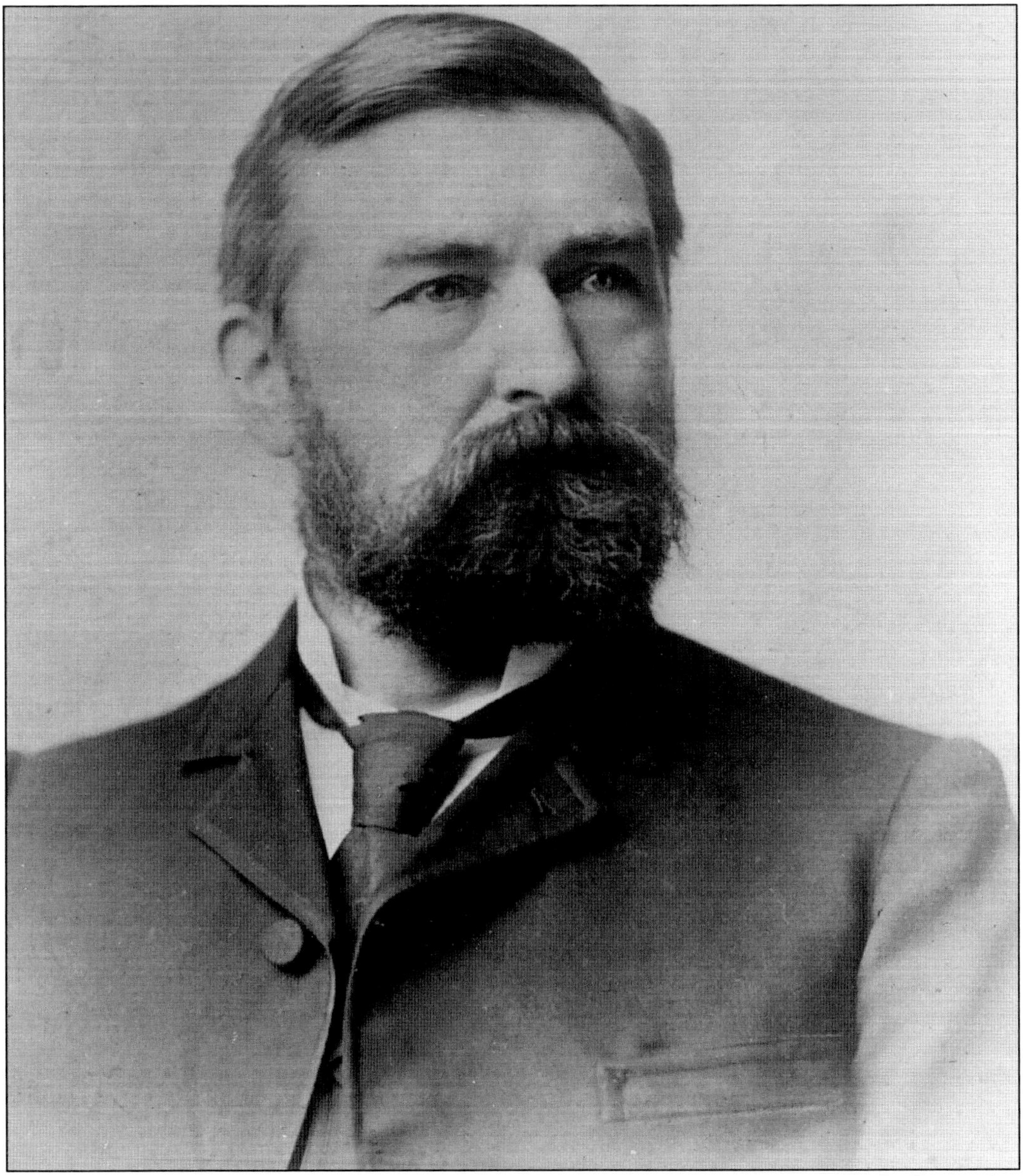

The National Ski Association was born in Ishpeming, Michigan, on February 22, 1905. This association was long talked about, but somehow lacked the man dynamic enough to get the job done, until Carl Tellefsen stepped forward and became the fledgling organization's first president. Tellefsen, from Trondheim, Norway, arrived in Ishpeming on March 14, 1888. George Newett, editor of Ishpeming's "*Iron Ore*" reported Tellefsen's debut this way, "Carl Tellefsen, a stranger employed at the Ishpeming National Bank, arrived too late to take part in the tournament, but he jumped 42 feet, 6 inches. He is an elegant rider who handles his skis gracefully and quickly." The jump referred to in the quote was an exhibition jump. Tellefsen joined the Ishpeming Ski Club, and played a leading role in getting the National Ski Association off the ground. Tellefsen had been a skier from his boyhood days in the early 1860s in his native Norway, and remained an active skier all his life until his death in Ishpeming in 1908. He was the first member elected to the U.S. National Ski Hall of Fame, in 1956.

Aksel Holter was the first secretary of the National Ski Association. A lifelong skier, he advocated the healthy aspect of exercise and fresh winter air. Holter later moved to Ashland, Wisconsin, where he set up a factory to manufacture skis. He was elected to the US National Ski Hall of Fame in 1956.

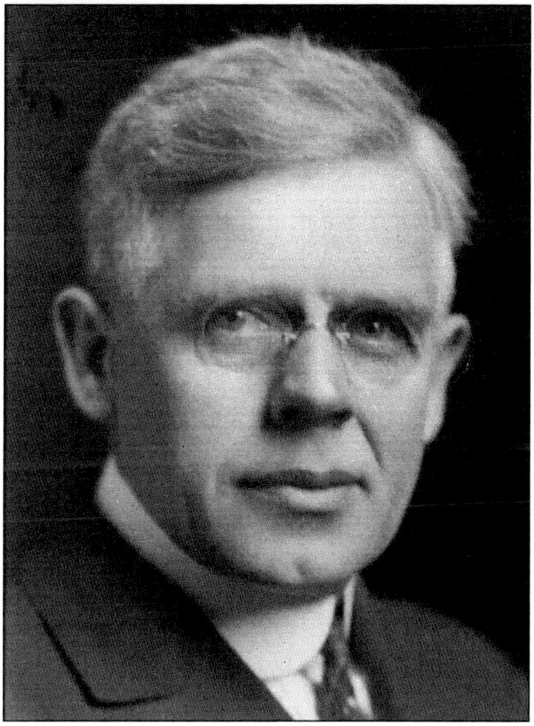

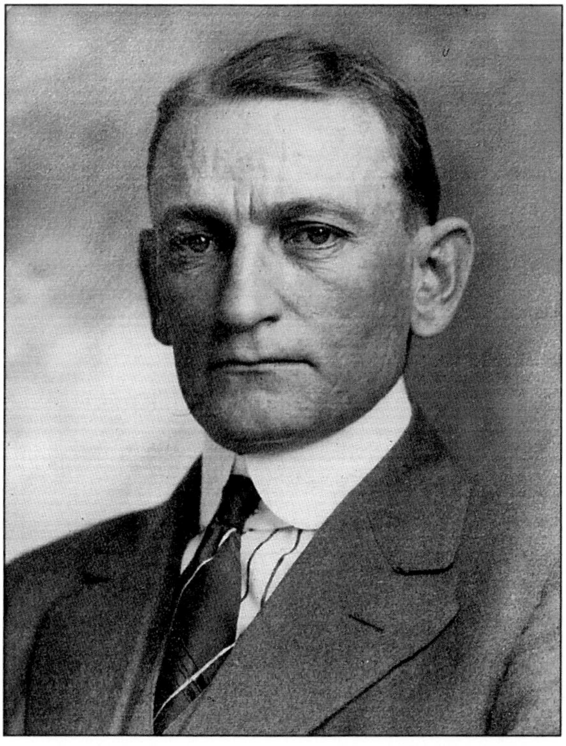

J. Simon Wahlman, an Ishpeming-born resident, was the first treasurer of the National Ski Association, organized February 21, 1905.

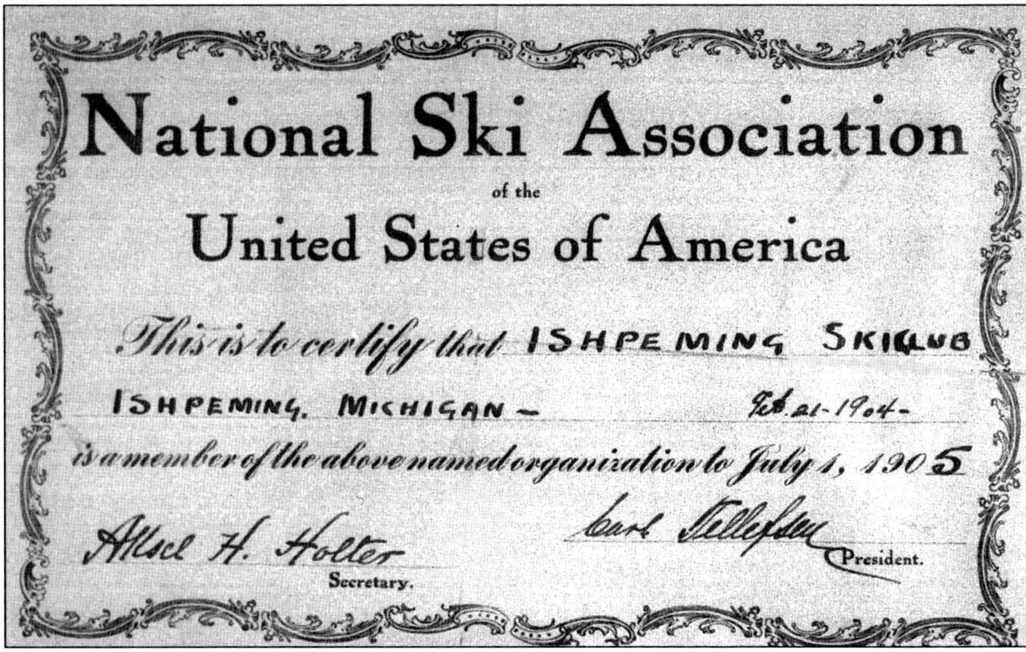

National Ski Association

of the

United States of America

This is to certify that ISHPEMING SKICLUB

ISHPEMING, MICHIGAN — Feb. 21-1904-

is a member of the above named organization to July 1, 1905

Aksel H. Holter
Secretary.

Carl Tellefsen
President.

The above certificate notes the entry of the Ishpeming Ski Club into the National Ski Association as one of its charter member clubs.

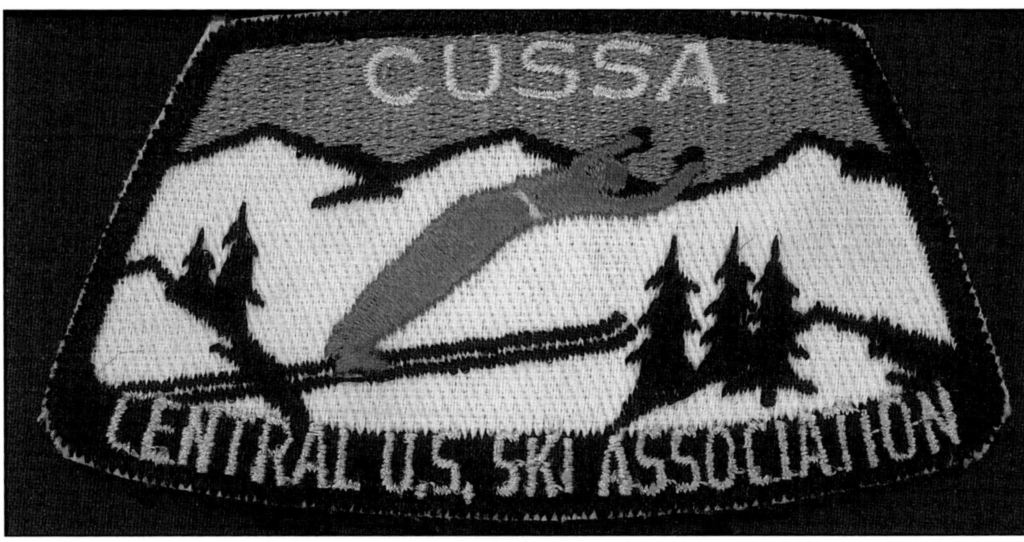

Until 1925, the National Ski Association (NSA) operated from a central division headquarters, and it was the leading and controlling factor in the development of skiing in the United States. The sport had grown rapidly in all areas of the country, and at the NSA Convention in 1925 in Canton, South Dakota, the policy of divisional organization was recognized. In 1924, the Eastern Division was formed in Saranac Lake, New York. In 1927, the Central Division became the home of the National Ski Association with Julius P. Blegen serving as its first president. The Central Division had 49 clubs in Minnesota, Wisconsin, Michigan, Illinois, South Dakota, and North Dakota.

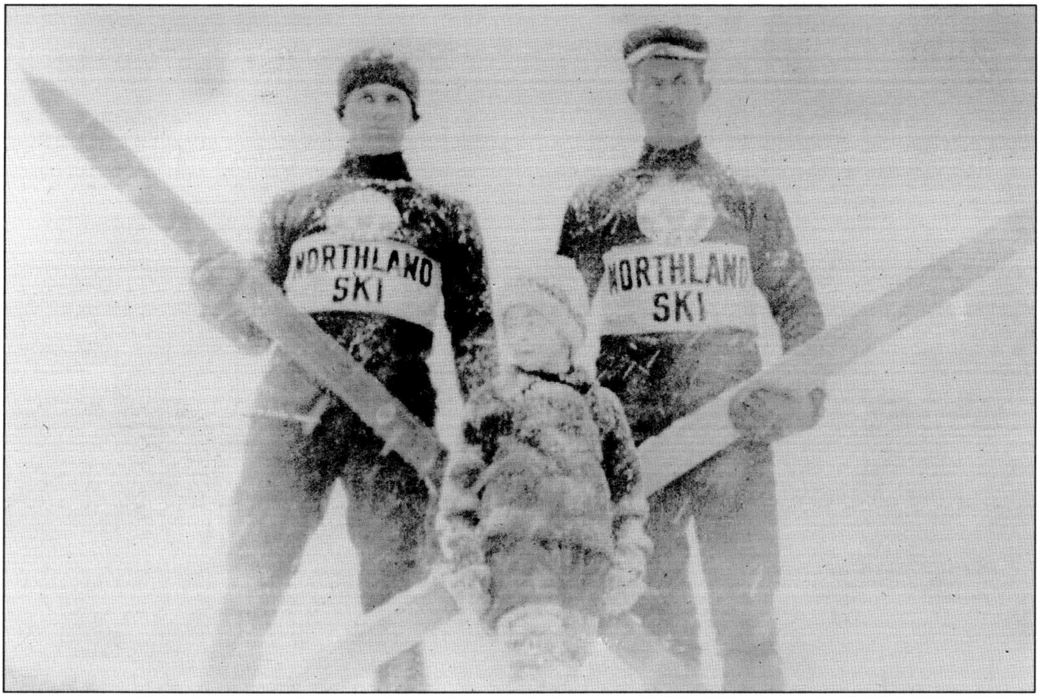

Pictured are Henry Hall (on the left), national ski jumping champion of 1920; Anders Haugen (on the right), former national ski jumping champion; and (in front) Joe Farmiloe, the smallest boy champion in the world.

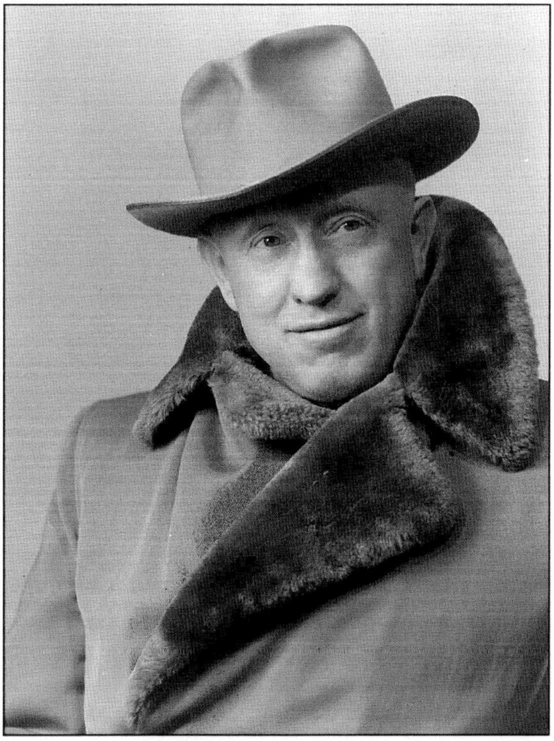

Arthur J. "Red" Barth of Milwaukee, Wisconsin, was one of the founders of the Central US Ski Officials "Judges" Association formed in 1935. He served as its first secretary. Art was editor of the *Central Ski Sport*, the oldest ski periodical in the country. He was an international ski jumping judge, served as chairman of the National Jumping Committee, as president of the National Ski Association in 1949, and was the first American Olympic Ski Jumping Judge in Europe. Arthur Barth was considered America's foremost ski jumping authority and was elected to the U.S. National Ski Hall of Fame in 1956.

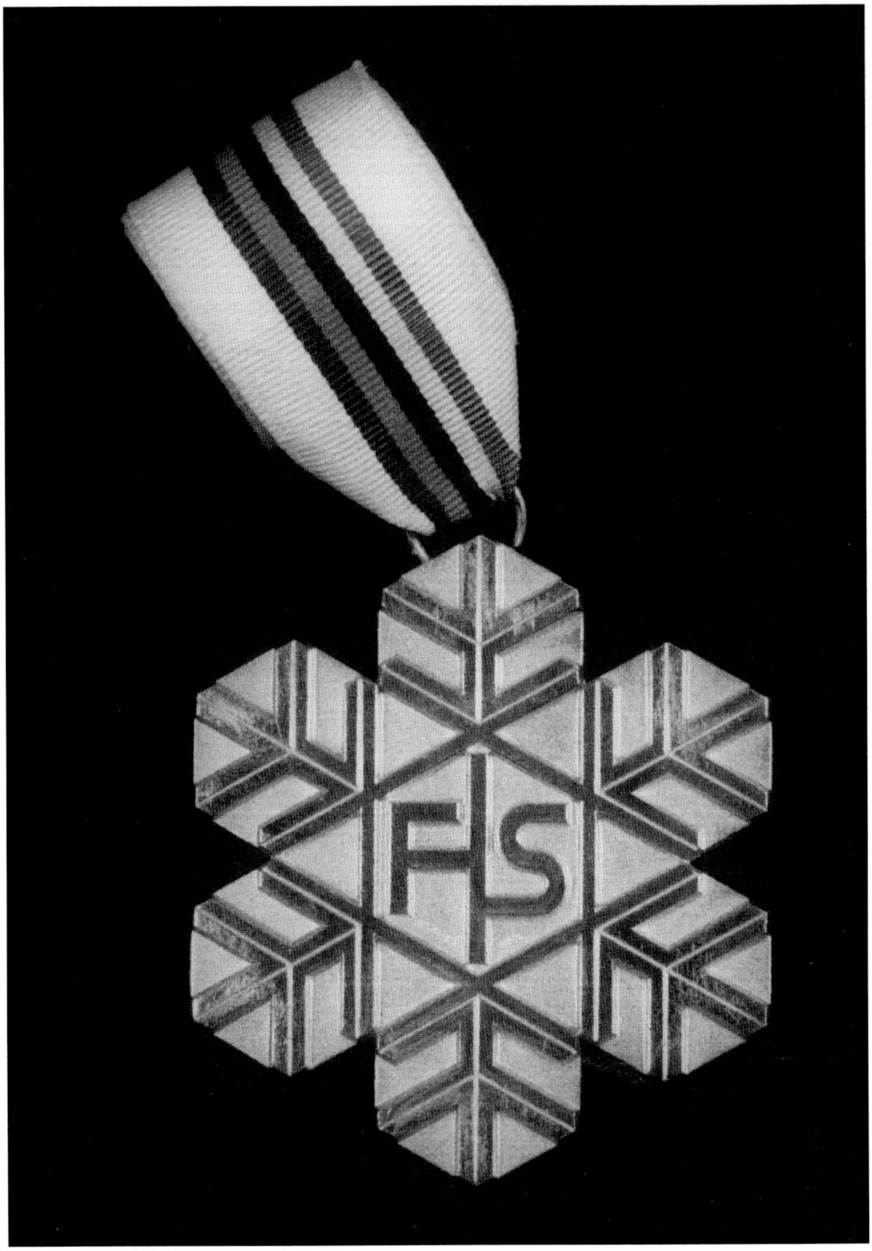

About 1900, international ski competition began to blossom, and an organization was needed to draw up uniform rules. At the invitation of the Norges Skiforbund, the first International Ski Congress met in Kristiana, Norway, on February 18, 1910. This original group consisted of ten European nations. When World War I broke out in 1914, international competition halted, as did the work of the fledgling international organization. Finally, at the International Ski Congress held at Chamonix, France, on February 2, 1924, the *Federation International de Ski* (FIS) was born. Its first president was Colonel Ivar Holmquist of Sweden, who served from 1924 until his retirement in 1934. He was replaced by Major N. R. Oestgaard of Norway.

This medal is on exhibit at the U.S. National Ski Hall of Fame and Museum.

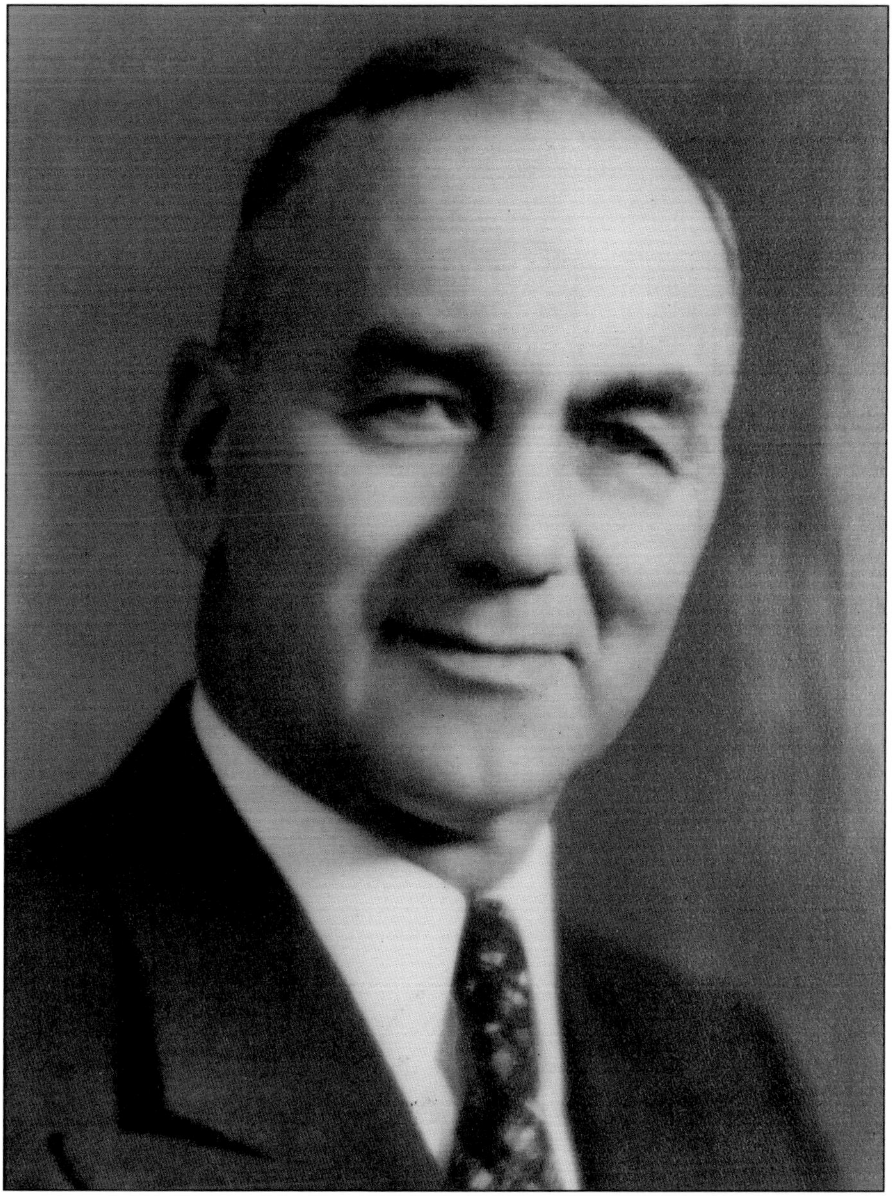

Julius Blegen was born near Oslo, Norway, in 1890, and emigrated to the United States in 1910. His specialty was cross-country skiing, and he was first class, winning the US Cross-Country Championships in 1911 and 1912, and qualifying for the US Winter Olympic Ski Team for the 1924 Olympics in Chamonix, France. He was unable to compete because of work commitments at the Minneapolis Parks and Recreation Department. Blegen was also a jumper and alpine skier. When the Central US Ski Association was formed in 1927, "Uncle Yoolius," as he was known to many, served as its first president until 1930, plus four years as association secretary, and in a number of Central and National committee positions. In 1945, the Central US Ski Association gave the National Ski Association (NSA) the Julius P. Blegen Award, which is awarded annually by the NSA to a member who has contributed outstanding service to the sport. It is the most prestigious award given by the national organization. He was elected to the US National Ski Hall of Fame in 1968.

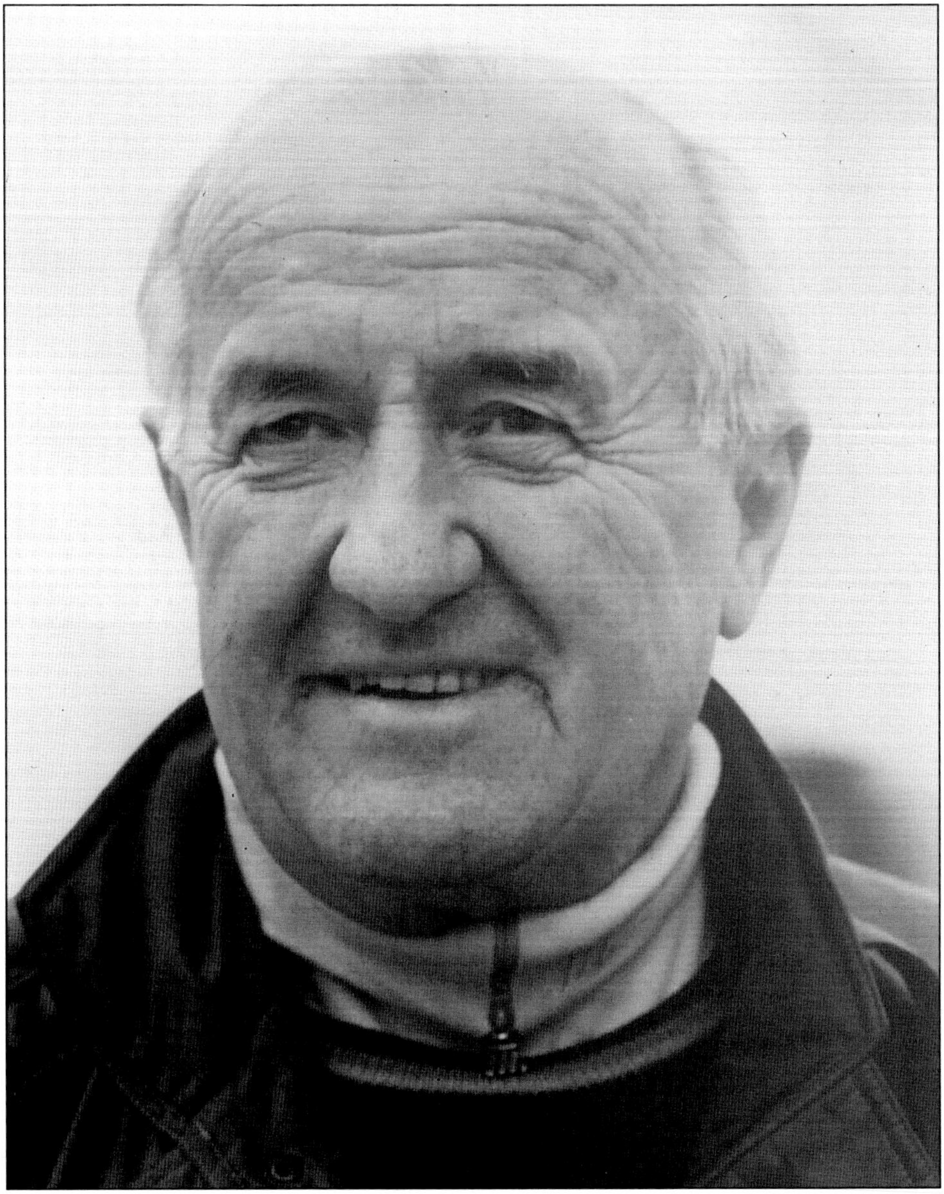

Marc Hodler was born on October 25, 1918, in Berne, Switzerland. As a college undergraduate, he was selected for the Swiss National Alpine Racing Team, but a serious accident while training for the 1938 World Championships ended his career as a competitor. He then turned to technical and administrative activities. From 1939 to 1948 he was the coach and trainer of the Swiss Alpine Team. From 1940 to 1951 he was vice-president of the Swiss National Ski Federation and was responsible for the first alpine competition at the Olympic Winter Games in 1948. Within the FIS, he presided over the downhill/slalom committees from 1946 to 1951. In 1948 he was elected to the FIS Council and became its president in 1951. He has been a member of the Swiss International Olympic Committee since 1963 and vice-president of the IOC since 1993, chairing the IOC Legal Committee. Marc has a law degree from the University of Berne and has a practice there. He was inducted into the U.S. Ski Hall of Fame in 1981.

Six

Olympic Movement

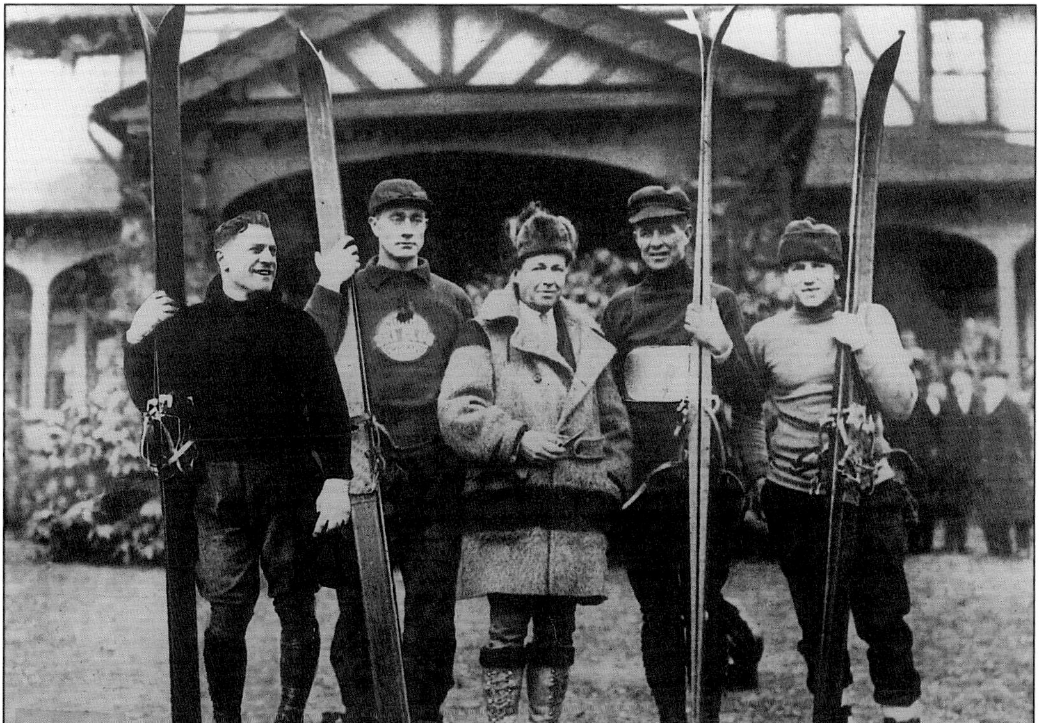

The 1924 Olympic Team is pictured here, from left to right: Ragnar Omtvedt, Harry Lien, Colonel George Emerson Leach (manager of the team), Anders Haugen, and Lemoine Batson.

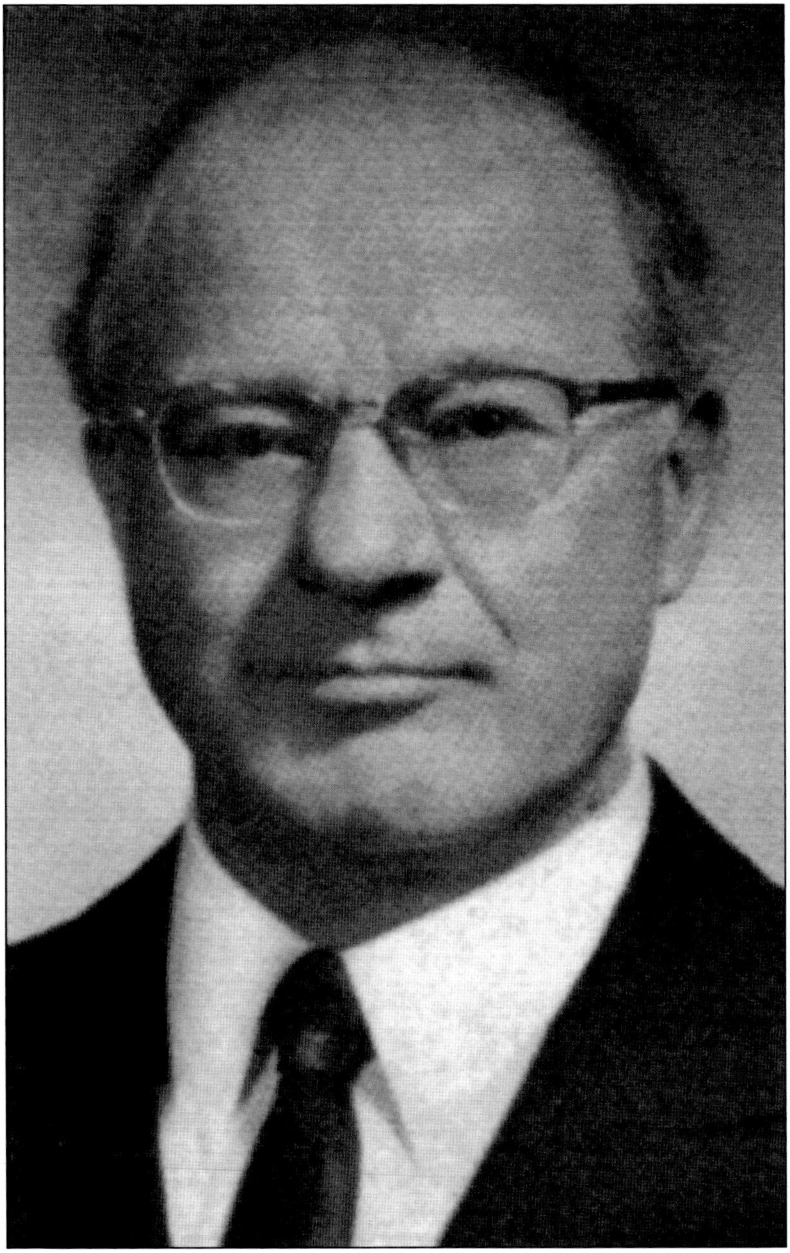

Avery Brundage was the amateur athletic czar for over forty years. He rose in the athletic administration of the Amateur Athletic Union, eventually becoming its president. After the 1938 Olympics at Amsterdam, Brundage became president of the US Olympic Committee, succeeding a young army general named Douglas McArthur. At the 1936 Olympic Games in Berlin, Brundage was elected to the International Olympic Committee, rising quickly in the organization's hierarchy for 20 tumultuous years, becoming its president in 1952. During his presidency, he faced all the issues besetting the modern Olympic movement – eligibility, commercialism, nationalism, politics, doping, and a good number more. Brundage's approach to his Olympic credo was unyielding, with no room for compromise, and as a result was unpopular within the Olympic movement.

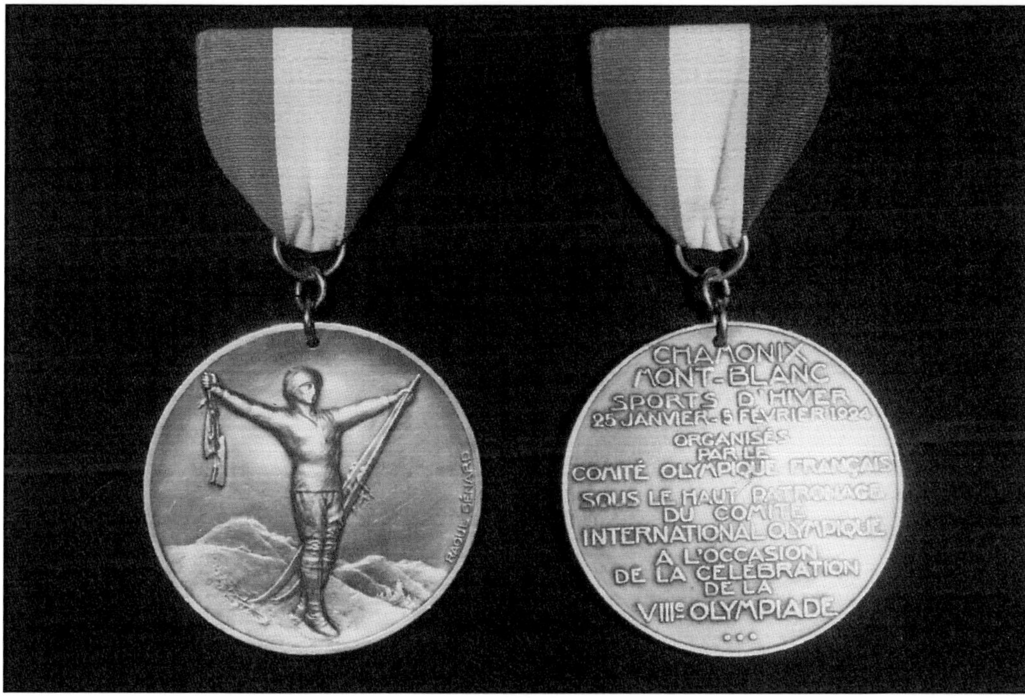

Pictured above is Anders Haugen's medal.

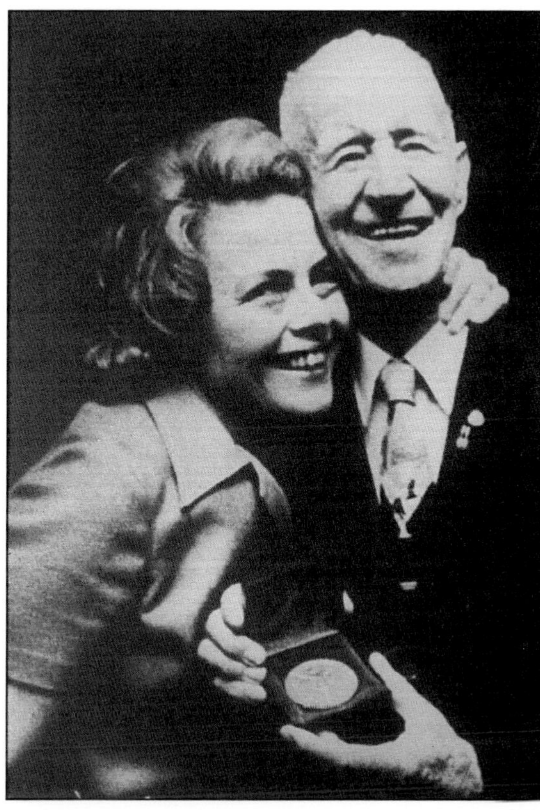

Anders Haugen was a member of the first United States Olympic Special Jumping Team that competed in the first Winter Olympic Games at Chamomix, France, in 1924. In the Olympic competition, Anders finished in fourth place according to the judges. Fifty years later, noted Norwegian ski historian, Jakob Vaage, noticed that there was an error in calculating the score of the event, and Thorlief Haug, who was awarded the bronze medal was actually edged out by Haugen by .075 of a point. Vaage contacted United States National Historian, William Banks Berry, and Anna Marie Magnussen, daughter of the now deceased Haug. In a ceremony in Olso, Norway, on September 12, 1974, Magnussen (on the left in photo) presented the bronze 1924 Olympic medal to Anders Haugen (on the right in photo). Although the error was corrected, the International Olympic Committee does not recognize this event, and still considers Thorlief Haug the bronze medal winner.

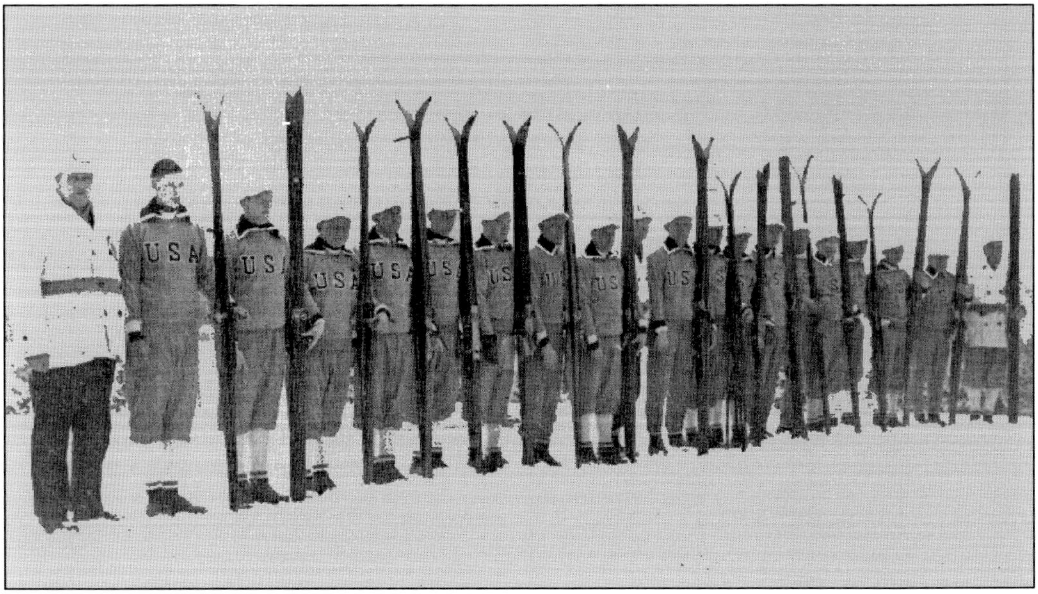

Pictured above is the 1932 American Olympic Ski Team. They are, from left to right: Alf Halvorson, (assistant coach), Richard E. Parsons, Rolf Monsen, Robert H. Reid, John M. Ericksen, James Harsh, Lloyd C. Ellingson, Pedar Falstad, Caspar Oimen, Prof. Charles A. Proctor, (manager), Roy Mikkelsen, Nils Backstrom, Olle Zetterstrom, Carl Holmstrom, John D. Steele, Edward J. Blood, Norton R. Billings, Erling N. Anderson, Lemoine Batson, and Julius P. Blegen, (head coach).

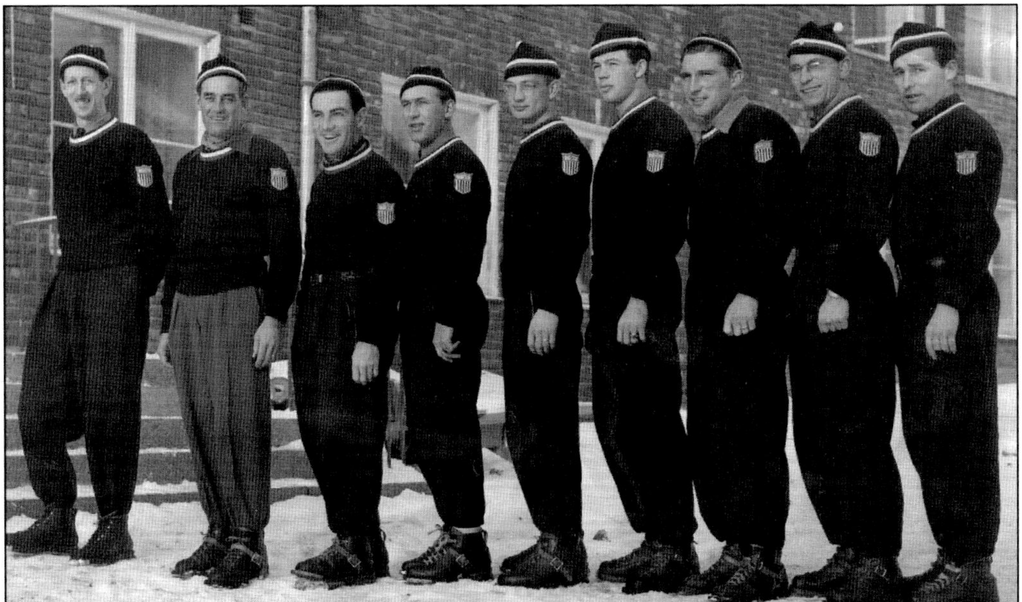

The 1952 Olympic Ski Jumping Team is pictured, from left to right: Major Hjalmer Hvam (Beaverton, OR), Coach Harold Sorensen (Colorado Springs, CO), Art Devlin (Lake Placid, NY), Art Tokle (Brooklyn, NY), Willis Olson (Eau Claire, WI), Keith Wegeman (Steamboat Springs, CO), Crosby Perry-Smith (Steamboat Springs), Wilbert Rasmussen (Ishpeming, MI), and Ralph Bietila (Ishpeming).

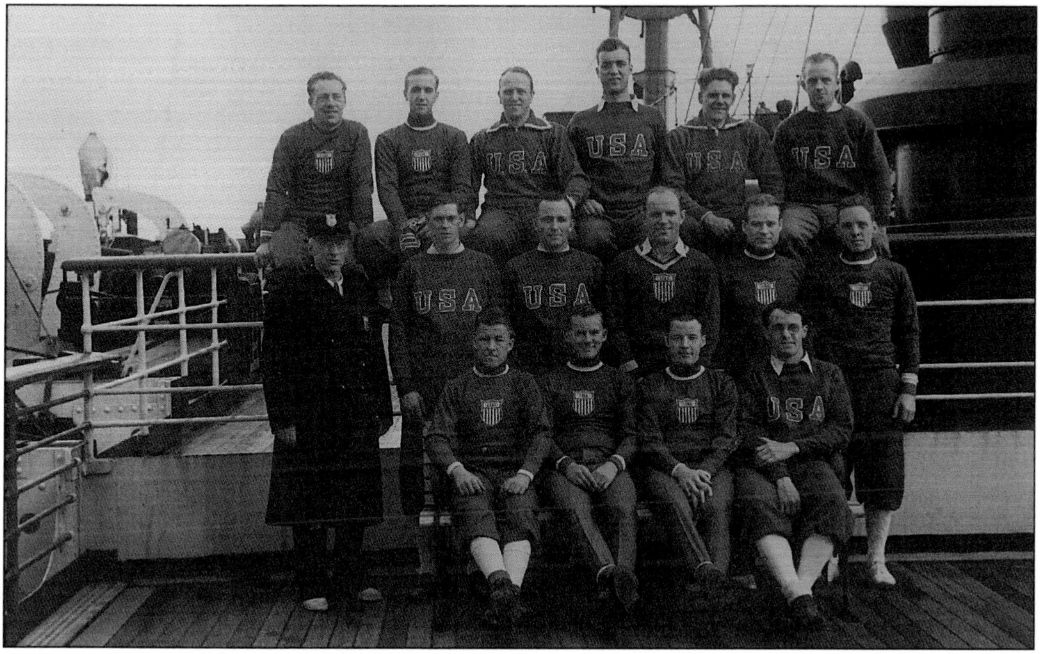

Pictured above is the 1936 Olympic Men's Team. They are, from left to right: (front row) Walter Bietila, Jimmy Hendrickson, Sverre Fredheim, and Edward Blood; (middle row) Dr. Hildebrant (in black coat), Richard Parson, Nils Backstrom, Roy Mikkelsen, Alex Bright, and Bob Livermore; (back row) Birger Torrissen, Ottar Satre, Rolf Monson, Warren Chivers, Casper Oimen, and Magnus Satre.

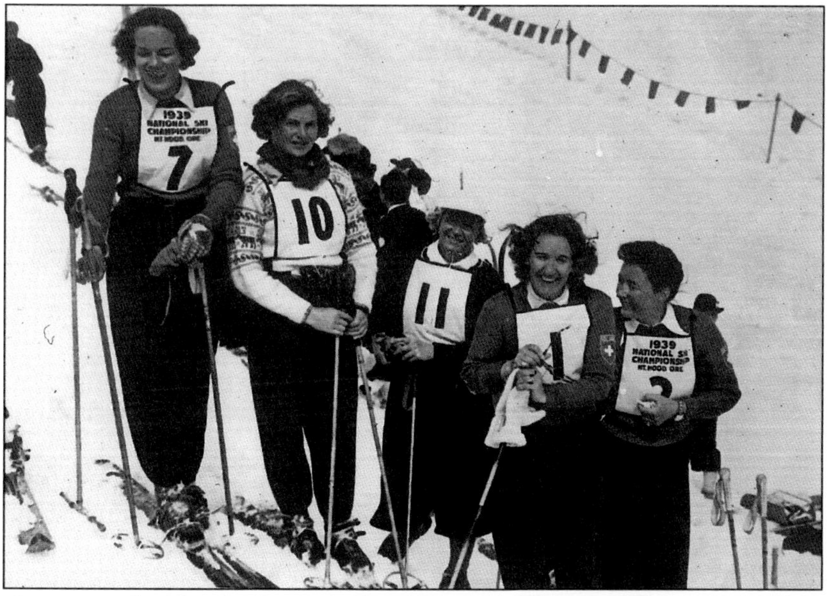

Pictured above at the finish line of the National Championships and Olympic team try-outs at Mt. Hood in 1939, is American Elizabeth Woolsey (number 11) with members of the British and Swiss teams. They are, from left to right: Doris Friedrich of Switzerland, Helen Palmer-Tomkinson of Great Britain, Woolsey, Nini von Arx-Zogg of Switzerland, and Erna Steuri of Switzerland.

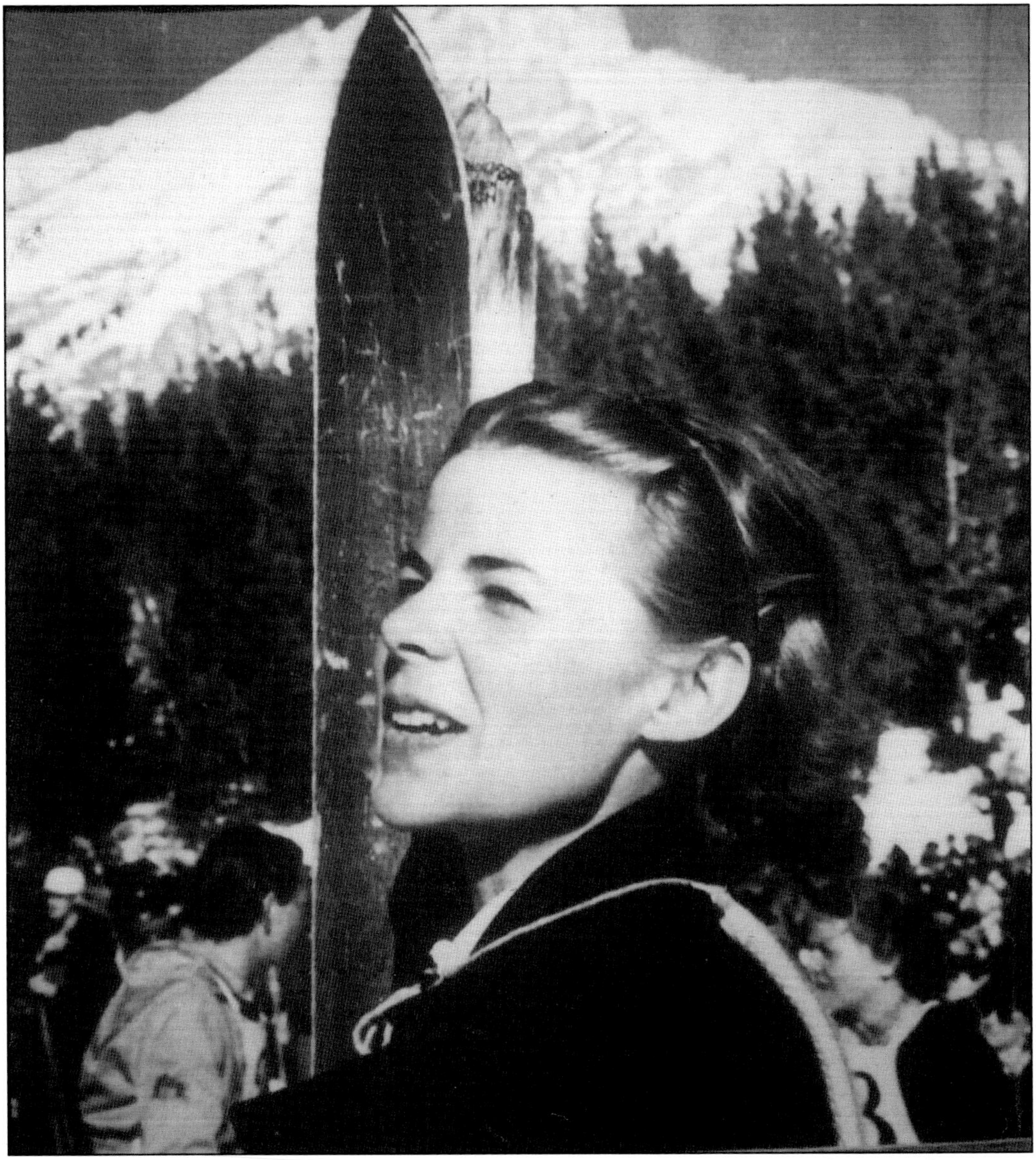

Grace Carter Lindley of Wayzata, Minnesota, was one of the top women skiers in the nation between 1936 and 1940. She was selected to represent the United States in 1936 at the FIS World Championships at Innsbruck, Austria, and was selected as a member of the 1936 United States Women's Olympic Team. She also won the first National Ski Association Slalom Championship at Stowe, Vermont, in 1938 and the National Women's Downhill Championship at Sun Valley in 1940. She was elected to the US National Ski Hall of Fame in 1966.

Barbara Hale Ferries, (above and below) born in Houghton, Michigan, was taught to ski at an early age by Fred Longsdorf of Michigan Technological University in Houghton. In 1960, she won the National Ski Association National Junior Girls' Slalom Championship as well as the National Junior Girls' Combined title. Rising to international stardom, Barbara placed third in the women's downhill in the 1962 FIS World Championships in Chamonix, France. She added a Roch Cup and Harriman Cup to her trophy case and was a member of the 1964 American Olympic team. Barbara Hale Ferries was elected to the US National Ski Hall of Fame in 1978.

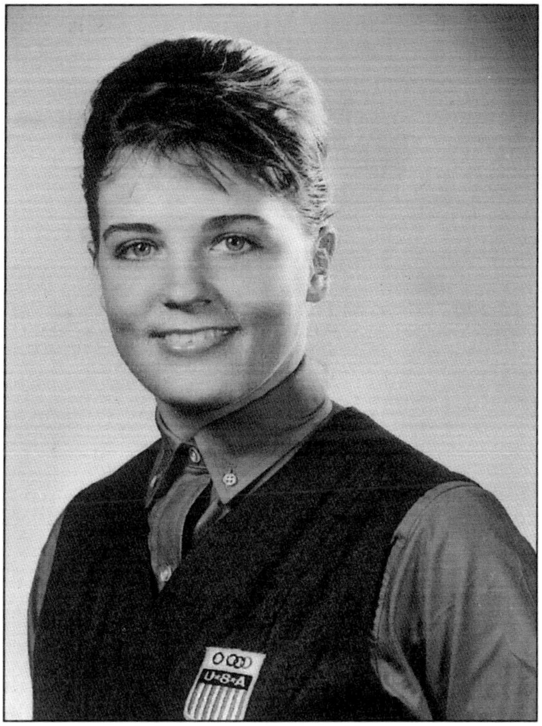

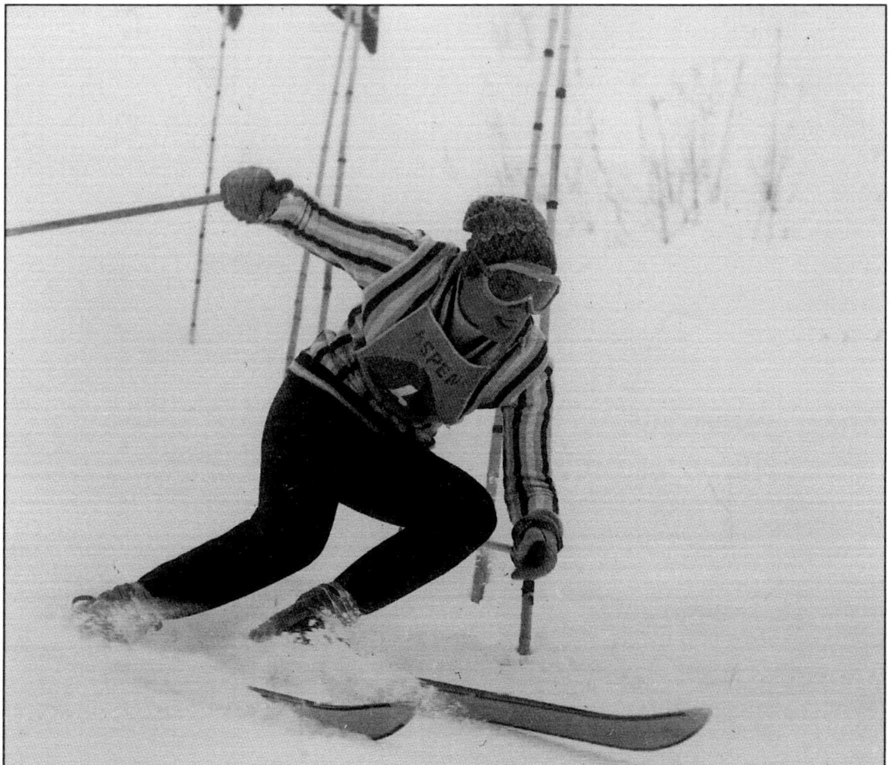

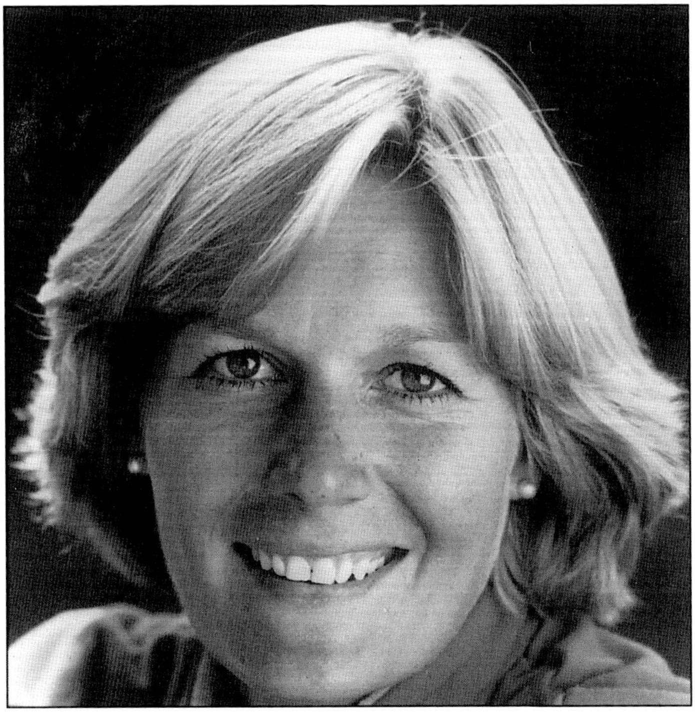

Cindy Nelson, of northern Minnesota, began skiing at the age of three and was first named to the US Ski Team in 1971. Cindy is known as one of the best international racers ever for the United States. She was elected to the US National Ski Hall of Fame in 1976.

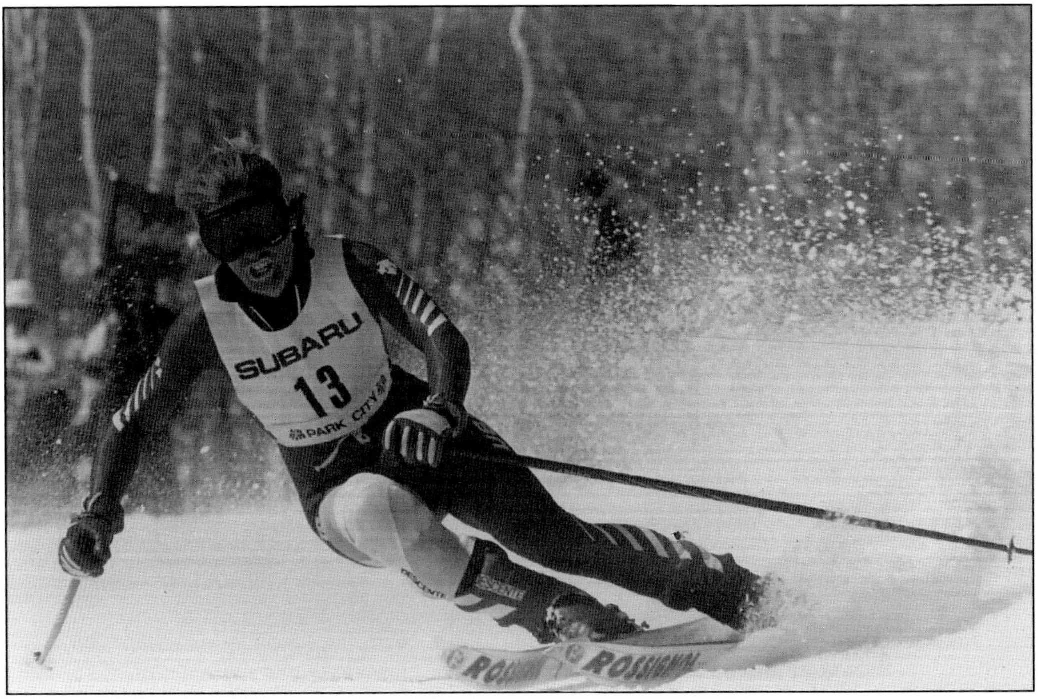

Eugene "Gene" Kotlarek began ski jumping when he was five. He was the Minnesota State High School Jumping Champion in 1957, winning the Junior National title the same year. In 1958, he was the North American Jumping Champion. Gene was selected for the 1964 Olympic Jumping Team and competed at Innsbruck, Austria. Kotlarek was a member of the 1966 FIS Team, and competed at the Holmenkollen in Norway, and followed this competition with a win in the National Jumping Tournament at Levenworth, Washington, in 1967. He was then named coach of the United States Ski Association's National Jumping Team from 1968 through 1970. Kotlarek was elected to the US National Ski Hall of Fame in 1982.

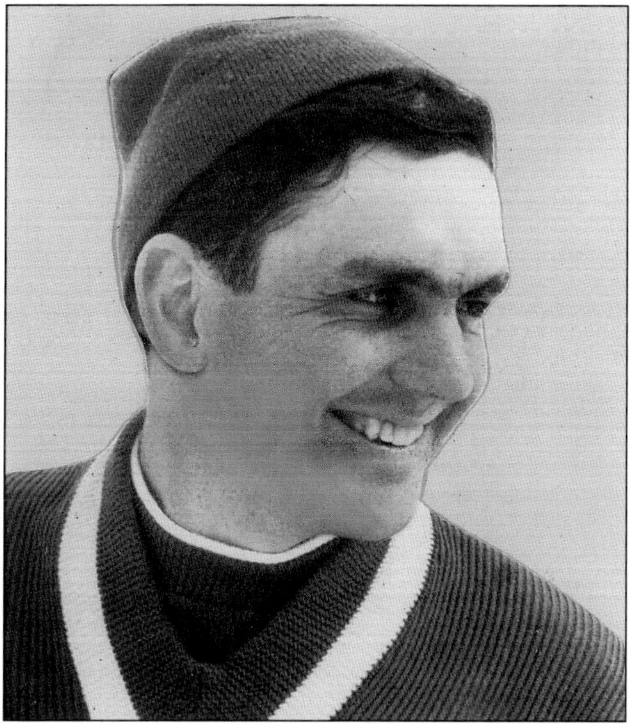

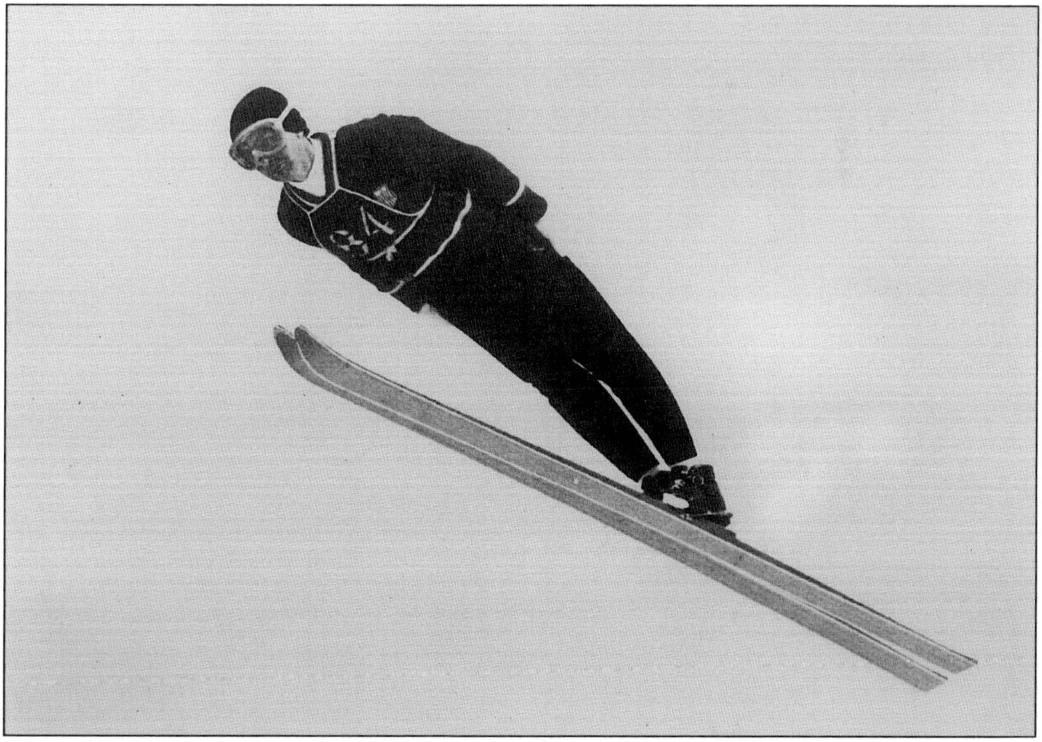

Eugene Kotlarek jumping at Iron Mountain, Michigan is pictured here.

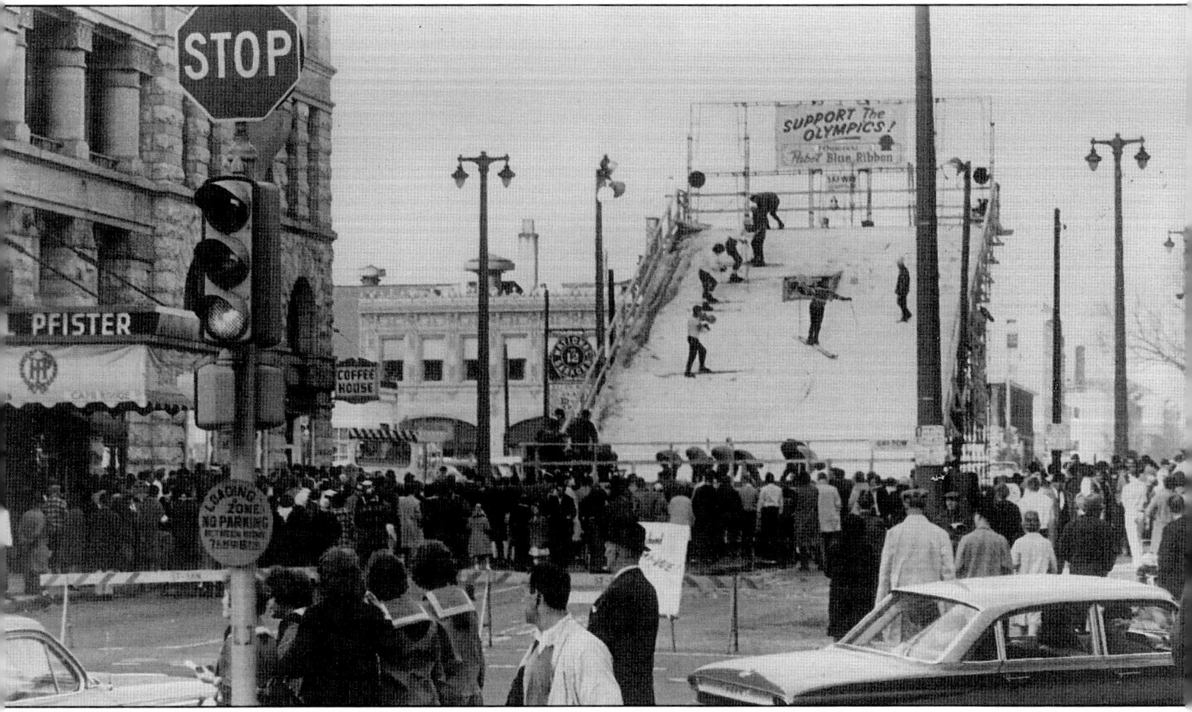

A ski ramp was constructed in downtown Milwaukee, Wisconsin, in the early 1960s showcasing alpine skiing to help raise funds to support the United States ski team at the Olympics.

Seven

Nordic Style

The Jumpers, the Hills, Cross Country

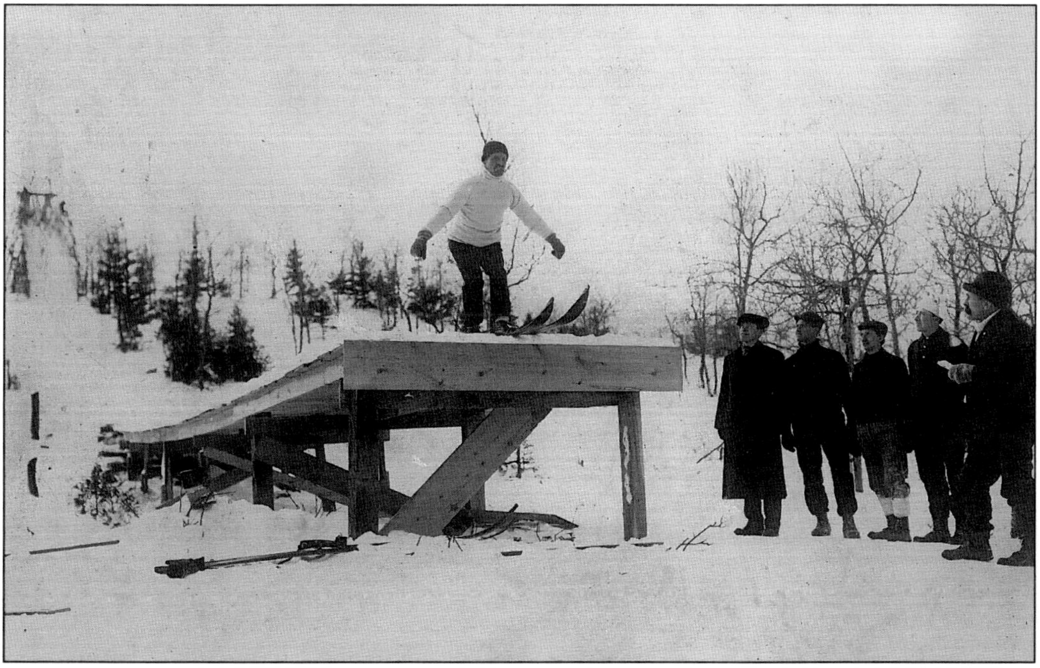

Gustave Bye on the first ski slide at Duluth, Minnesota, in the early 1900s is pictured above.

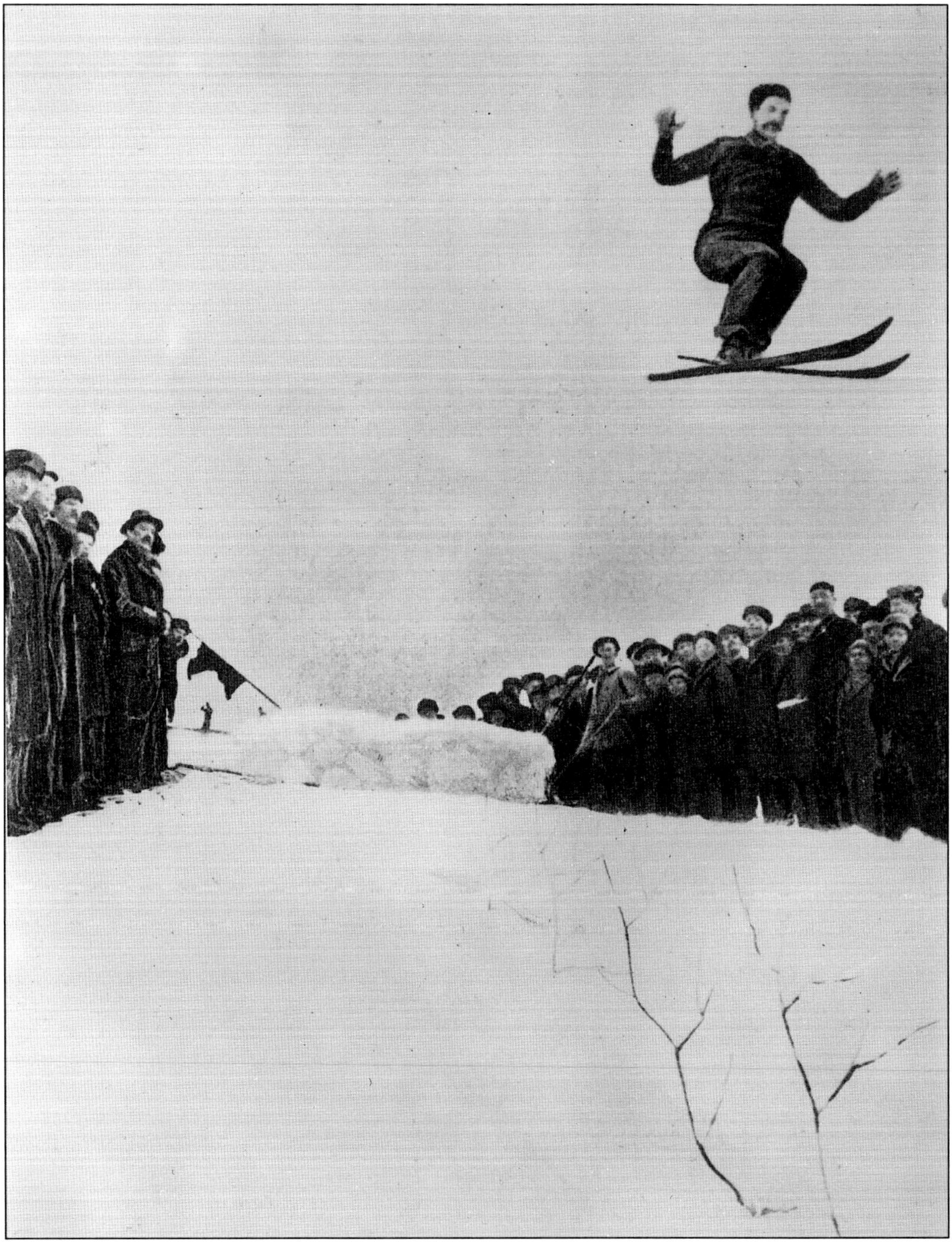

This photo shows Ole Mangseth ski jumping in 1907. Note the height and early style – more nerve than technique.

Jackson Hill, east of Ishpeming, Michgan, was used by several early ski jumpers.

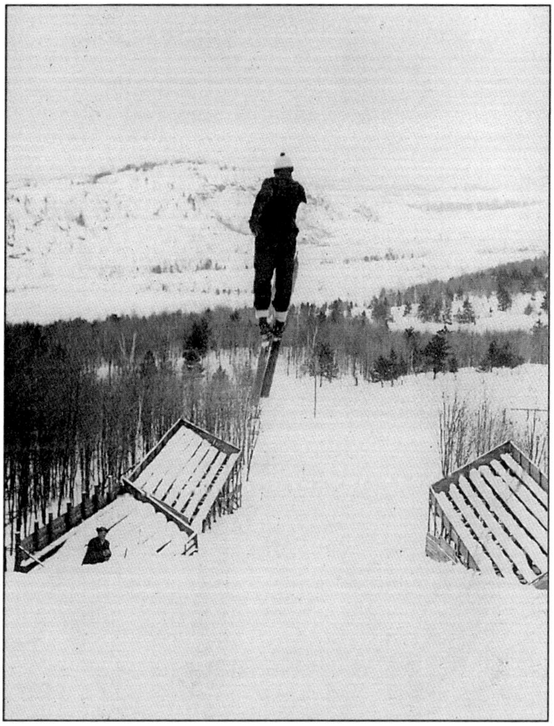

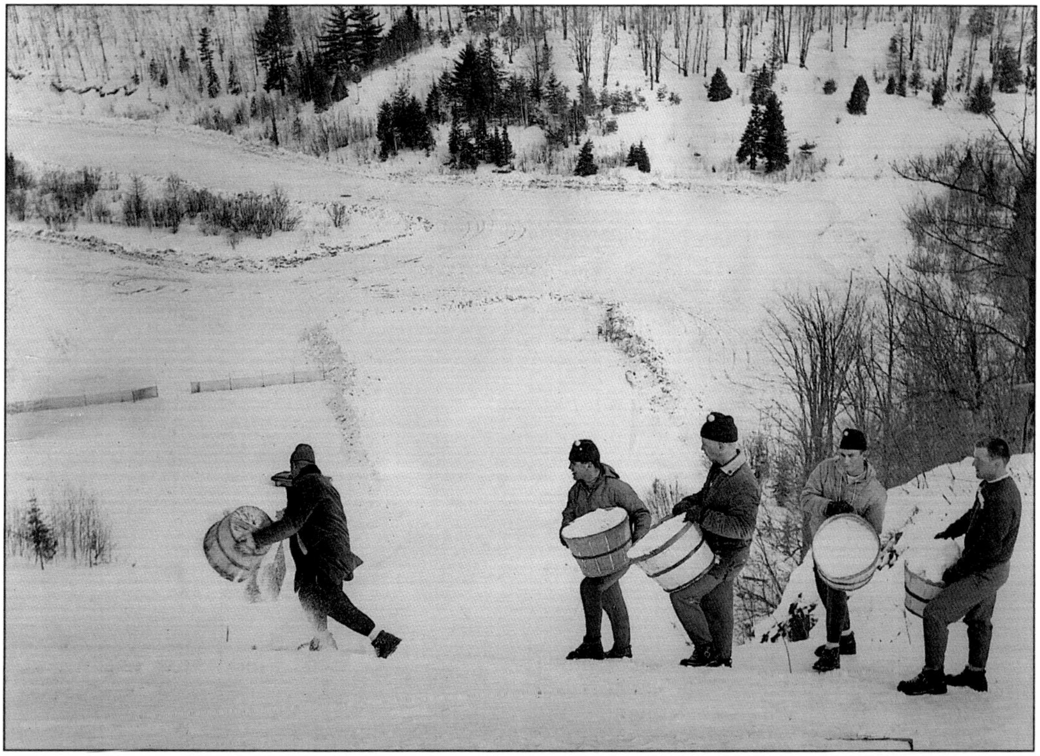

Ski jumpers in the Midwest preparing their ski hill for the season are pictured above.

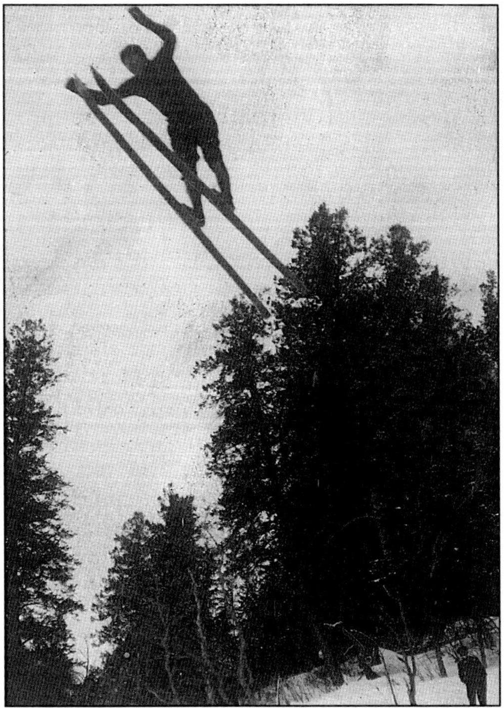

Pictured at left is Henry Hall executing a new world record jump of 203 feet, at Steamboat Springs, Colorado in 1917. This is an example of one of the earliest ski jumping styles. Henry was a native of Ishpeming, Michigan. When he made his record leap at Steamboat Springs, ski fans stuck a flag into his hand and carried him back to his hotel. He was the first American to establish a recognized world ski jumping record.

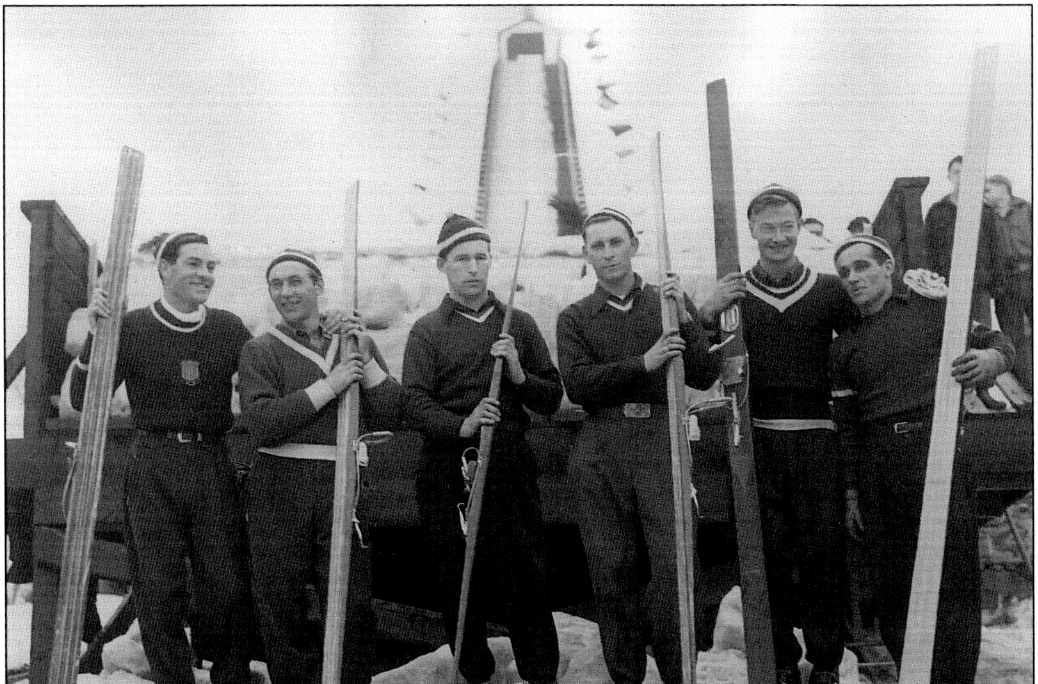

The Iron Mountain, MI, Kiwanis Ski Club jumping meet (c. 1950). Shown left to right are: Art Devlin (Lake Placid, NY), Art Tokle (Rockaway, NJ), Ralph Bietila (Ishpeming, MI), Wilbur Rasmussen (Negaunee, MI), Billy Olson (Eau Claire, WI), and Joe Perrault, (Ishpeming).

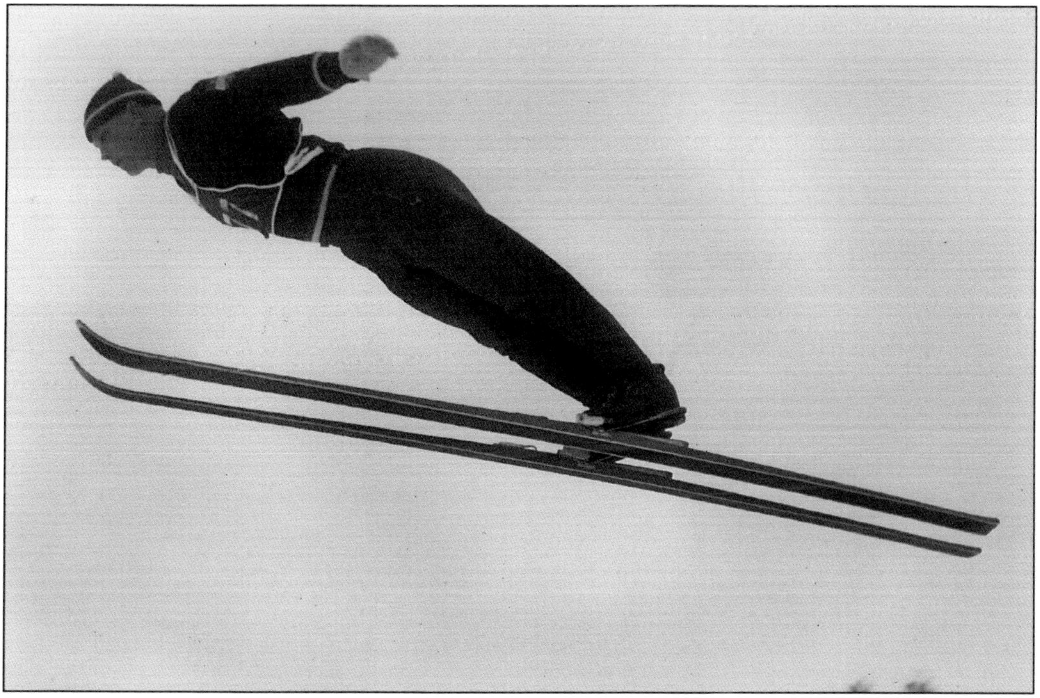

Rudy Maki is pictured above performing the classic jackknife style of the 1950s, still considered by many as the most beautiful of all ski jumps. Rudy was elected to the US National Ski Hall of Fame in 1982.

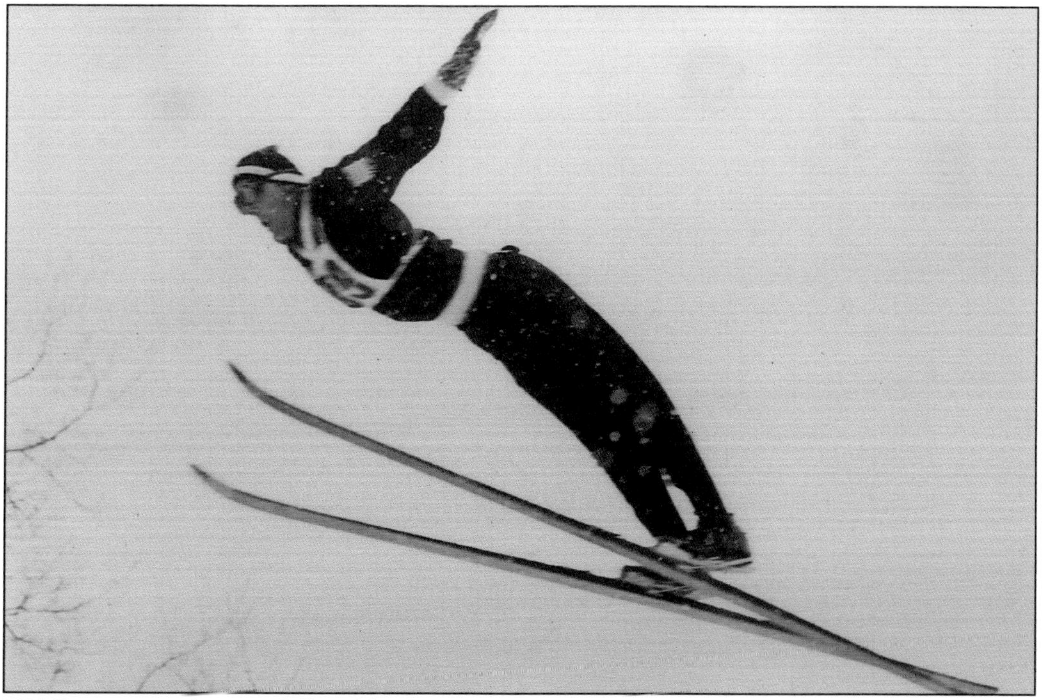

Wil Rasmussen doing a full jackknife style. He was elected to the US National Ski Hall of Fame in 1988.

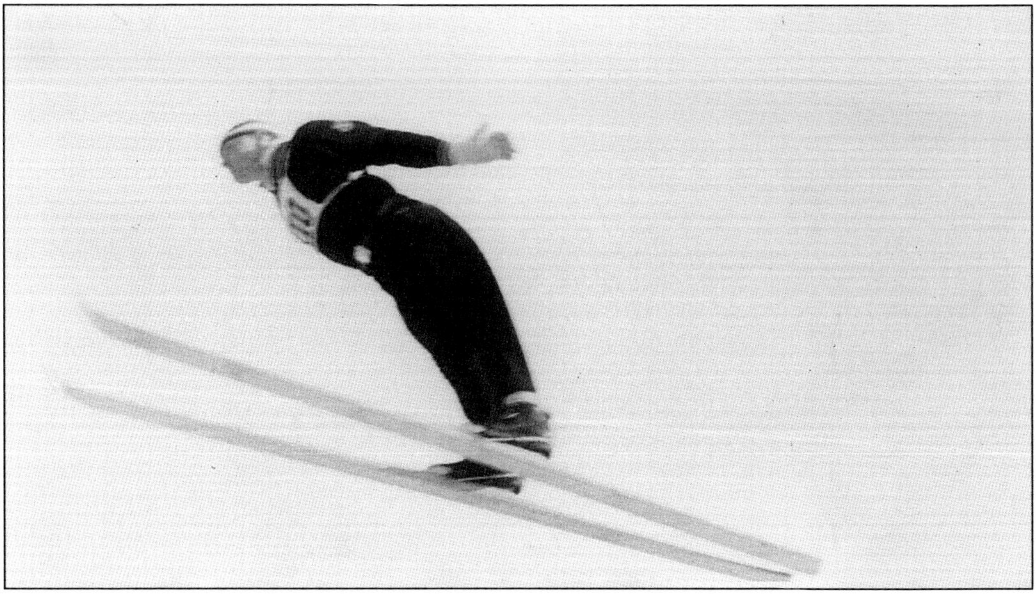

Coy Hill is pictured here, demonstrating an adaptation of the style Germans used, which involved a lot of drag on the body. He was elected to the US National Ski Hall of Fame in 1974.

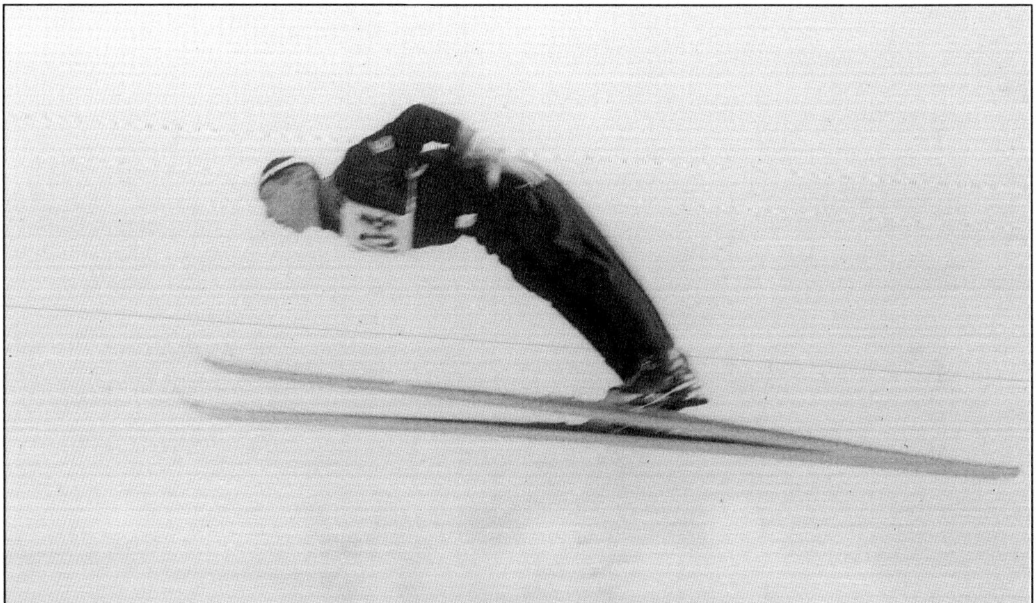

Ray Gauthier is shown above, doing the extreme jackknife on February 17, 1957.

All skiers on pages 65–66 are from Ishpeming, Michigan.

Pictured at right is Reed Zuehlke of Eau Claire, WI, in 1978. Skiing on plastic was a fairly new innovation, which allowed skiers the opportunity to train on actual jumping hills in the off-season.

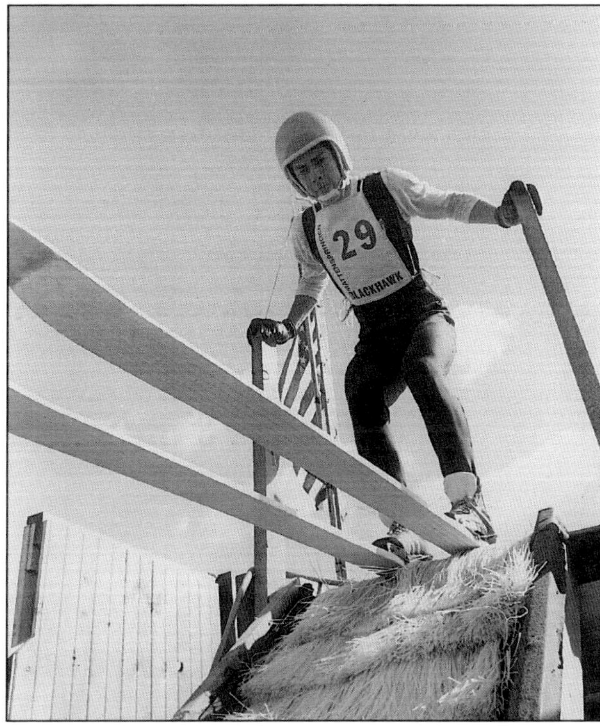

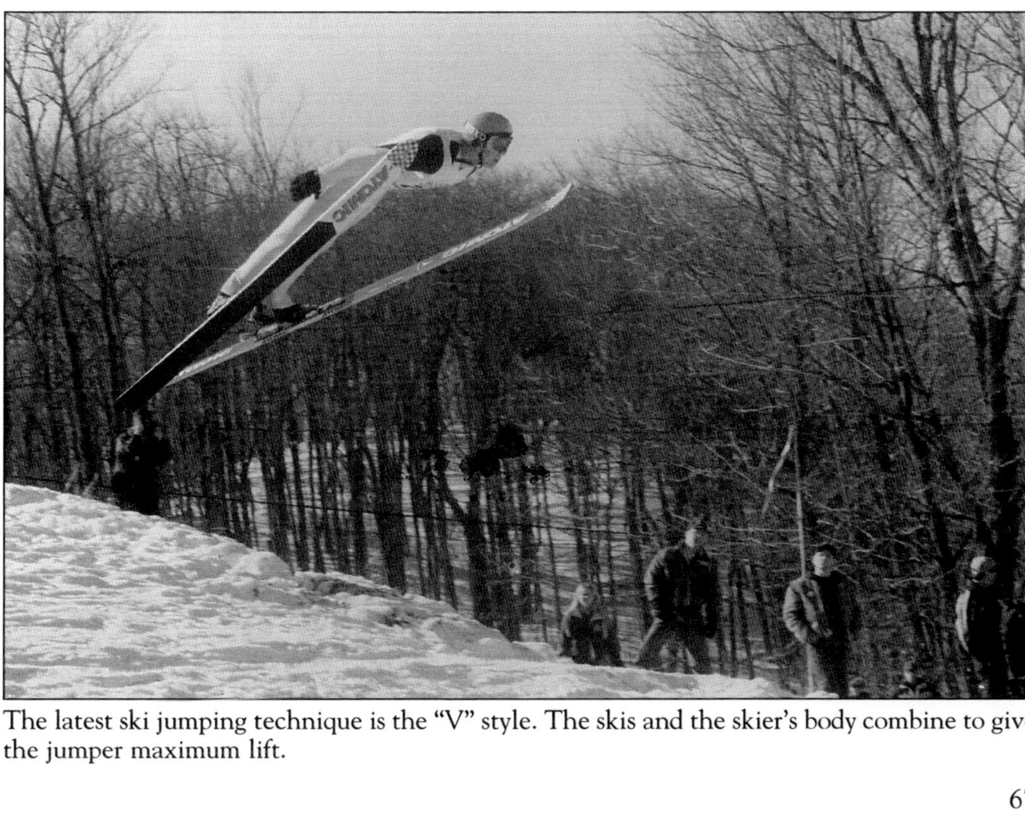

The latest ski jumping technique is the "V" style. The skis and the skier's body combine to give the jumper maximum lift.

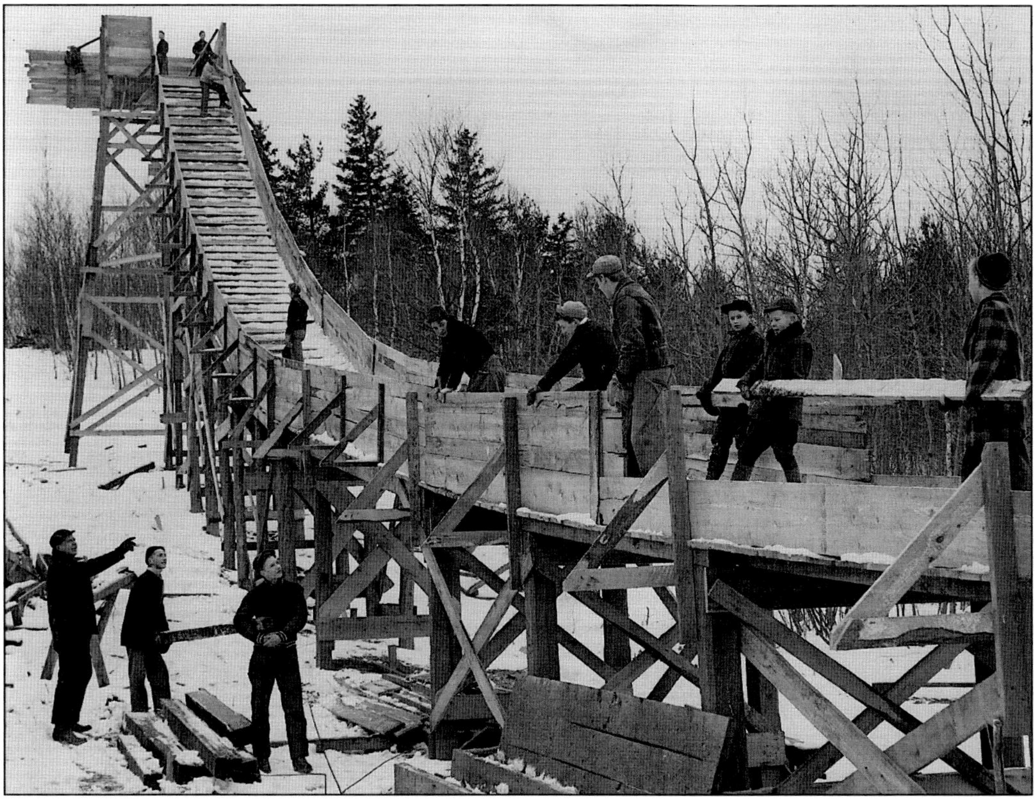

The Chester Bowl in Duluth, Minnesota, was completed in December of 1944.

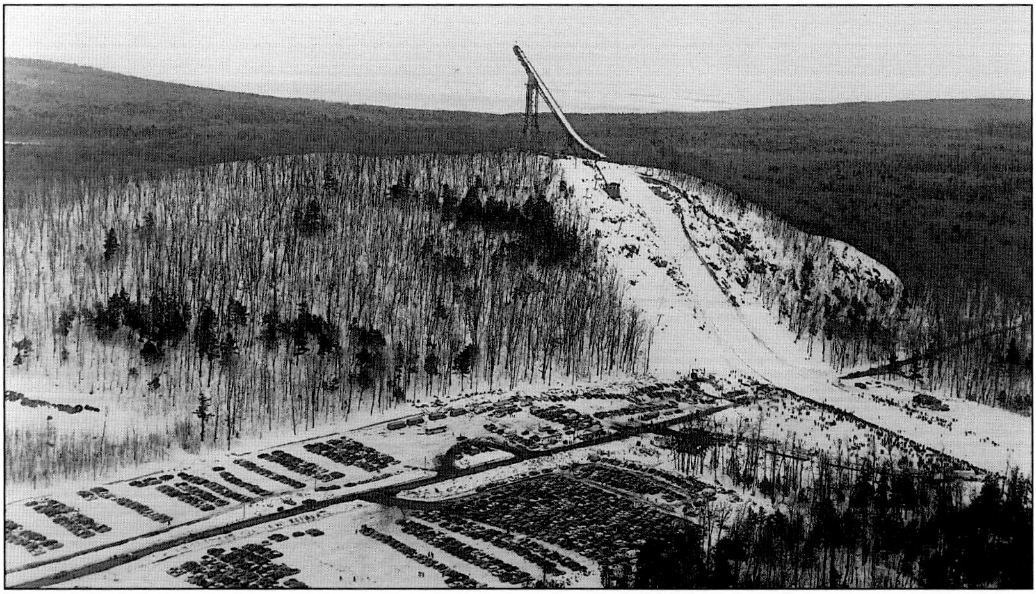

Copper Peak, the only ski flying hill in North America, is located in Gogebic County, Northern Michigan. A large ski jumping facility is classified as a "K120" hill. Anything over that size is considered a "ski flying" hill.

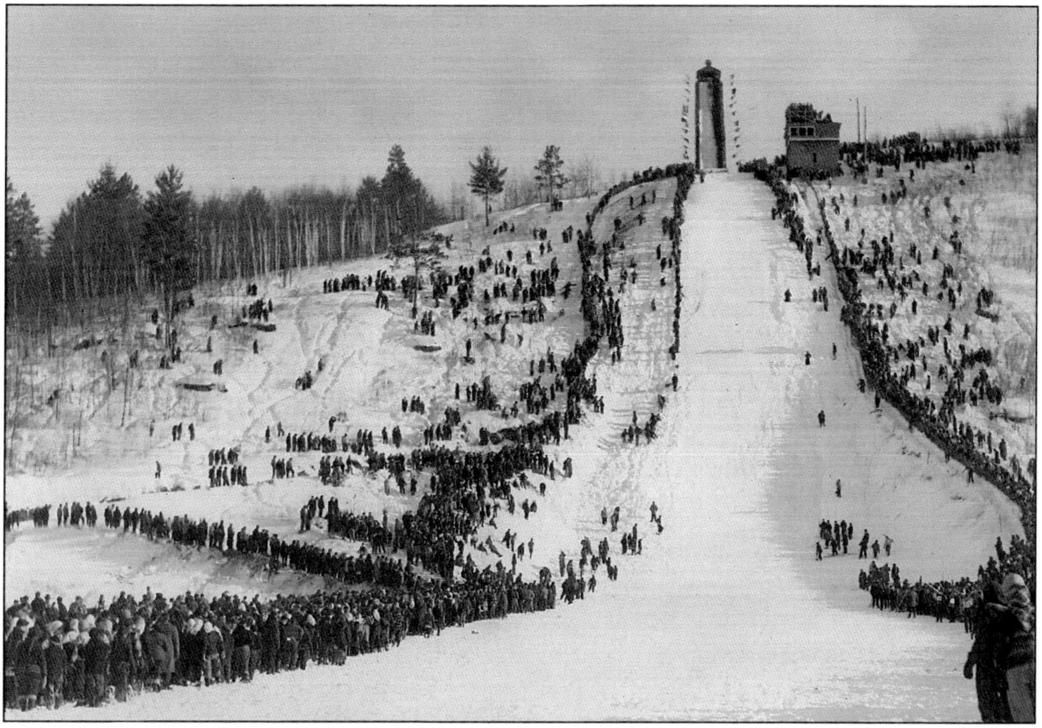

This is an early photo of Pine Mountain Ski Area near Iron Mountain, Michigan.

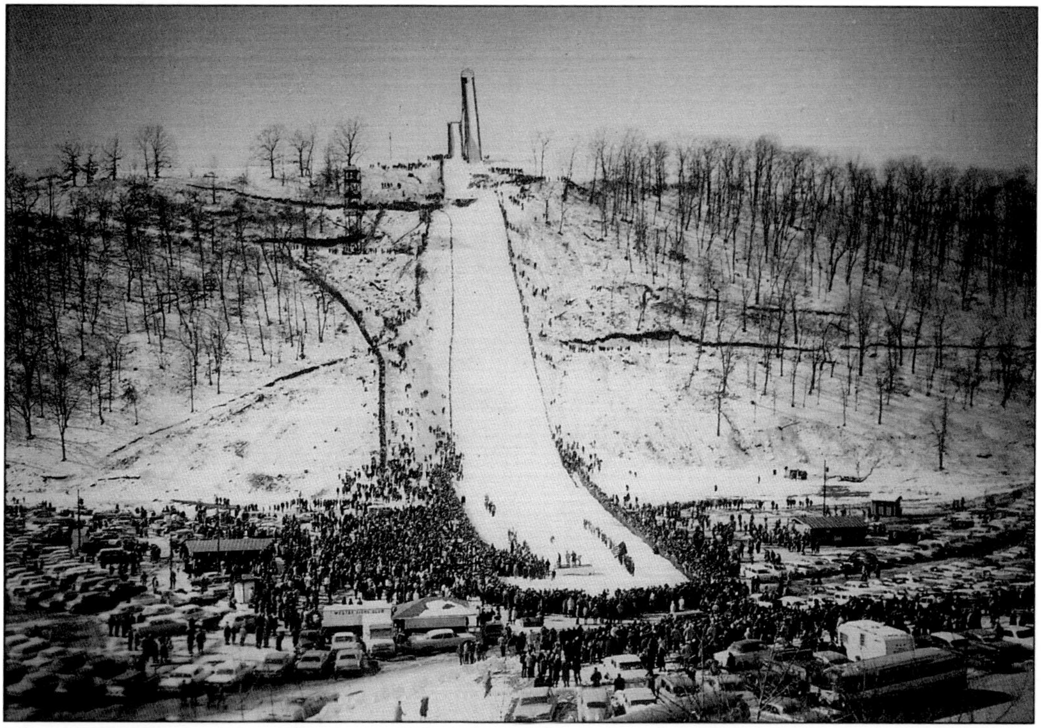

The photo above shows the Snowflake Ski Club of Westby, Wisconsin. A record jump of 318 feet was set here in 1963.

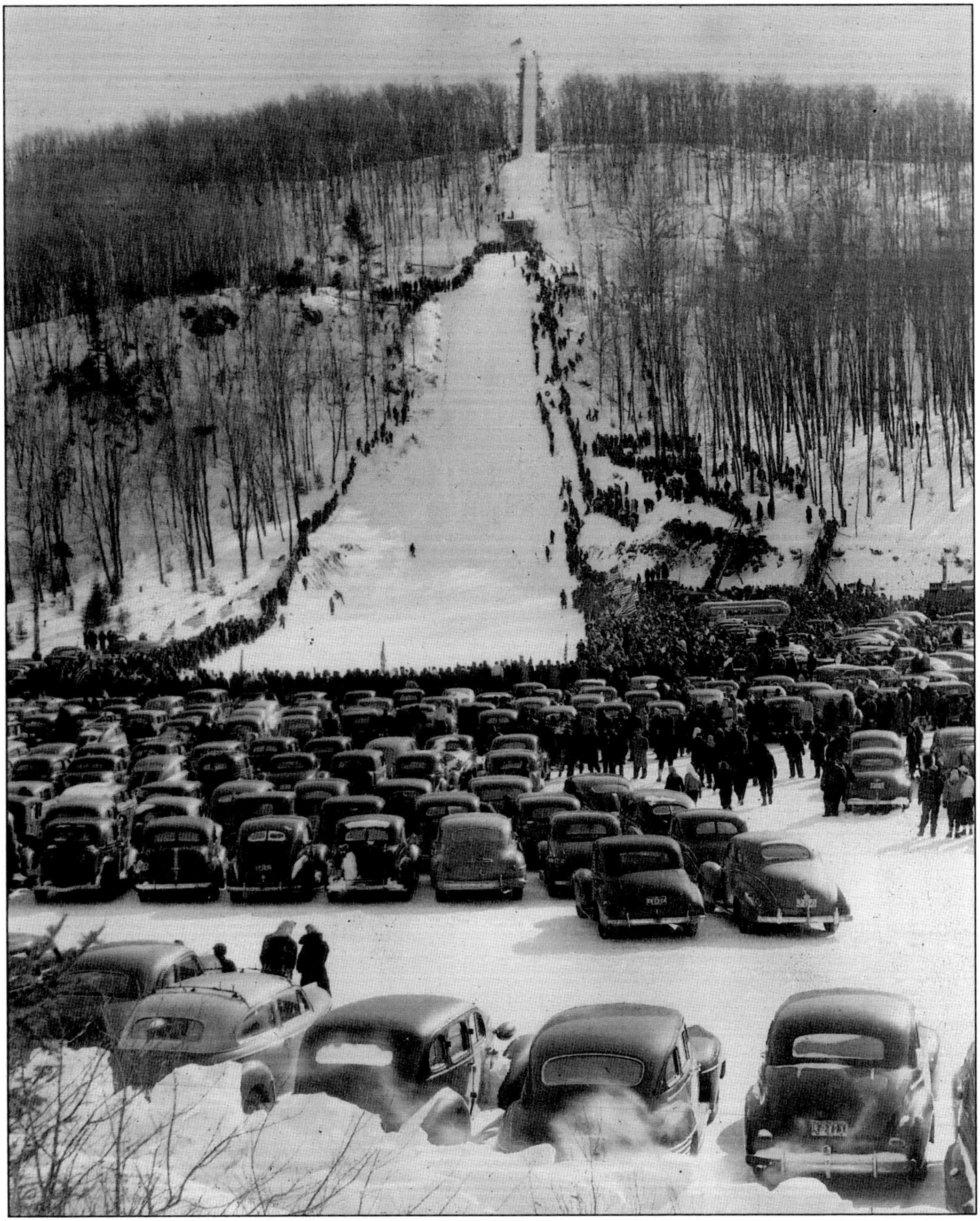

A 1946 tournament at Suicide Hill in Ishpeming, Michigan, is pictured here.

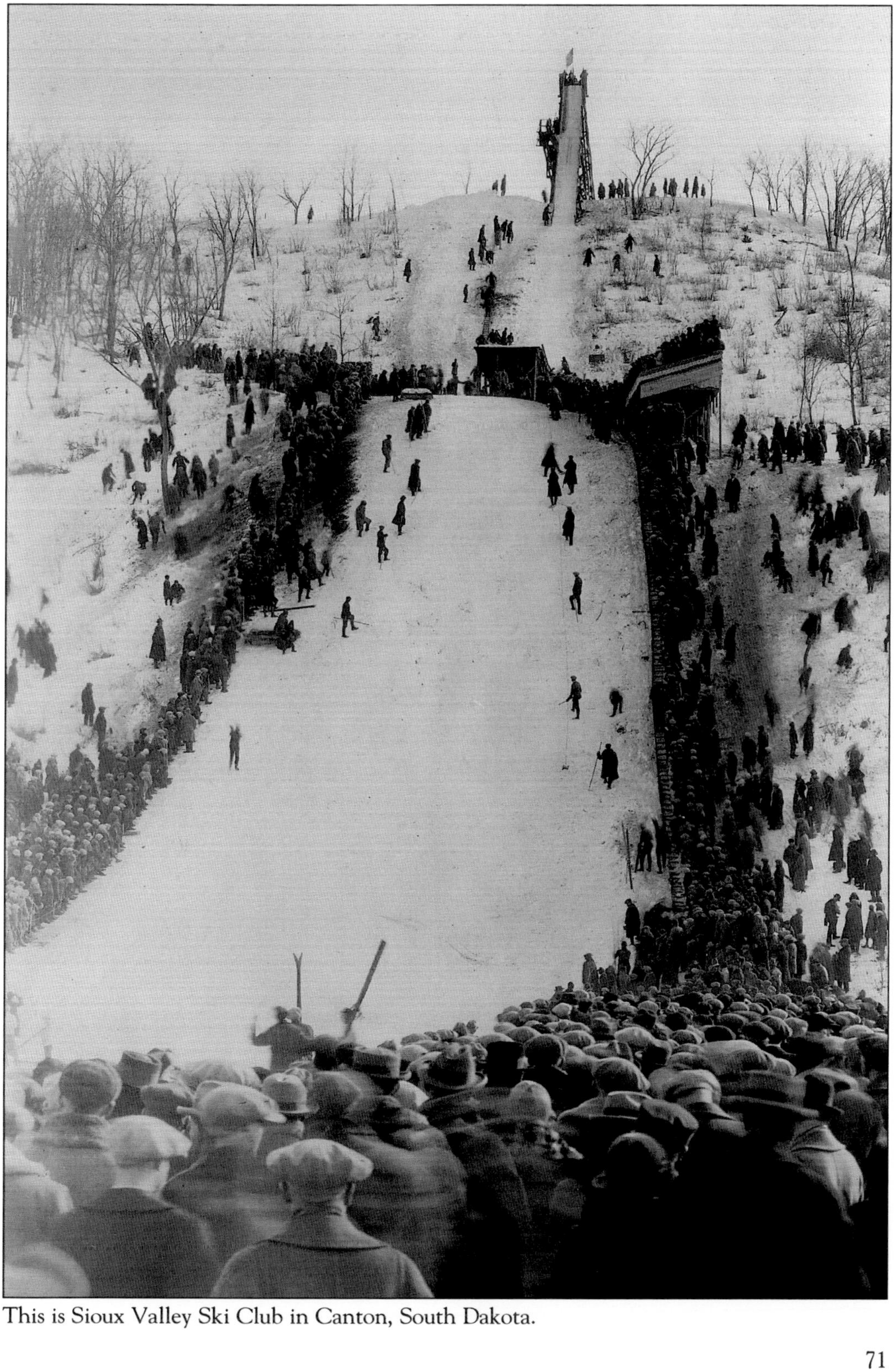

This is Sioux Valley Ski Club in Canton, South Dakota.

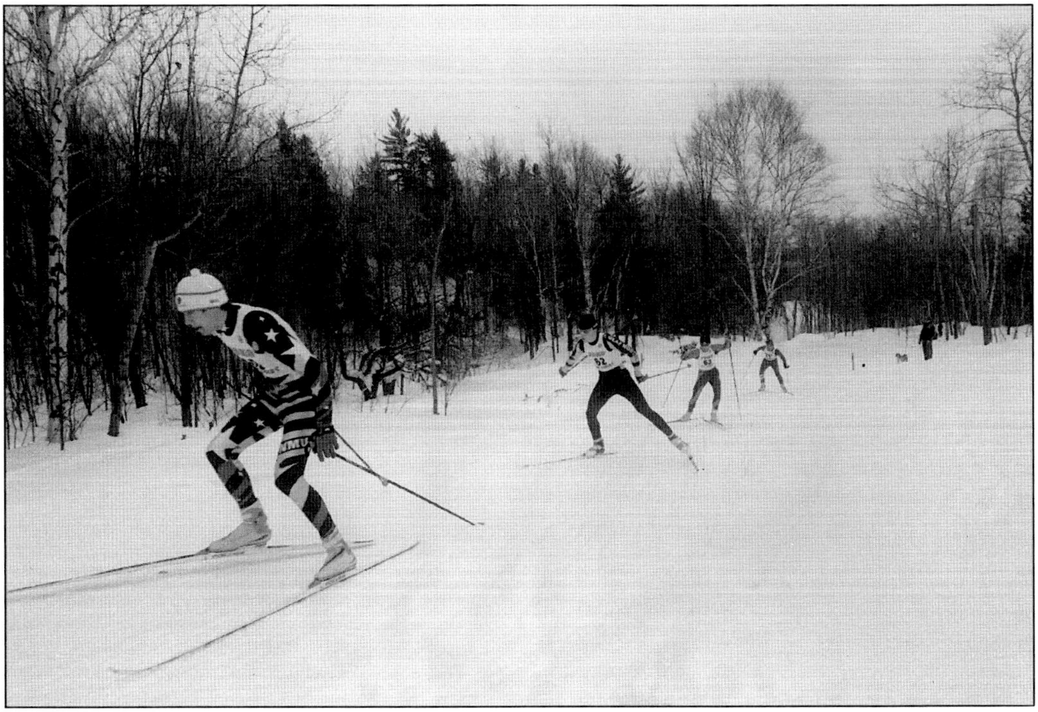

Cross-country ski racers using a very speedy skating technique, using longer ski poles and groomed, wider trails, are pictured above.

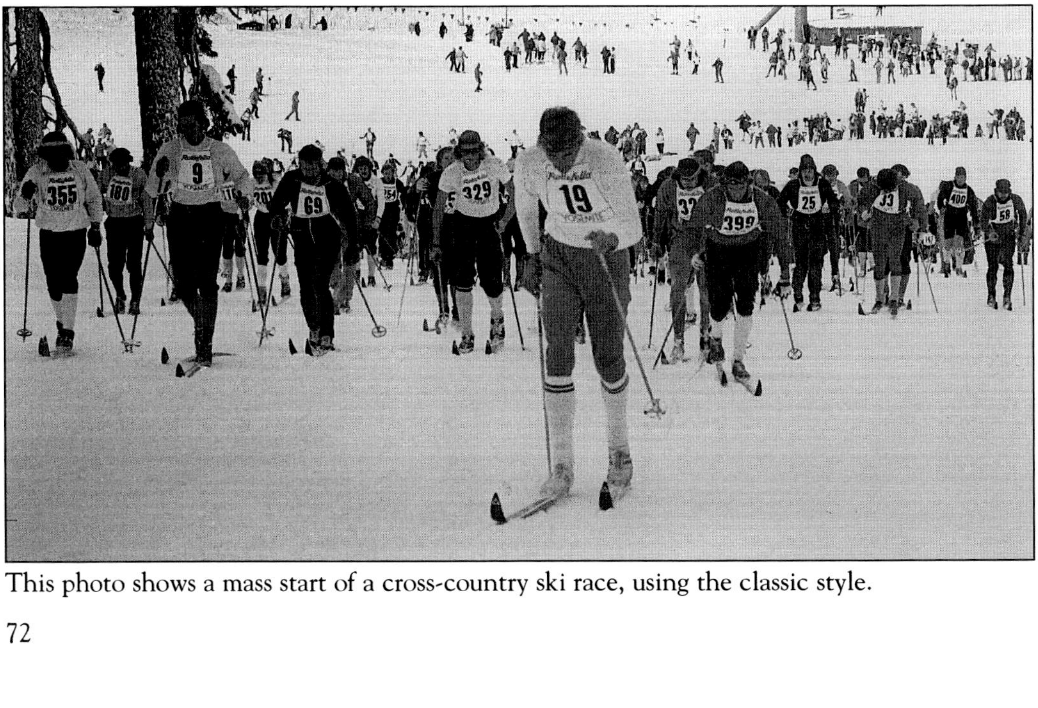

This photo shows a mass start of a cross-country ski race, using the classic style.

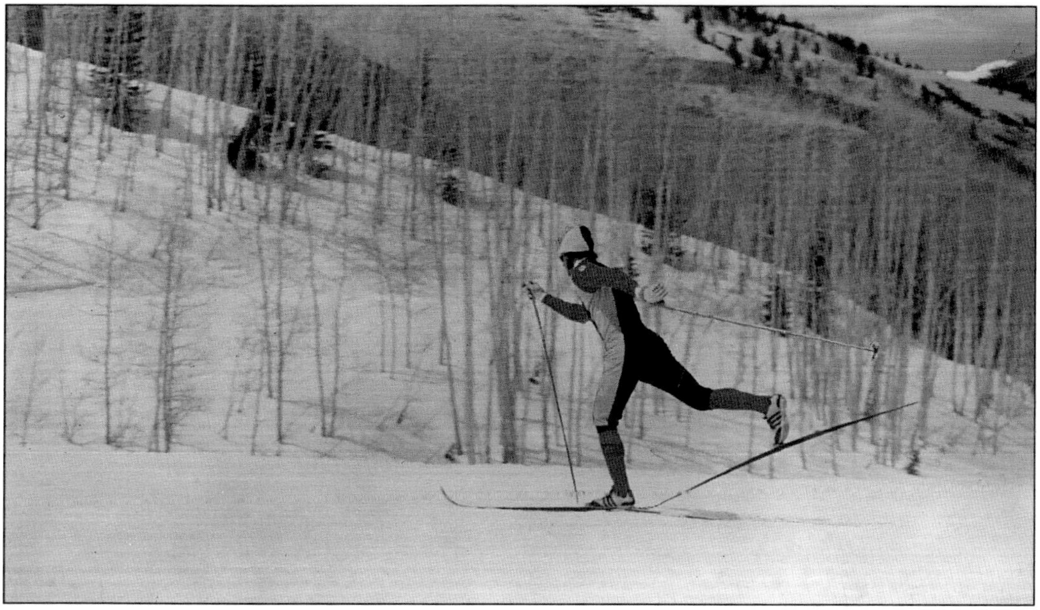

Bill Koch is shown doing the classic style, consisting of a high kick, with skis straight forward in the typically groomed parallel ski track.

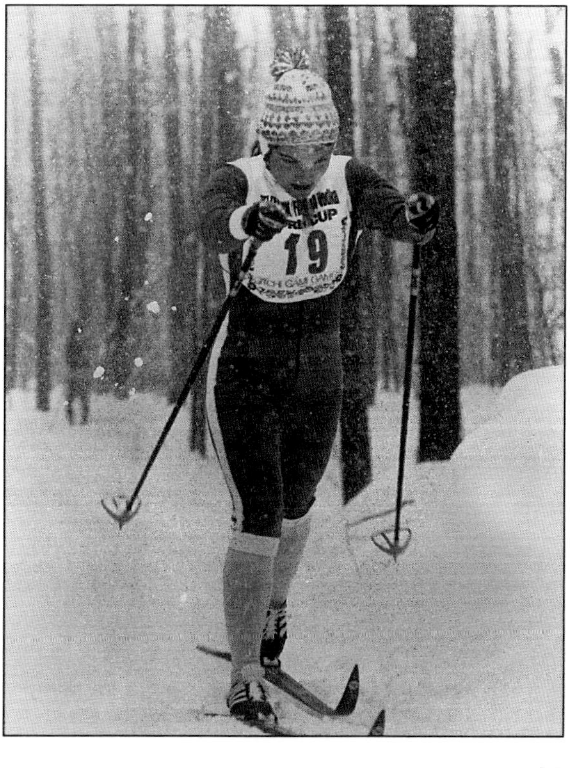

This photo demonstrates cross-country ski racing, "double poling," on the classic ski track, in fresh snow conditions.

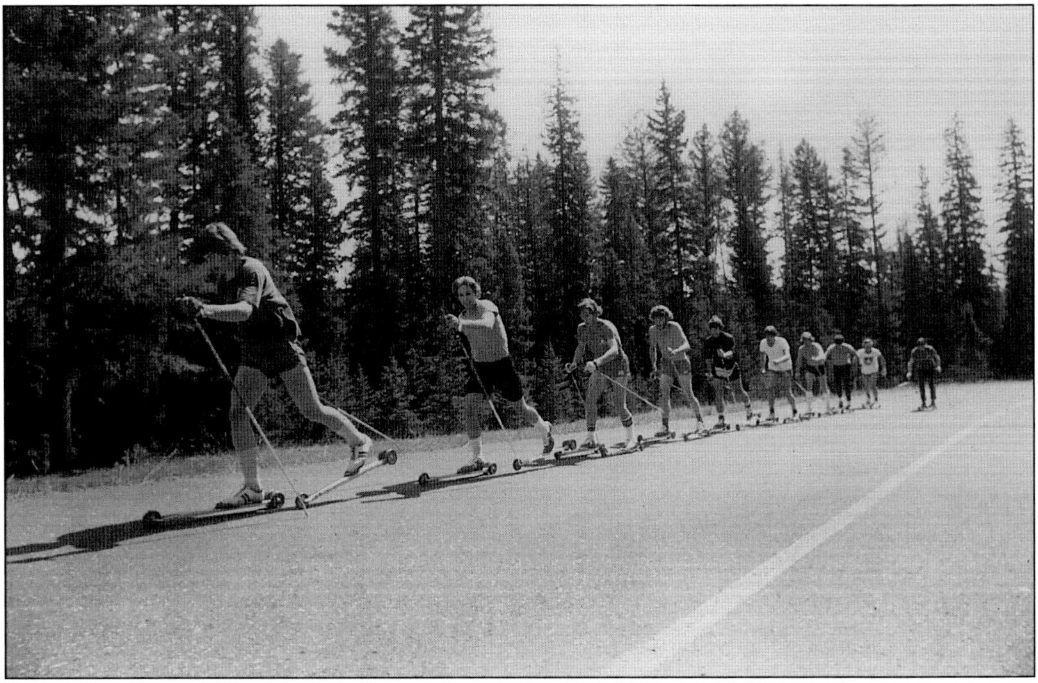

Pictured above is summer training on roller skis along back roads of asphalt or concrete. (Some of the larger wheeled skis were also used on well-maintained gravel roads).

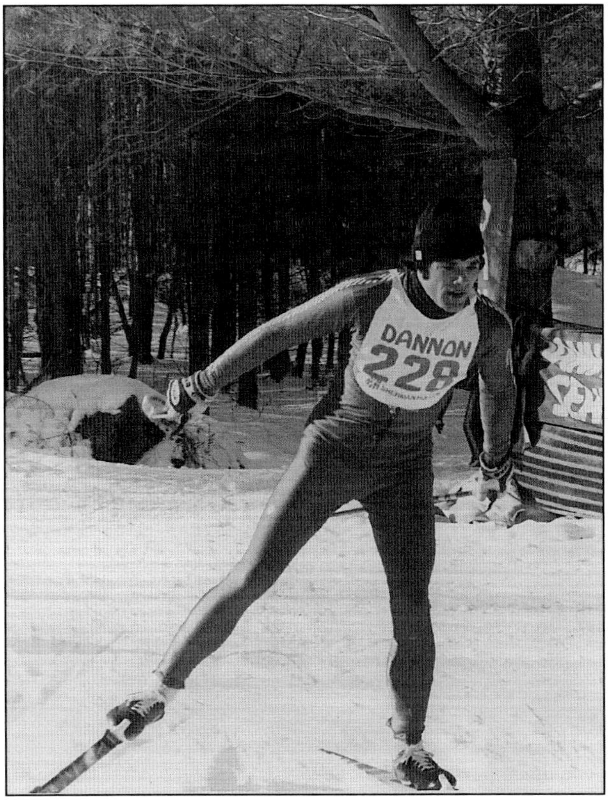

This is a Skating Style racer in action.

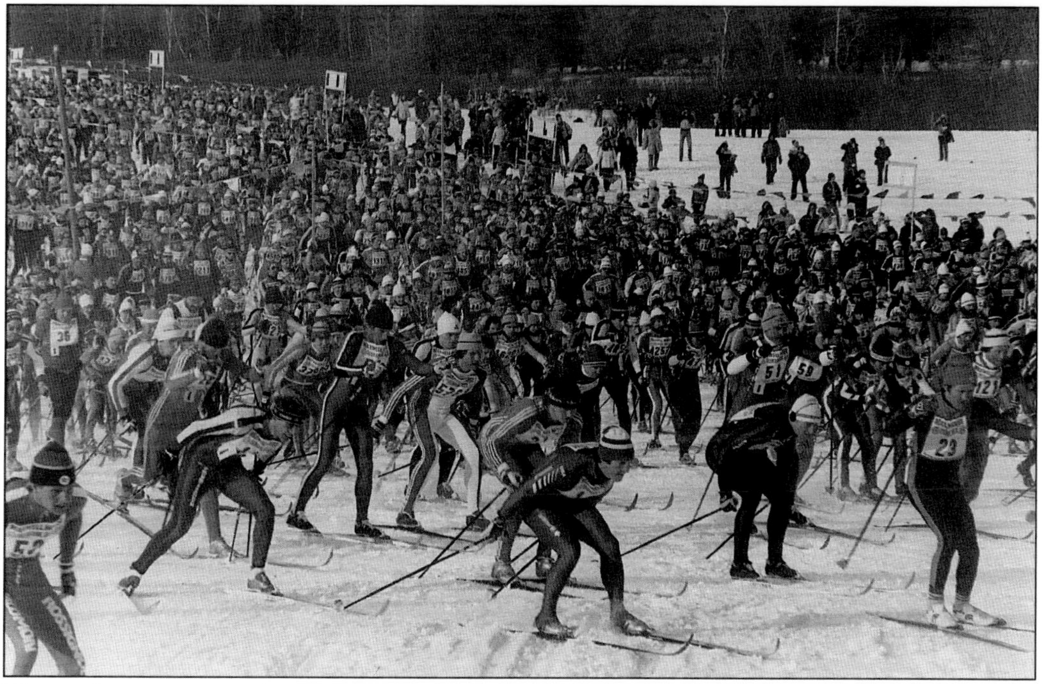

This is the mass start of cross-country American Berkebeiner ski race in Hayward, Wisconsin, in 1983. This well-known race started in 1973, when 53 skiers traveled 52 kilometers from Hayward, Wisconsin, to Telemark Resort in neighboring Cable.

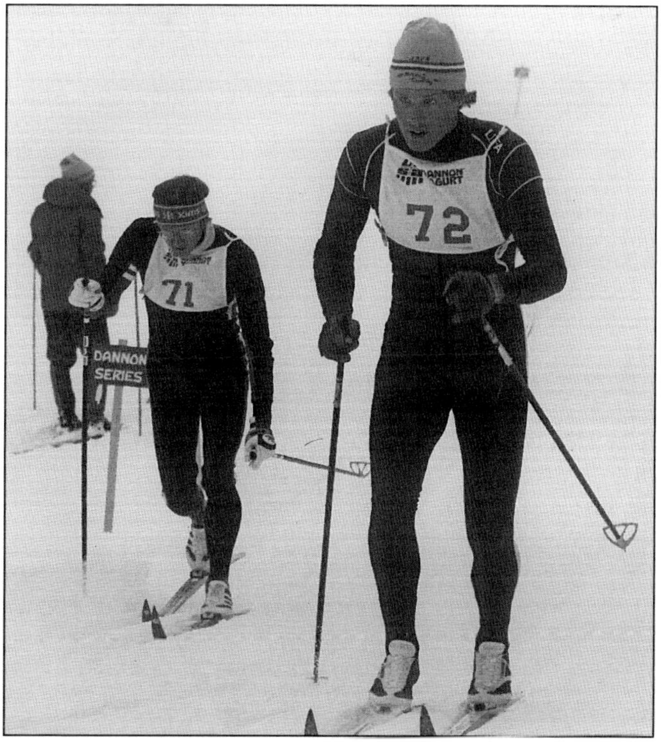

The photo at right demonstrates the Classic Style.

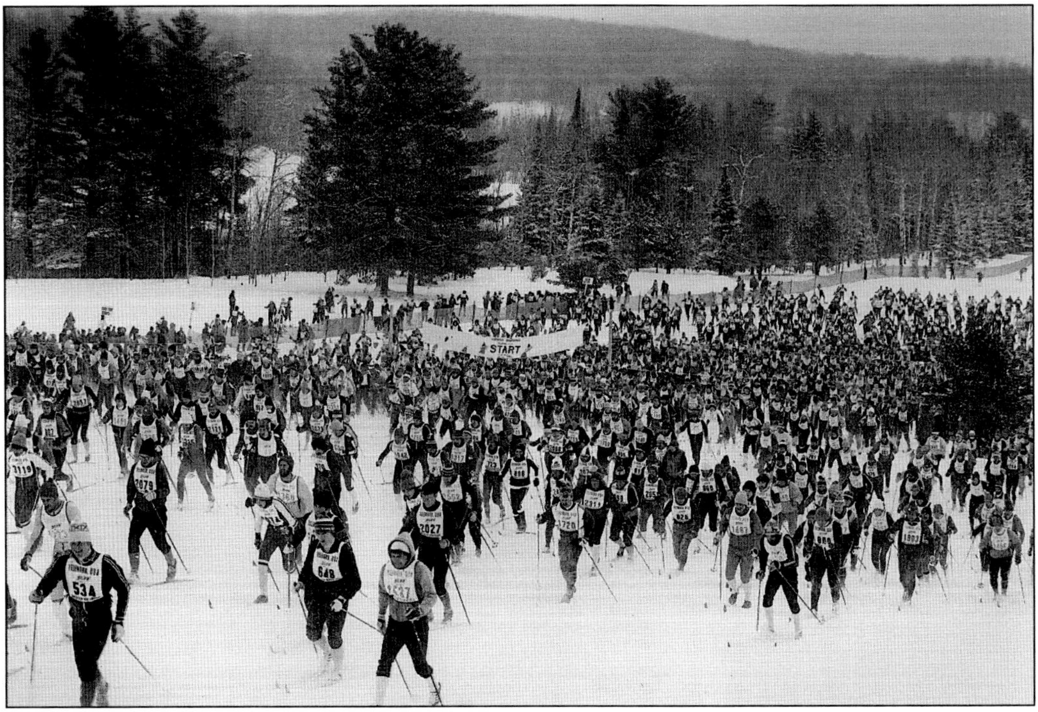

This is a mass start at the 1977 American Birkebeiner.

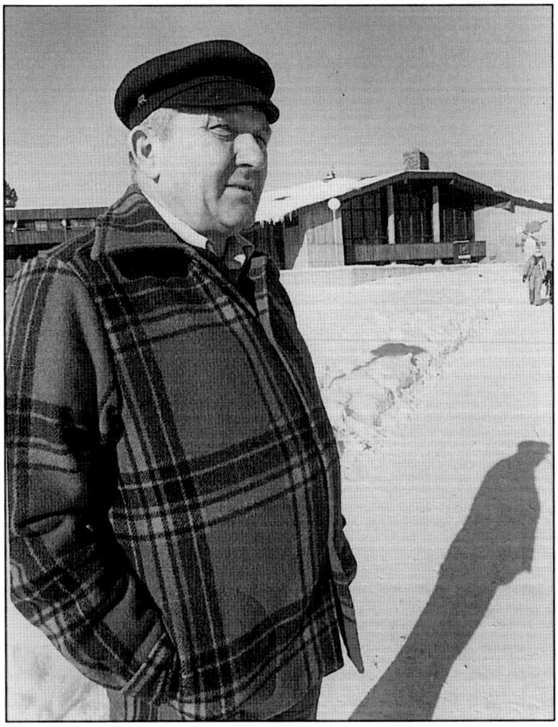

Anthony "Tony" Wise of Cable, Wisconsin, proved to be a ski promoter and innovator. He looked at a small hill in Wisconsin, and envisioned a first-class ski resort on it. He named the hill Mount Telemark. It is now a first-class resort, complete with T-bars and chair lifts and a fine wooded cross-country course. He founded and promoted the American Birkebeiner, fostered the World-Loppet Cross-Country Race Series, and brought international acclaim to his beloved Telemark. Anthony "Tony" Wise was elected to the US National Ski Hall of Fame in 1988.

Eight

Offspring Organizations

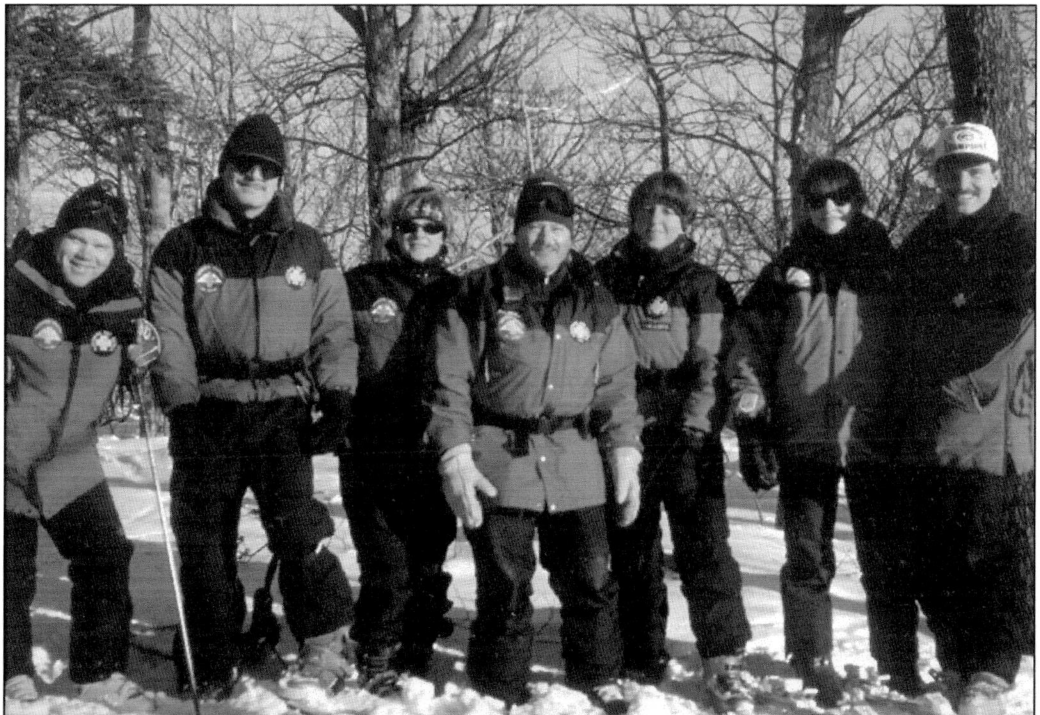

Pictured above is a Sunday evening shift for the local ski patrol at Marquette Mountain, Michigan (c. 1990s). They are, from left to right: Don Koski, Andrew Bek, Leslie Bek, Fred Tibbitts, Susan Johnson, Ann-Marie Lakenen, and Rich DeMerse.

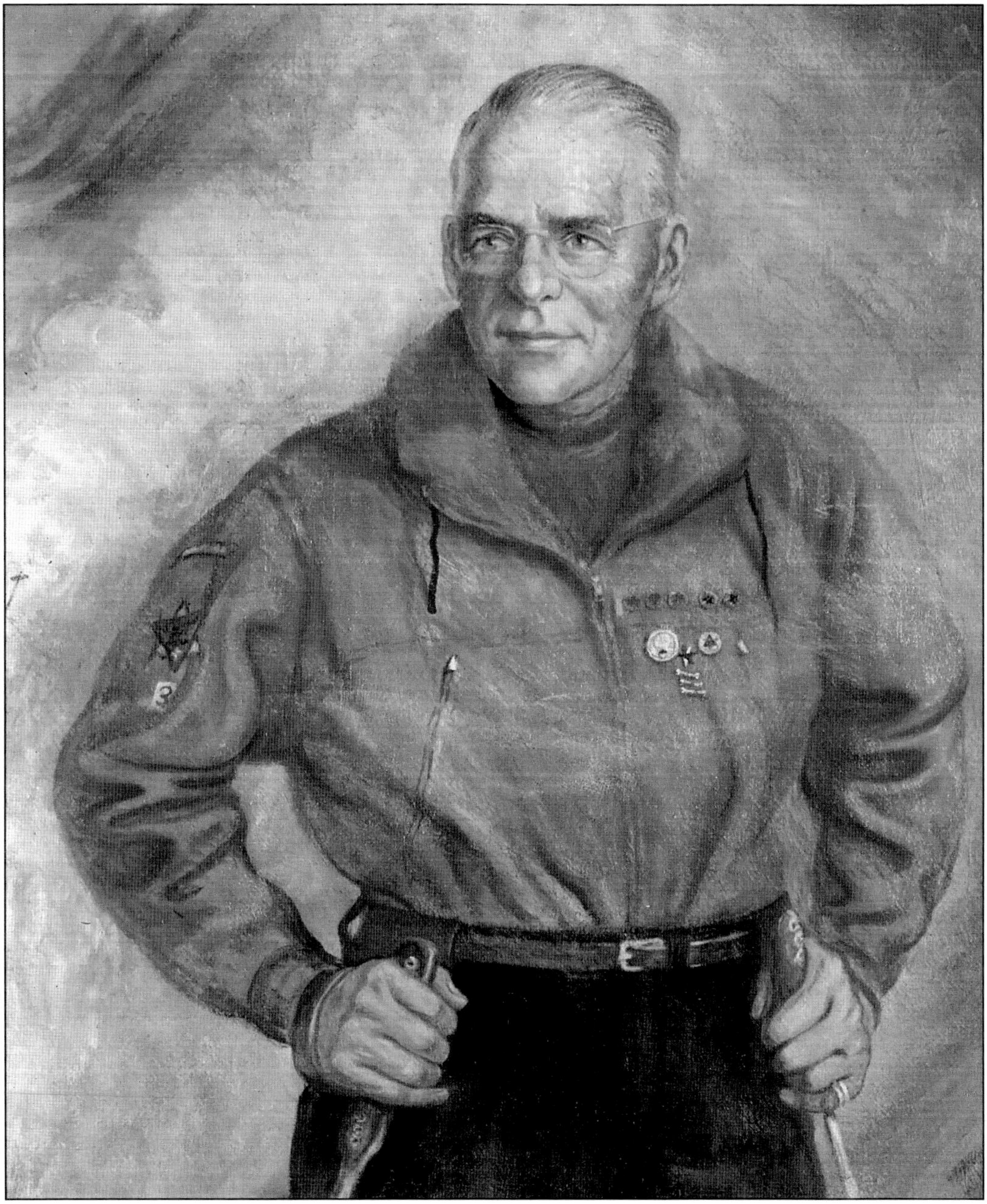

Charles Minot "Minnie" Dole was a member of the Amateur Ski Club of New York, where he chaired the original committee to investigate skiing accidents and safety in skiing. His interest in safety prompted him to organize and head a ski patrol for the National Alpine Races in Stowe, Vermont, in 1938. Impressed with Dole's measures, the National Ski Association President, Roger Langley, requested that ski patrols be formed on a national basis. Therefore, the National Ski Patrol was born, and Dole served as its National Director from 1938 until 1950.

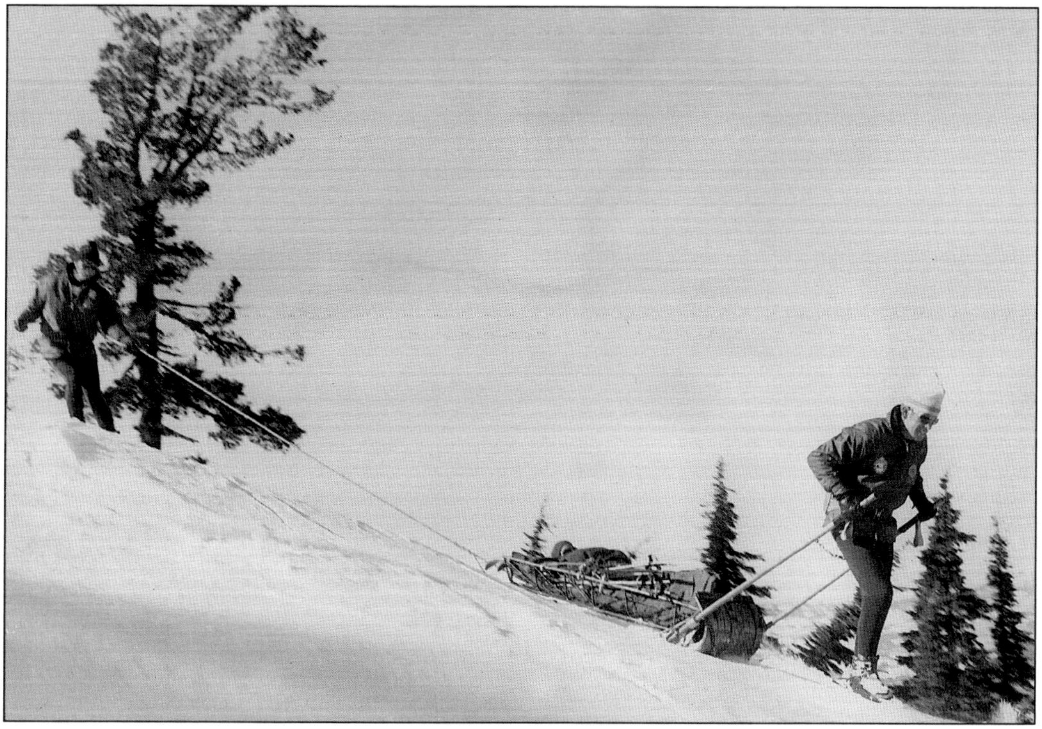

The National Ski Patrol is pictured here, exercising a toboggan rescue.

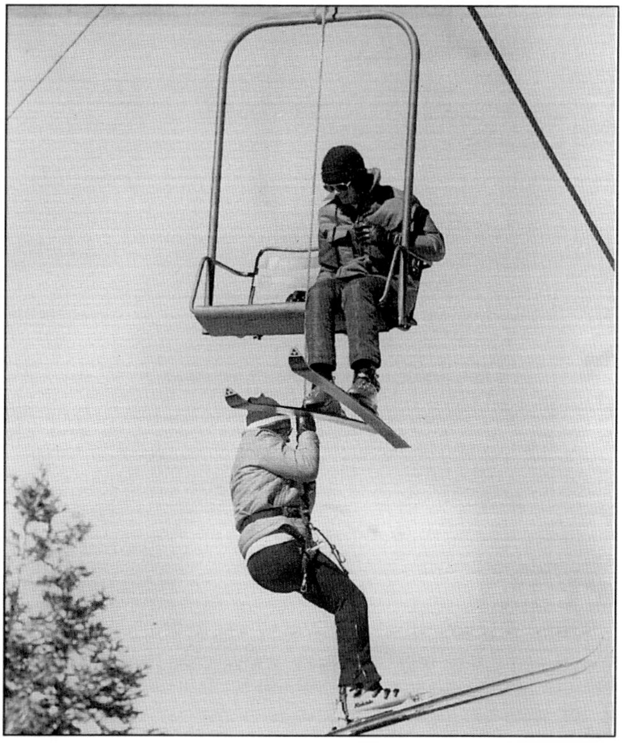

These two are practicing an evacuation from a chair lift.

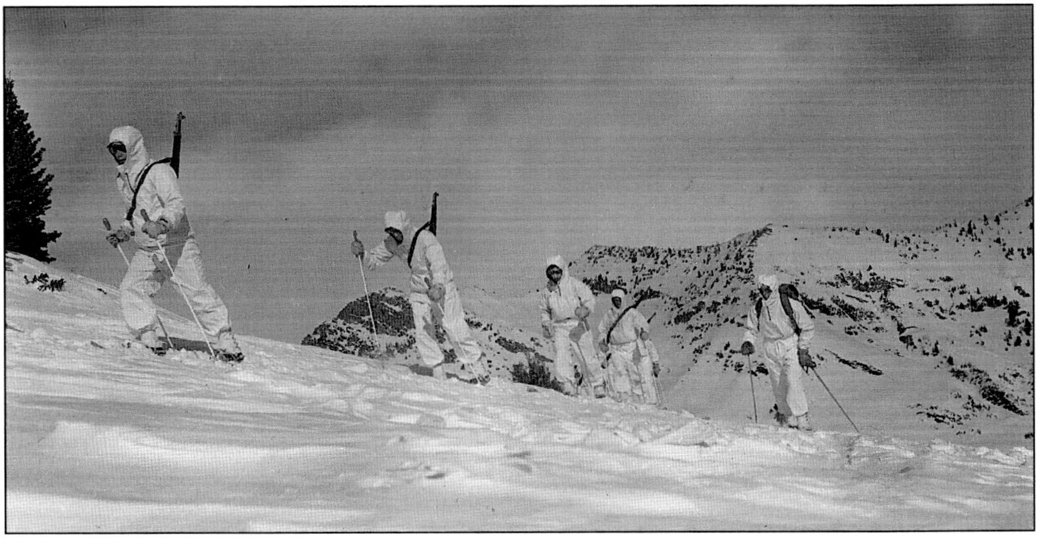

In 1940, with the war raging in Europe, Charles "Minnie" Dole approached the War Department in Washington to suggest the possibility that American troops train in mountain and winter warfare. Since the United States had not entered the war yet, the project was put on temporary hold. Dole and John E. P. Morgan continued to work with the War Department to make their winter warfare group a reality. Forming a National Volunteer Winter Defense Committee, using the National Ski Patrol system as a nucleus, they convinced the army to purchase 200 pairs of skis. The winter warfare group became a reality. It was headquartered at Camp Hale in Colorado, and eventually was named the 10th Mountain Infantry Division.

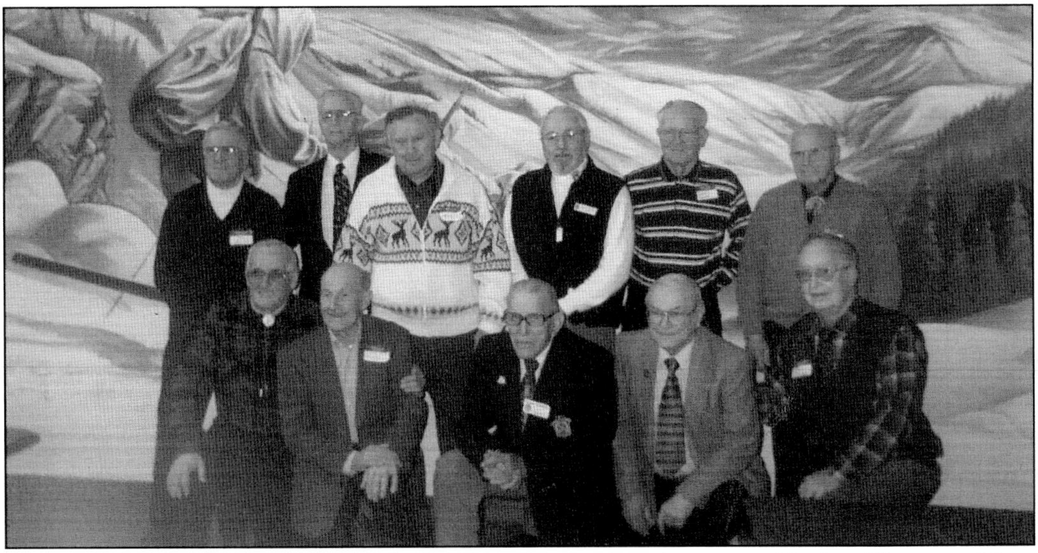

Pictured are several members of the 10th Mountain Division, U. P. Chapter. They are, from left to right: (front row) Paul Perrault (Ishpeming, MI), Uno Isaacson (Lake Linden, MI), Eugene Kestimaki (Marquette, MI), Lawrence Korpi (Marquette, MI), and Lavern Trepp (Iron Mountain, MI); (back row) James Lawson (Ishpeming, MI), Floyd Erickson (Lansing, MI), Walter Cook (Marquette, MI), Andy Lucas (Copper City, MI), Wilhart Etelamaki (Palmer, MI), and Erwin Hollmann (Peshtigo, WI). (This picture was taken February 19, 1999, Belvedere Day.)

The shoulder patch of the 10th Mountain Division was approved on June 7, 1944, and the "Mountain" tab was approved on November 22, 1944. The blue background is indicative of an infantry unit, which it was, and the crossed bayonets form the Roman numeral ten, which was the division's number. The patch itself is in the shape of a powder keg, which is symbolic of the unit's explosive power. The unit distinguished itself in Italy. This proud unit returned to the United States in August, 1945, and was deactivated in November, 1945. The 10th was reactivated as the 10th Infantry Division in July 1948, and still proudly wears the patch without the tab.

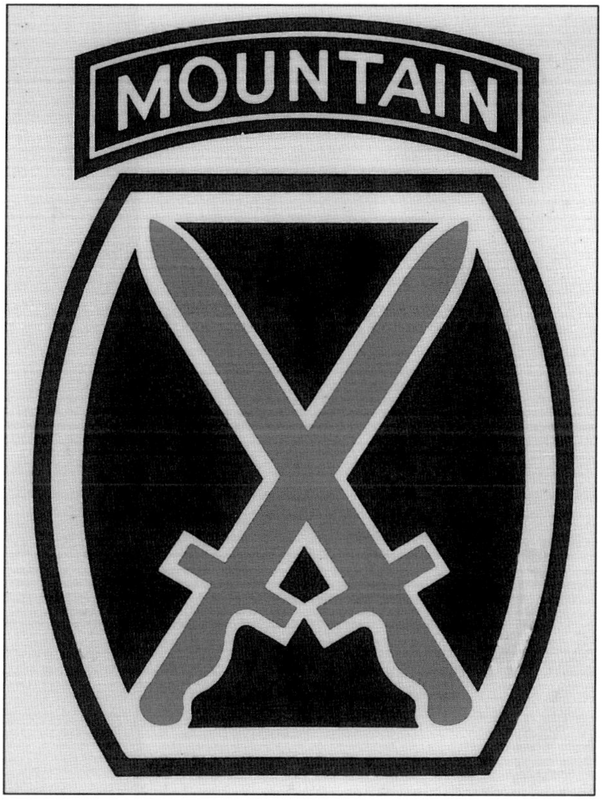

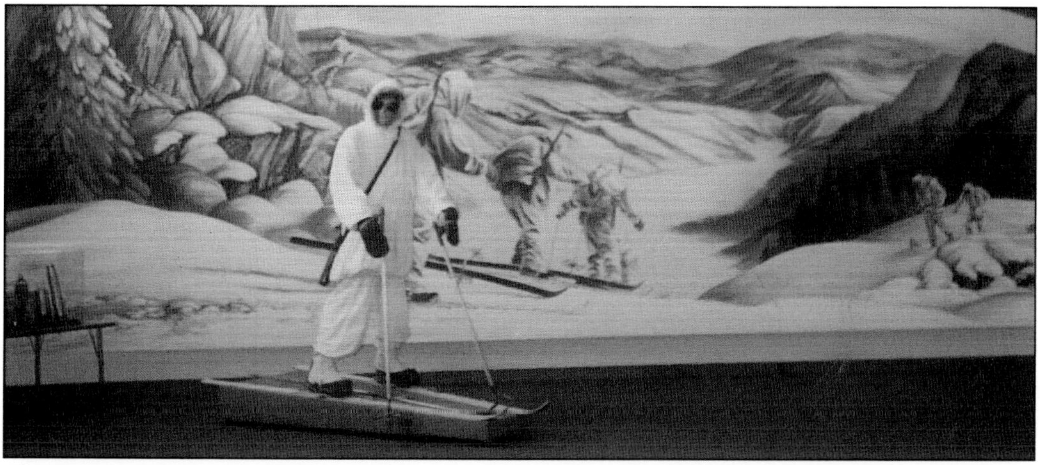

This exhibit of the 10th Mountain Division is located at the US National Ski Hall of Fame and Museum in Ishpeming, Michigan. The mural is by Ishpeming artist Roger Junak.

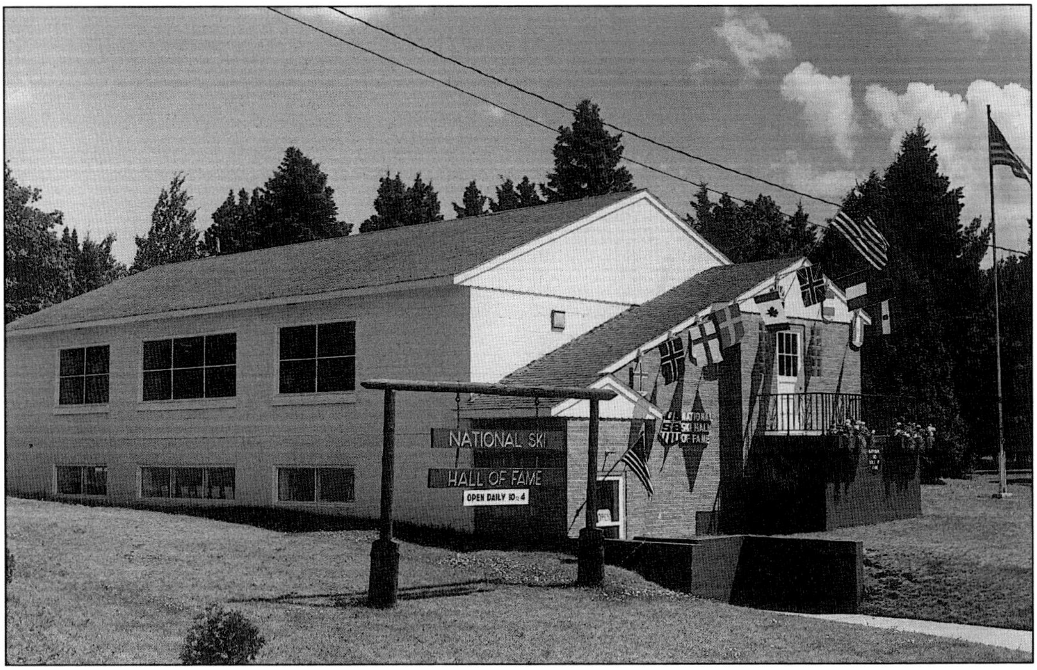

The original building of the U.S. National Ski Hall of Fame and Museum was dedicated in 1954.

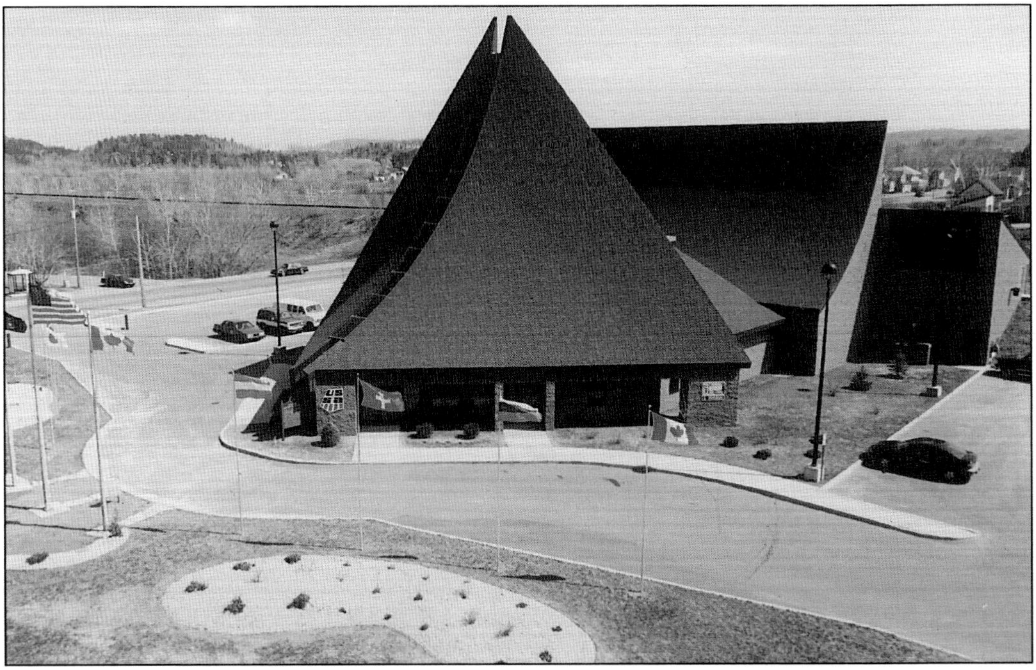
The present headquarters of the U.S. National Ski Hall of Fame and Museum was dedicated in 1992.

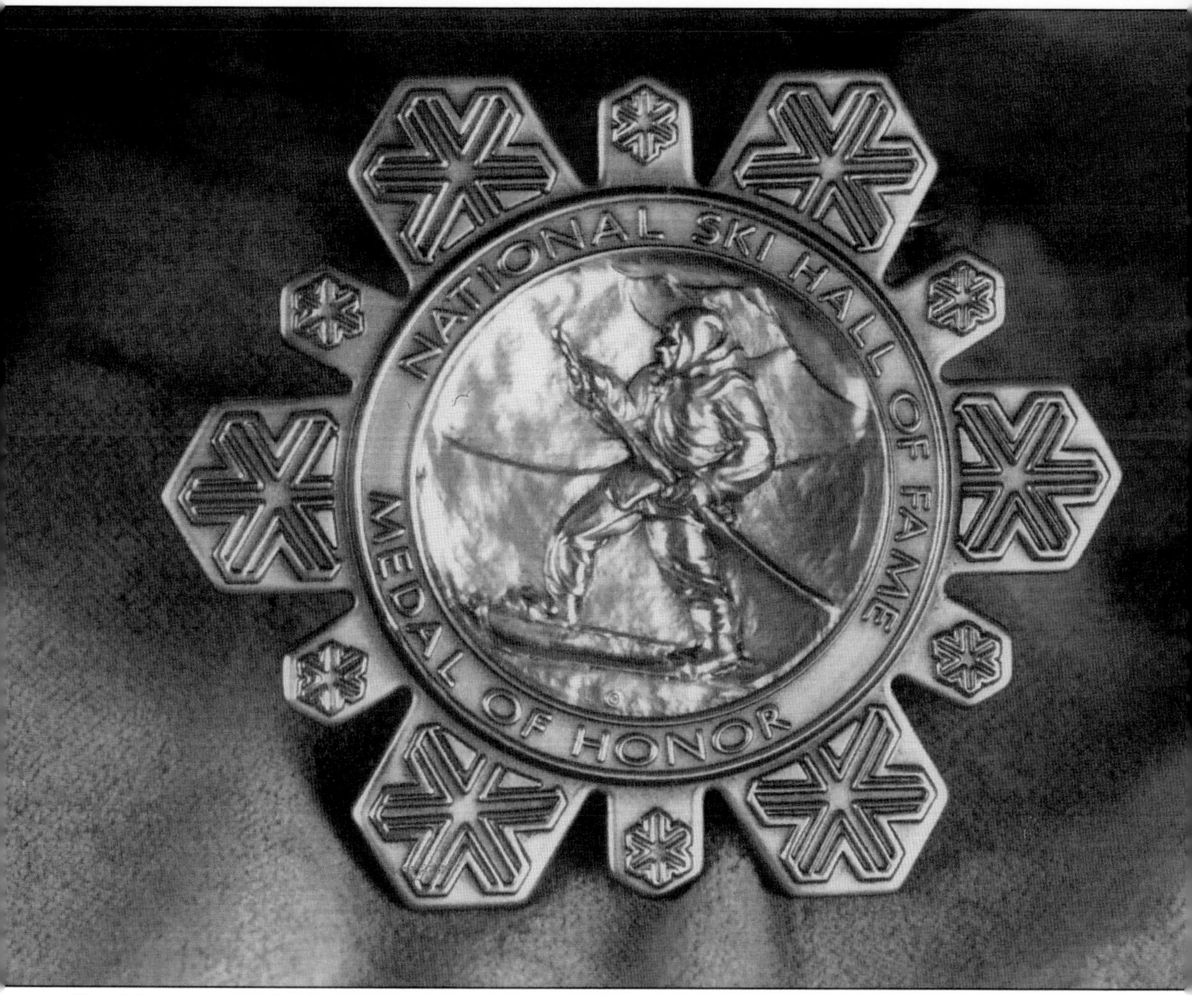

The U.S. National Ski Hall of Fame Honored Member Medallion was the brainchild of then USSA National Historical Committee Chairman, J. H. "Red" Carruthers. He stated that this new medal must be the "medal of medals," and available only to those elected to the Hall of Fame. A local committee was chaired by Martin Dolan, who enlisted the help of the Art and Design Department at Northern Michigan University, under the guidance of Professor Mike Gorski. He interested his students in a competition to design the medal, and the winning design was submitted by Mark Martin. The medal is a three-inch snowflake design in an antique gold finish. The Medal of Honor and its companion lapel pin were awarded for the first time on February 22, 1986, to the five Honorees of the Class of 1986. All previously elected Honored Members received their medals by mail later in the year.

More than three hundred enshrinees own this very special medal.

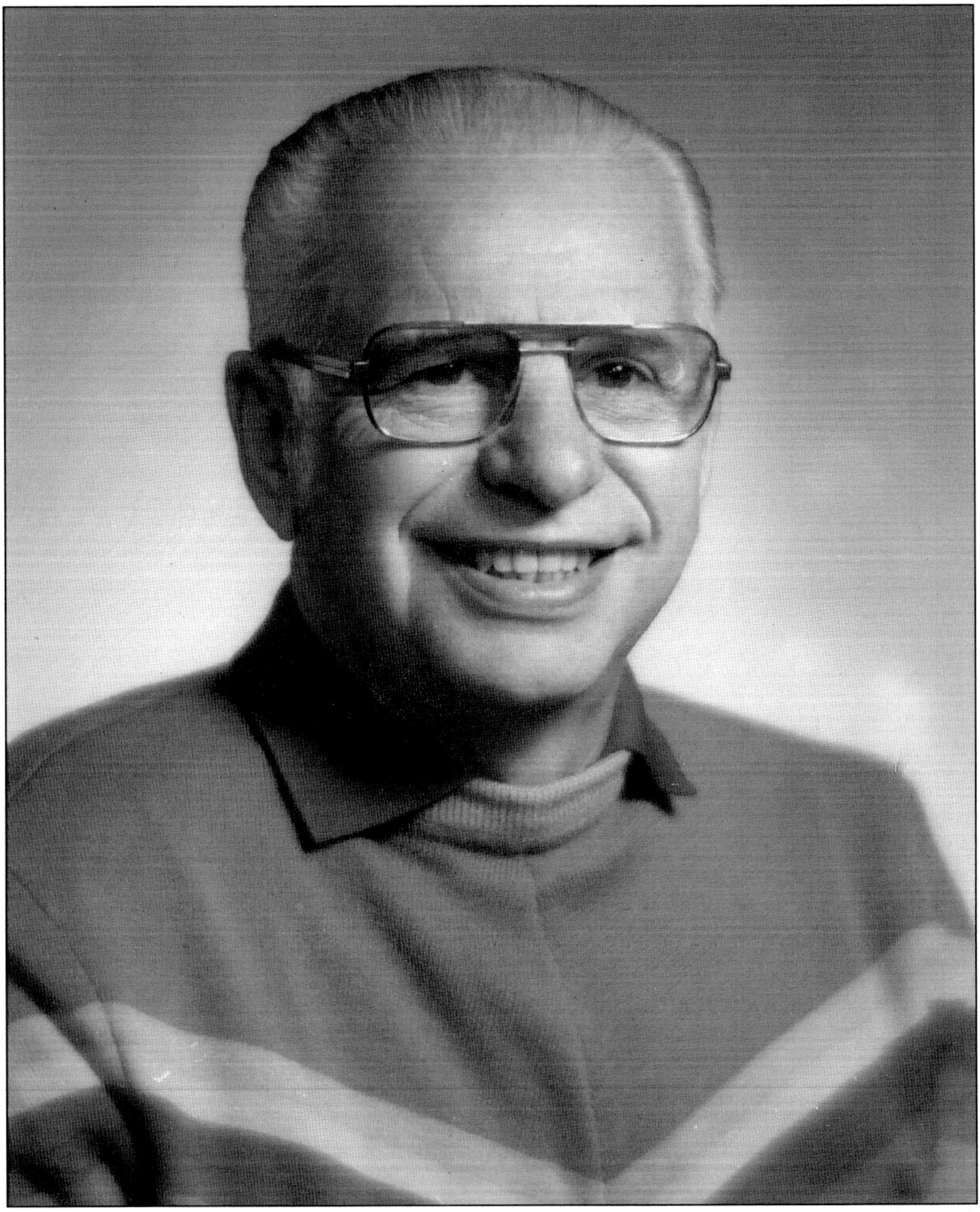

During the Battle of the Bulge in World War II, Paul Leimkuehler was wounded by shrapnel, which resulted in the loss of his left leg. After helping the staff in the limb and brace shop at Virginia's McGuire General Hospital while waiting for his own artificial limb, he went into the prosthetic field on his own. Leimkuehler's first "3-tracker" equipment for handicapped skiers was made with one pair of boots and a pair of old skis and poles. A fellow amputee, Stan Zakas, helped him adapt the equipment, and when the public was informed of this new invention through the media, the two friends received over 200 requests on how to get started. In 1957, when Leimkuehler began to manufacture the equipment, classes were held, clubs were formed, and the sport blossomed.

Paul Leimkuehler is pictured at right in 1981, ski racing on his three-track ski equipment (one ski and two ski outriggers). After hearing of this skiing equipment for amputees in 1956, the following year Leimkuehler not only manufactured skis for the physically challenged, but lectured and demonstrated the techniques, giving the physically challenged a chance to enjoy the sport of skiing.

He was elected to the U.S. National Ski Hall of Fame in 1981.

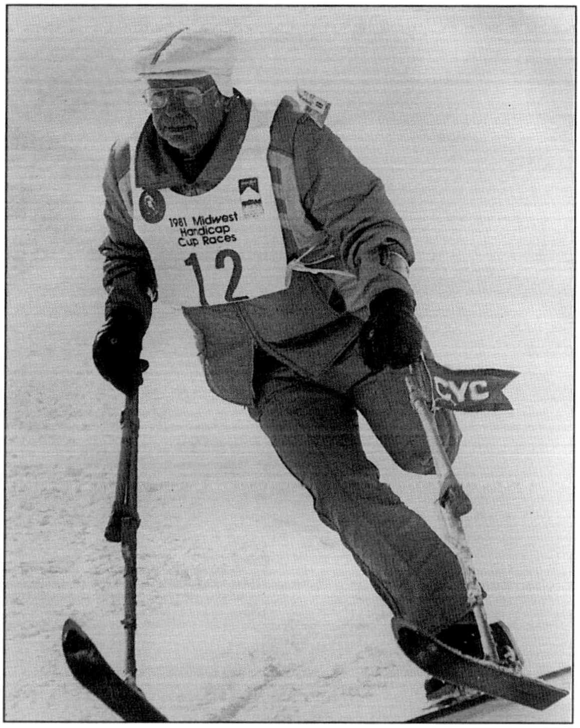

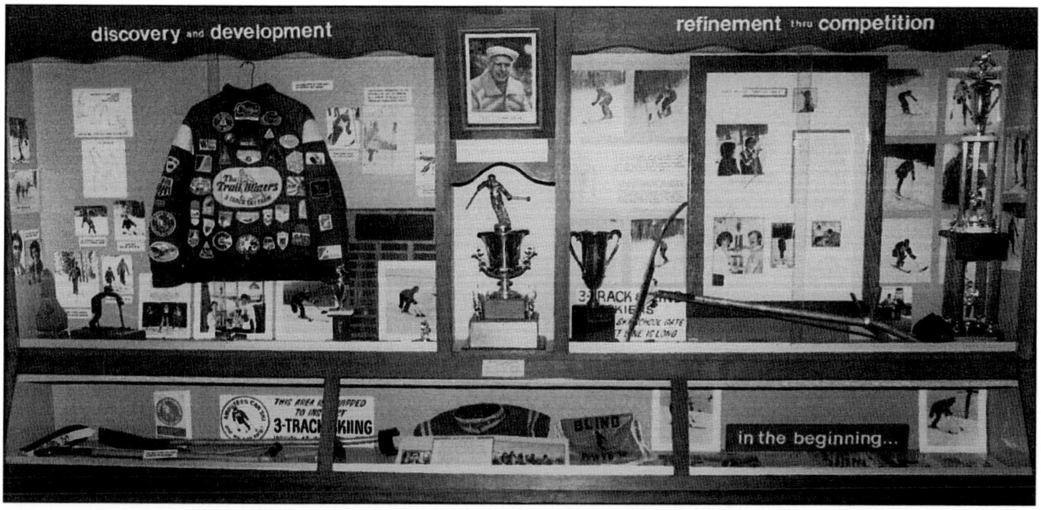

This case, donated to the U.S. National Ski Museum, displays equipment, artifacts, and awards of the amputee skiers in the Midwest.

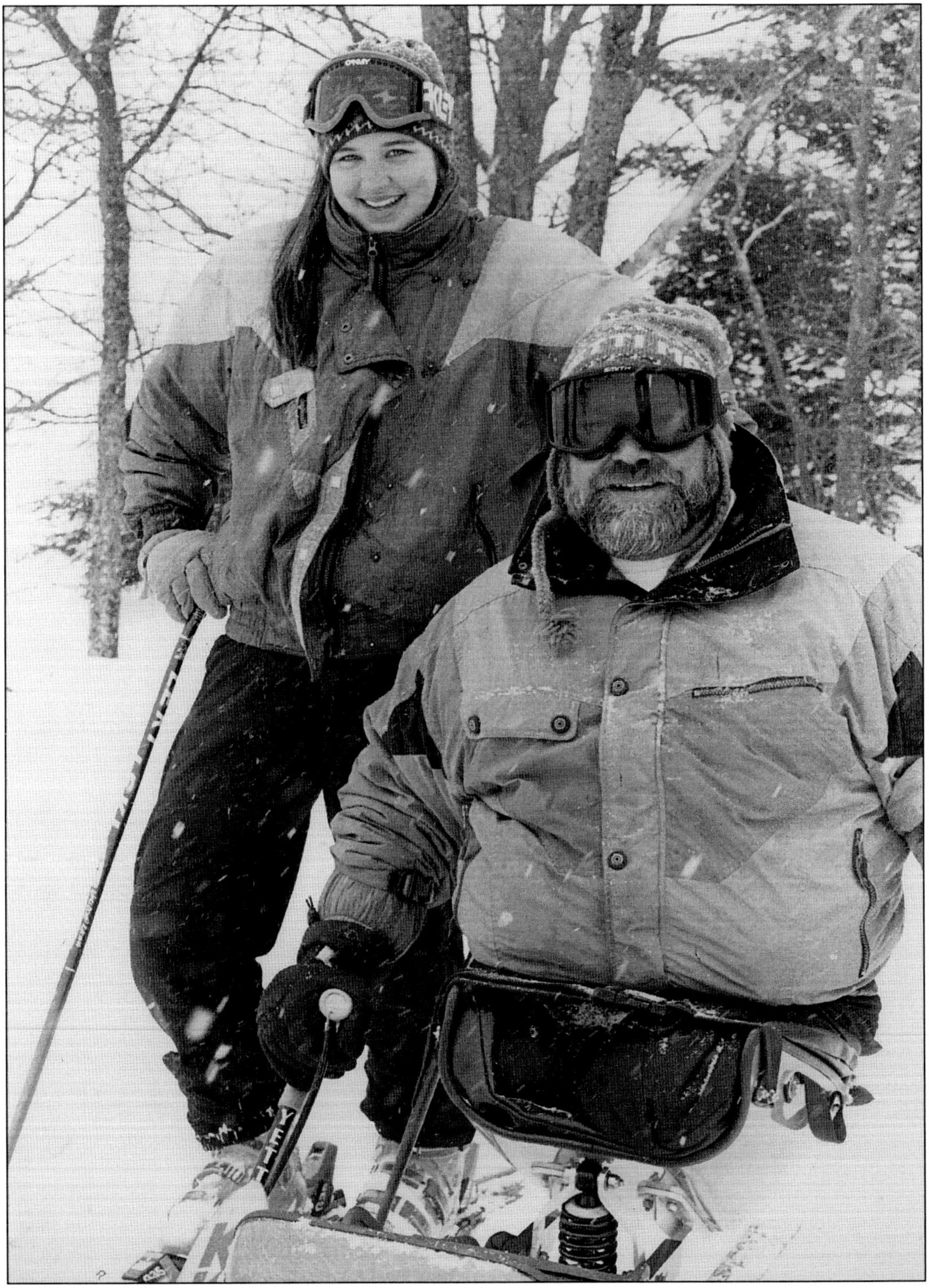

Professor Jim Dehlin of Northern Michigan University in Marquette, Michigan, and his daughter Kristin are pictured here enjoying a day of skiing together. Jim lost his legs during the Vietnam conflict and took up skiing afterwards using the mono ski.

Nine

Ski Personalities

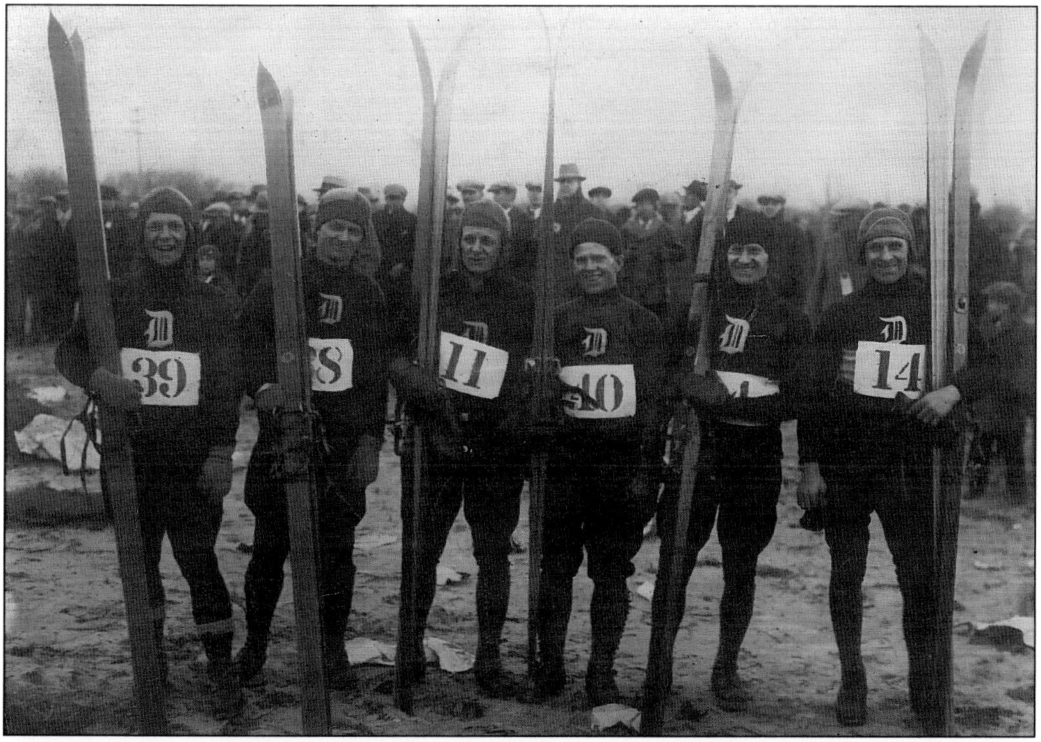

Pictured above are skiing pioneers, the Hall brothers. They are, from left to right: Magnus, Arthur, Clarence, George, Carl, and Henry. The Hall brothers were originally from Ishpeming, Michigan. When the Hall family moved from Ishpeming, their residence became the home for the famous Bietila skiing family.

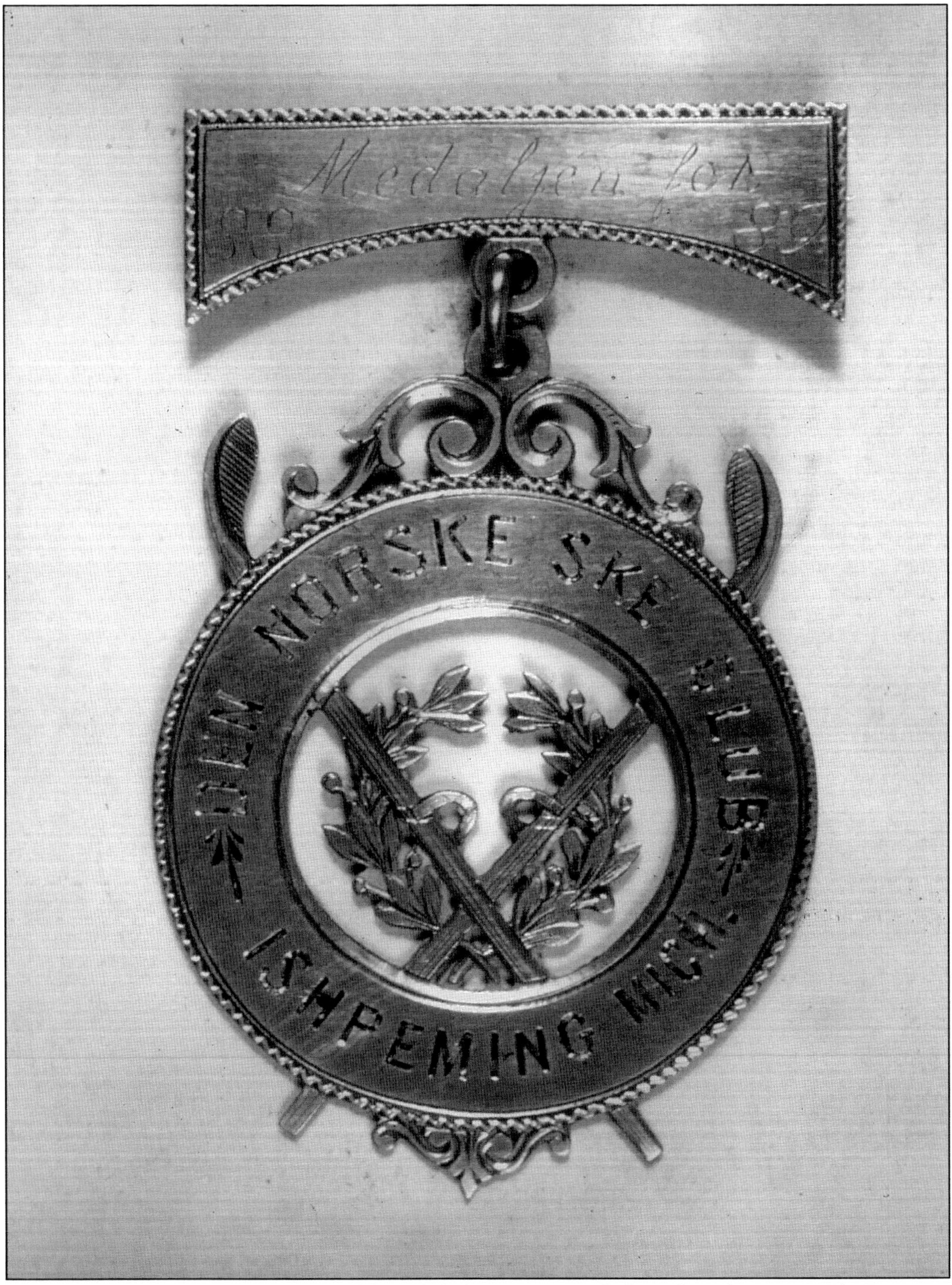

Ole Sundlie won the first place gold medal that was awarded in the Ishpeming Ski Jumping Competition. First prize had to be won two years in succession in order to keep it. Ole captured first place in 1888 and 1889.

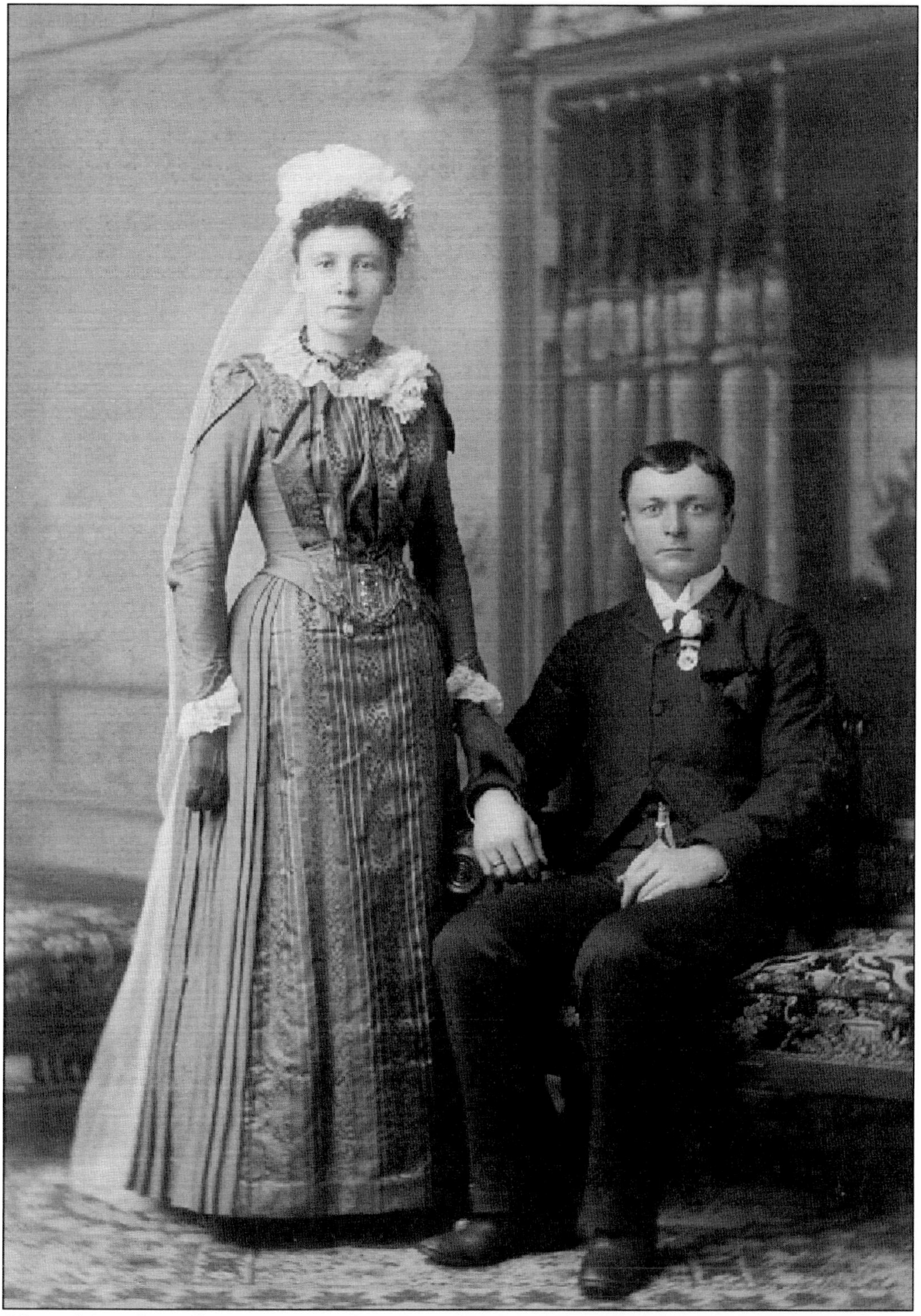

Ole and Sigrid Sundlie were married on December 16, 1890, which was also the birthday they shared. (Note that Ole is wearing his first place gold medal).

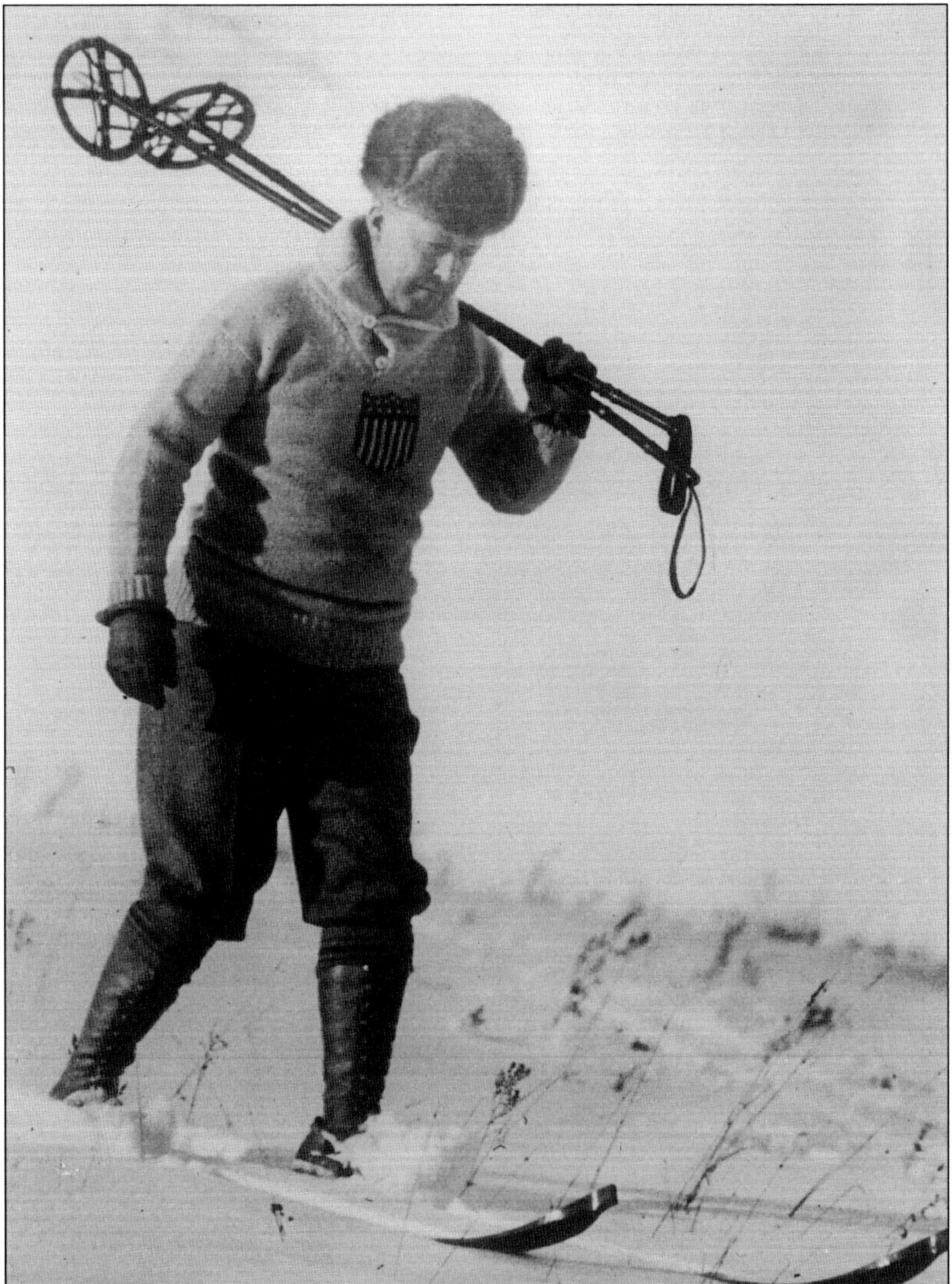

Colonel George Emerson Leach (1876–1955) was the mayor of Minneapolis, Minnesota, when it was known as the "Ski Capital of America." He also represented the National Ski Association as a United States delegate to the first International Ski Congress. Leach was a tireless worker, also managing the 1924 U.S. Oymplic Team in Chamonix, France.

Willis S. Olson, more affectionately known as "Billy the Kid" Olson, was born in Eau Claire, Wisconsin, in 1930. As a teenage ski jumper, he was equal to any slate of strong international jumpers that competed in Mid-America. He is the only American to win all four different National Ski Association ski jumping titles. Billy won Class C in 1948, Class B in 1949, and Class A in 1958. When he reached the age of 32, he entered the Veterans Class and won that title three times in 1965, 1966, and 1968. His longest jump of 393 feet was made in Obersdorf, Germany. He was elected to the US National Ski Hall of Fame in 1972.

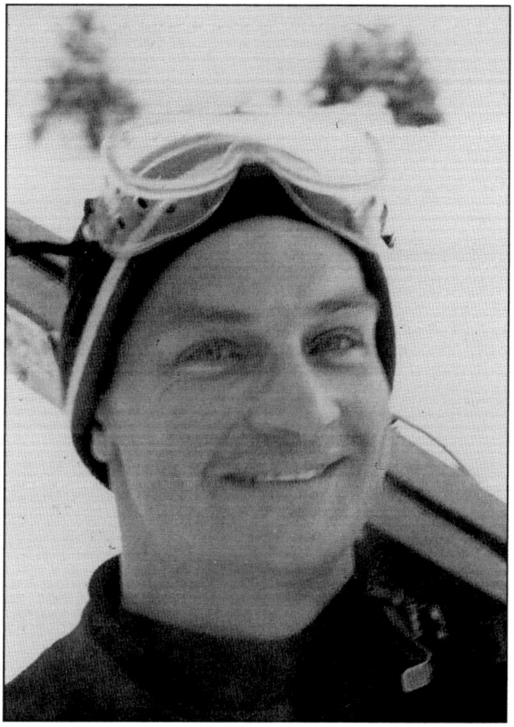

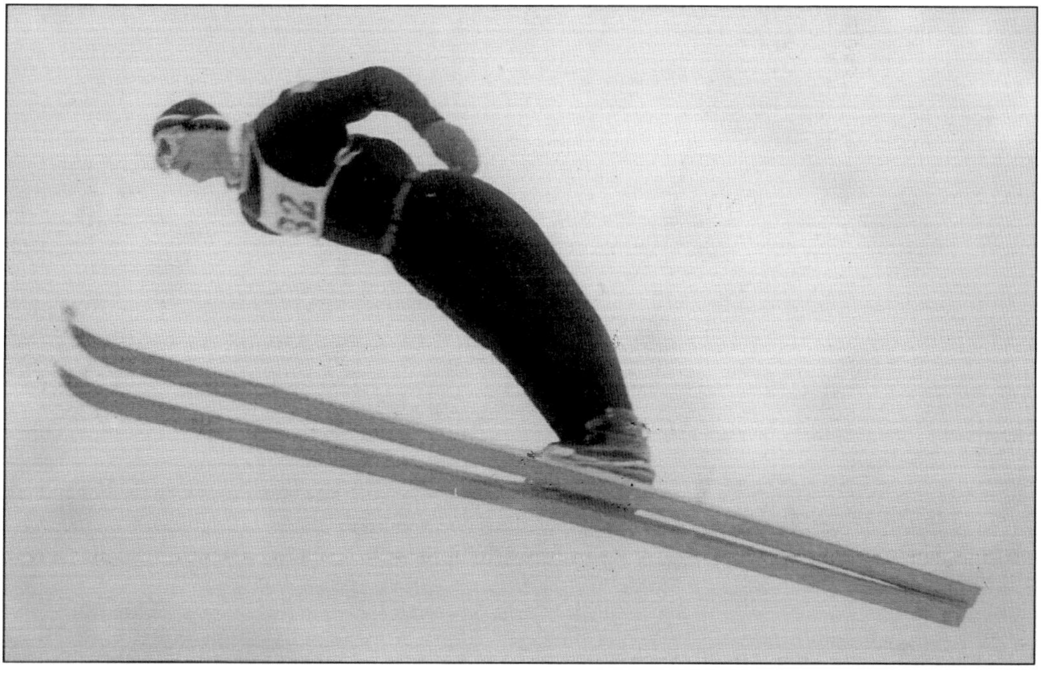

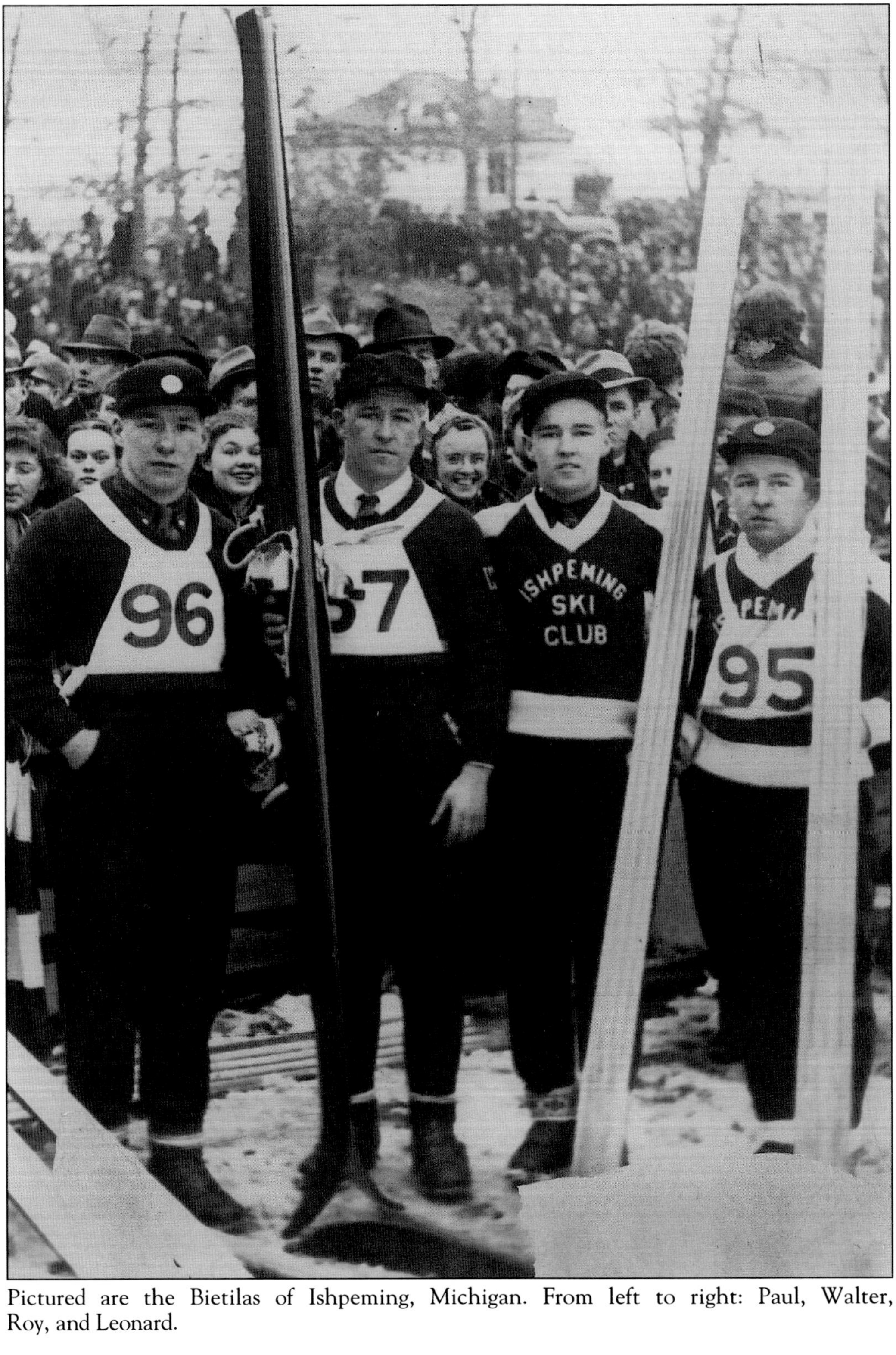

Pictured are the Bietilas of Ishpeming, Michigan. From left to right: Paul, Walter, Roy, and Leonard.

Eugene Wilson from Coleraine, Minnesota, has had a distinguished ski jumping career. He finished in the top three places in 69 of 80 major jumping meets, according to National Ski Association statistics at the end of the 1947 season. Such is the remarkable record of Eugene (Gene) A. Wilson, whose skisport career spanned three decades, from 1933 to 1963.

He was elected to the US National Ski Hall of Fame in 1982.

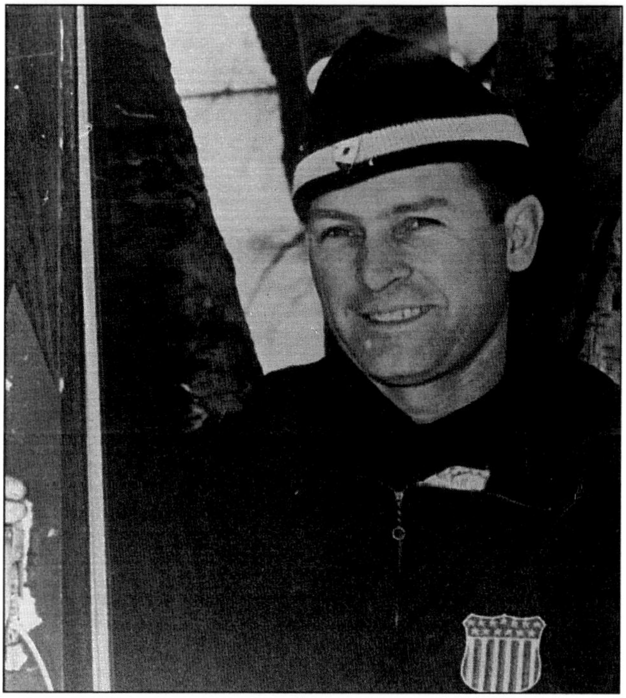

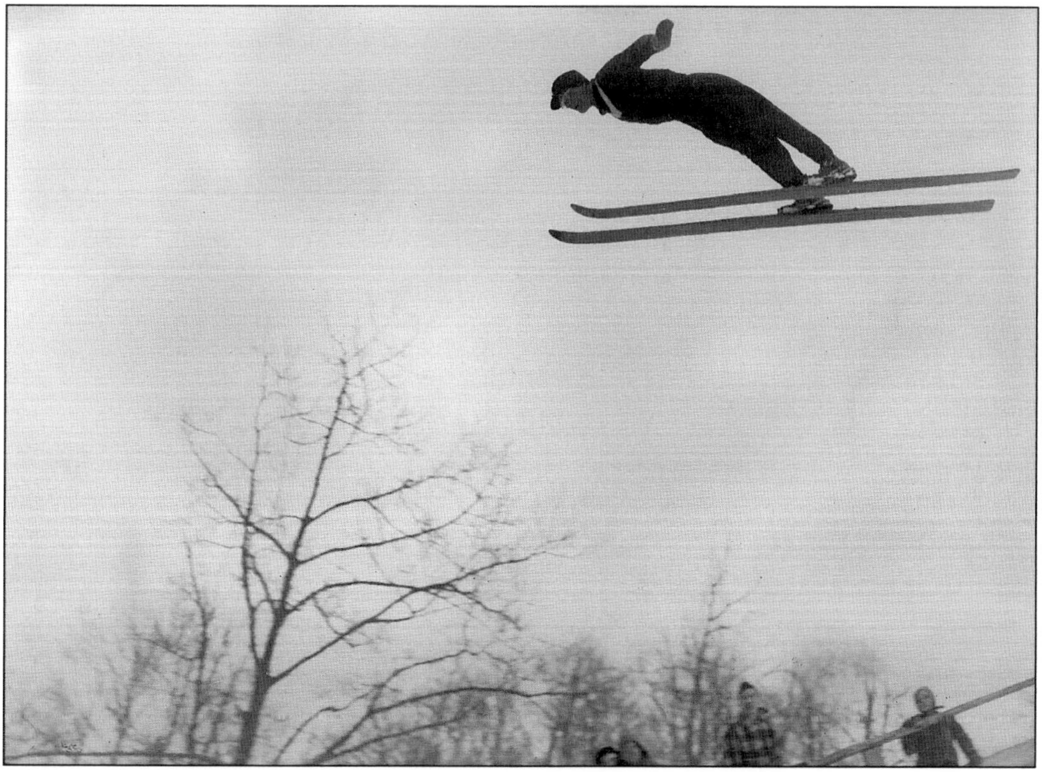

Eugene was a strong contributor to the new, apparently effortless, ride in which he seemed to virtually float through the air.

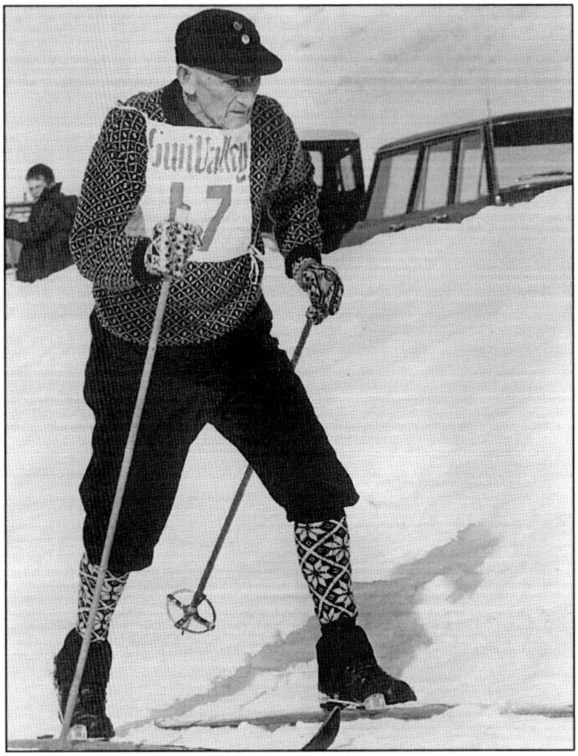

Herman "Jack Rabbit" Smith-Johannsen emigrated to Cleveland, Ohio, from his native country of Norway in 1899. He sold heavy machinery, but became disenchanted with what he considered the wasteful practices of the companies in the United States. He then moved to Piedmont, Quebec, Canada, skiing and trapping in the wilds, where the Cree Indians, whom he taught to ski, nicknamed him "Chief Jack Rabbit." He had a hand in cutting some of Canada's most famous ski trails, and was also credited with upgrading the Lake Placid area, where he revised the trail and slope system. "Jack Rabbit" continued to ski, entering competitions on both sides of the border, and at the age of eighty was considered a geriatric marvel. He lived to be 111 years of age, and was elected to the National Ski Hall of Fame in 1969.

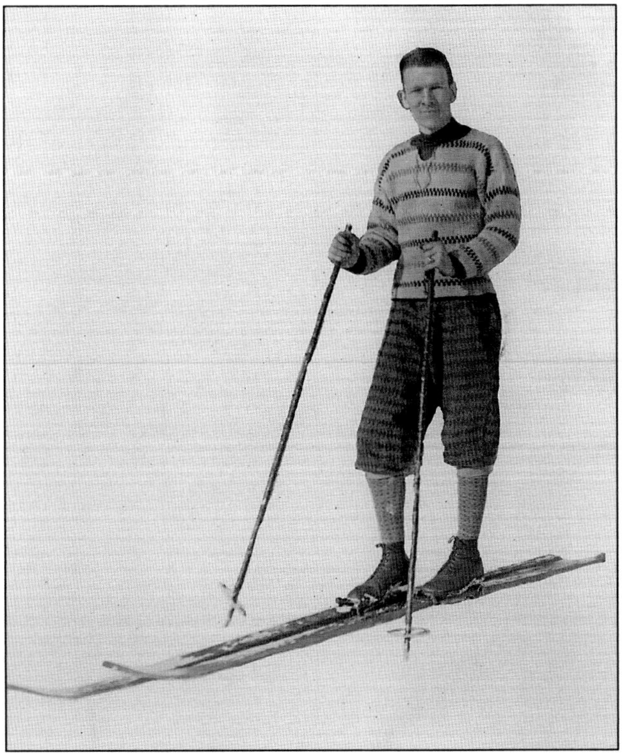

In 1958, Harold Grinden became the third person in the United States to be elected to the Hall of Fame by national convention action. Grinden was cited for more than thirty years of devoted service to the sport of skiing on a local, divisional and national basis. In 1952, Grinden was honored by the Central US Ski Association, when the group awarded him their divisional medal for outstanding service. In 1954, he was awarded the Julius Blegen award by the National Ski Association for his contributions to the sport. Grinden had a long service record as a ski official and was recognized for years as a "four events judge" in the sport. The "Flash Card System" used in open scoring of ski jumping competition was created by Harold.

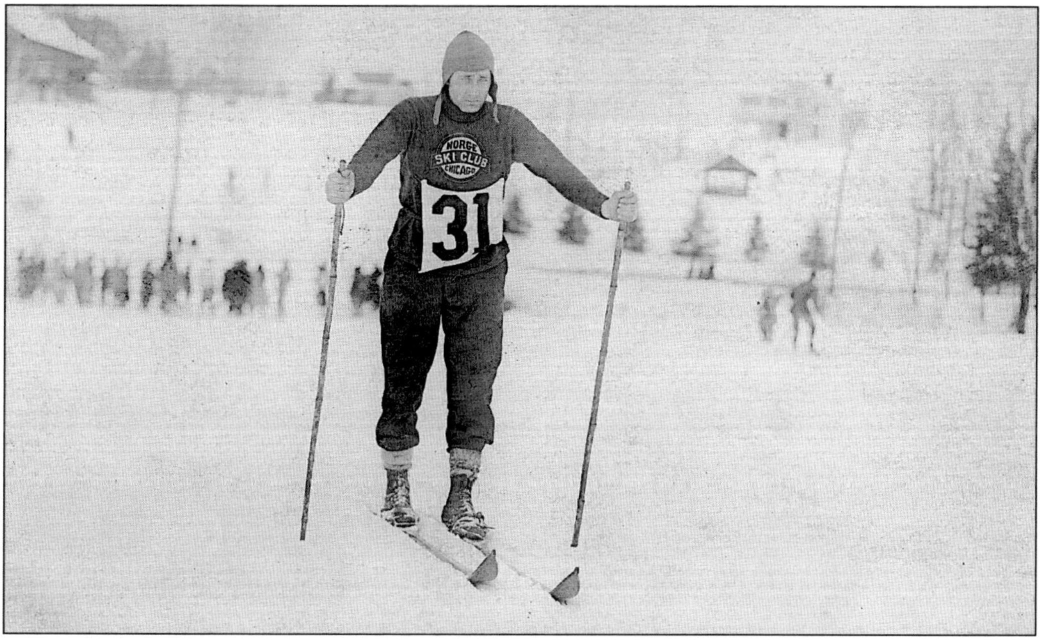

In 1924, Harry Lien represented the United States at the first Winter Olympic Games at Chamonix, France. After three years of inactive skiing, Harry participated in the Norge Annual Meet in 1937, placing second. In 1946, he constructed three ski hills in Hayward, Wisconsin, drawing skiers from Chicago, Minneapolis, Duluth, and Iron Mountain for training.

Harry was elected to the U.S. National Ski Hall of Fame in 1969.

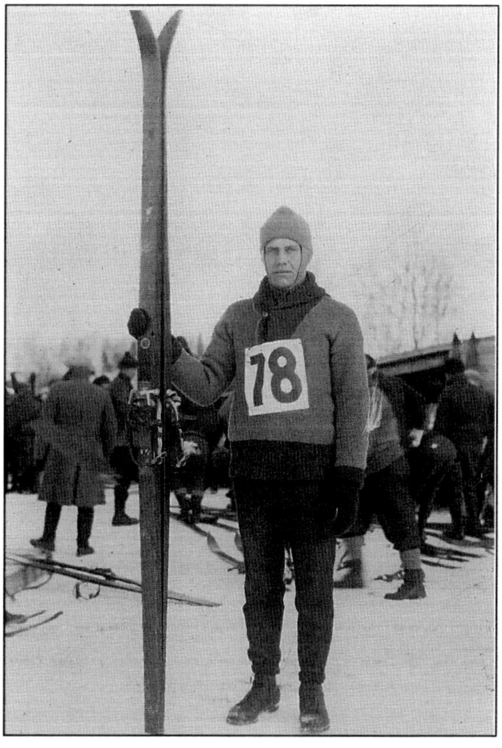

Casper Oimoen was born in Norway in 1906. He came to the United States in 1923 and settled in Minot, North Dakota. He then proceeded to take the ski jumping sport by storm. His spectacular career spanned nineteen jumping seasons.

Based on his amazing athletic achievements, Casper was elected to the U.S. National Ski Hall of Fame in Ishpeming, Michigan, in 1963. He was the twenty-fifth person to be so honored.

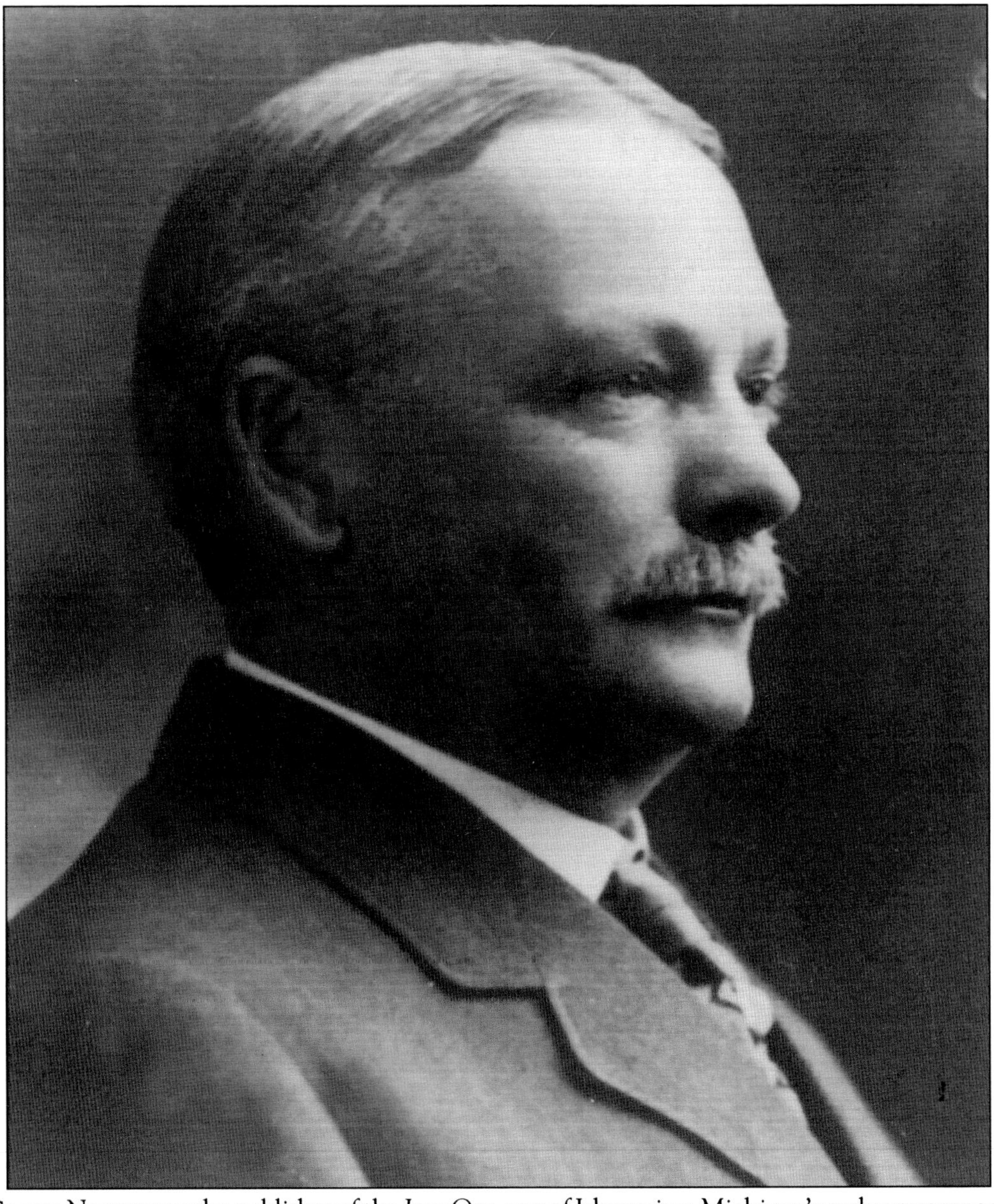

George Newett was the publisher of the *Iron Ore*, one of Ishpeming, Michigan's early newspapers. Newett's accounts of early ski jumping events in the Upper Midwest did much to add to early skiing's popularity in the region, and led him into joining with the group of Ishpeming citizens to form the National Ski Association in February, 1905. Newett drew national attention to himself and the area when he wrote a bold political editorial about Theodore Roosevelt, the 1912 candidate for US president of the Progressive "Bull Moose" party. His statements about Roosevelt's lying, cursing, and frequent drinking of alcohol resulted in a lawsuit filed by the candidate. A trial held in Marquette, Michigan, in May of 1913, brought Roosevelt and numerous character witnesses to Northern Michigan, who defended the twenty-sixth president's reputation. Roosevelt won the case and accepted a settlement of six cents!

Newett was elected to the US National Ski Hall of Fame in 1970.

Paul Joseph Perrault, known to everyone as "Jumping Joe", moved to Ishpeming, Michigan, at an early age where his interest in skiing developed. Joe was a member of the Olympic Teams of 1948 and 1952. Perhaps his greatest day in skiing, and one of the first triumphs for American ski jumping took place on Saturday, February 26, 1949, at Pine Mountain Ski Hill in Iron Mountain, Michigan. He jumped 297 feet, a new North American distance record, just three feet short of the elusive 300-foot barrier. This was one of the most exciting days in American ski jumping history.

Joe Perrault was elected to the US National Ski Hall of Fame in 1971.

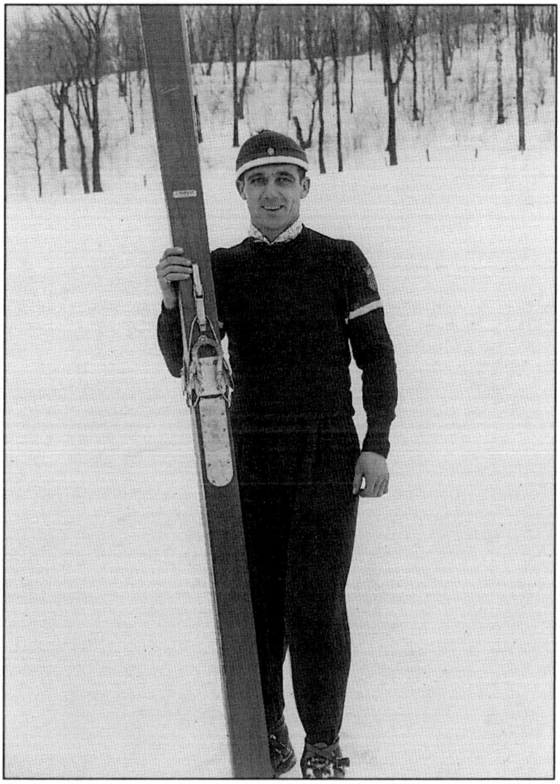

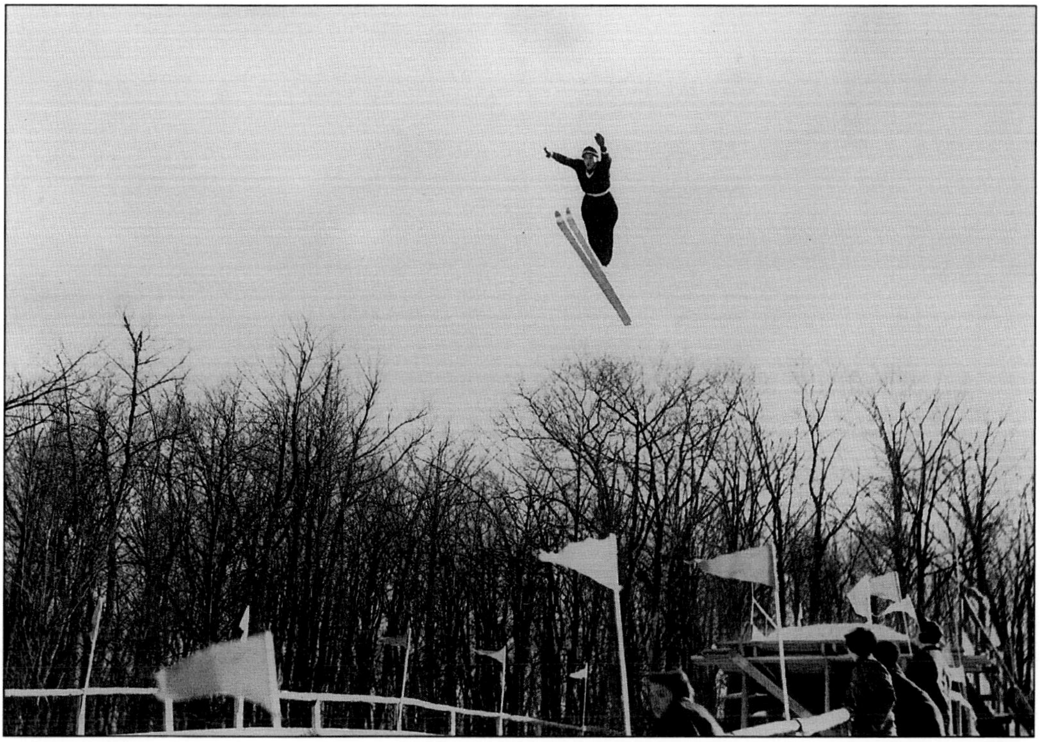

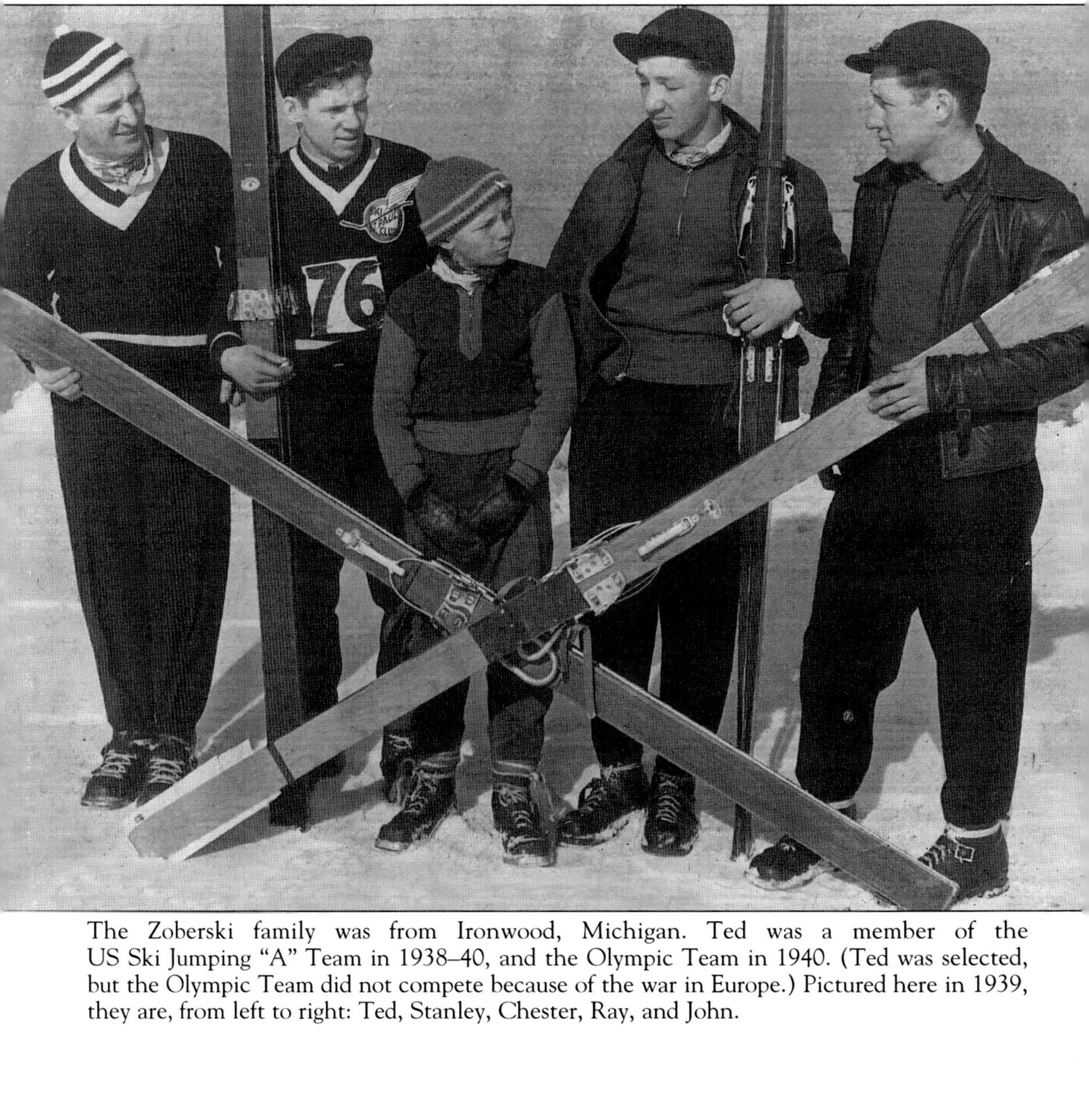

The Zoberski family was from Ironwood, Michigan. Ted was a member of the US Ski Jumping "A" Team in 1938–40, and the Olympic Team in 1940. (Ted was selected, but the Olympic Team did not compete because of the war in Europe.) Pictured here in 1939, they are, from left to right: Ted, Stanley, Chester, Ray, and John.

Relatively little is known of Asario Autio except that he was an "Iron Man" on cross-country skis. A native of Finland, in the early 1900s, Autio emigrated to the United States, settling in Ely, Minnesota. In 1907, he entered the first National Ski Association sanctioned National Cross Country Championships in Ashland, Wisconsin, and won it easily, becoming the first National Ski Association Cross Country Champion. He was the first person awarded the Gale Cotton Burton Memorial Trophy when it was initiated, and was posthumously awarded the National Ski Association Bronze Plaque for his cross-country feats in 1966.

Asario Autio was elected to the US National Ski Hall of Fame in 1966.

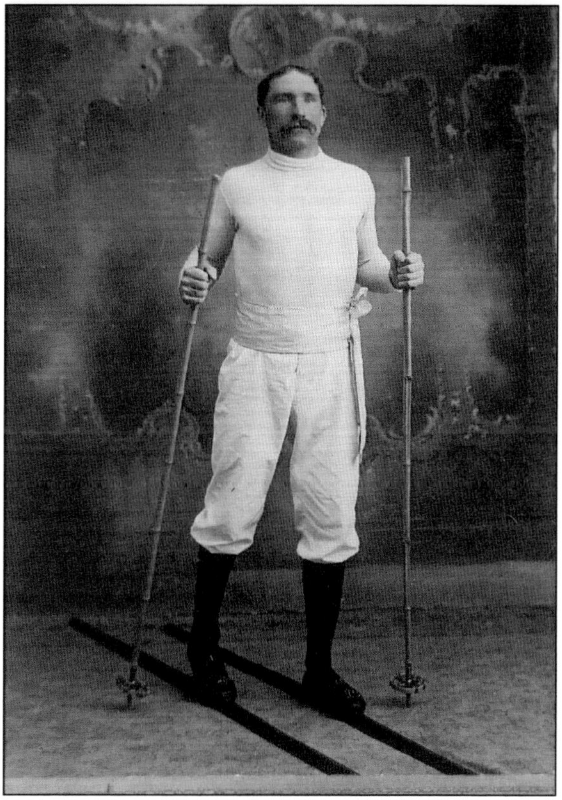

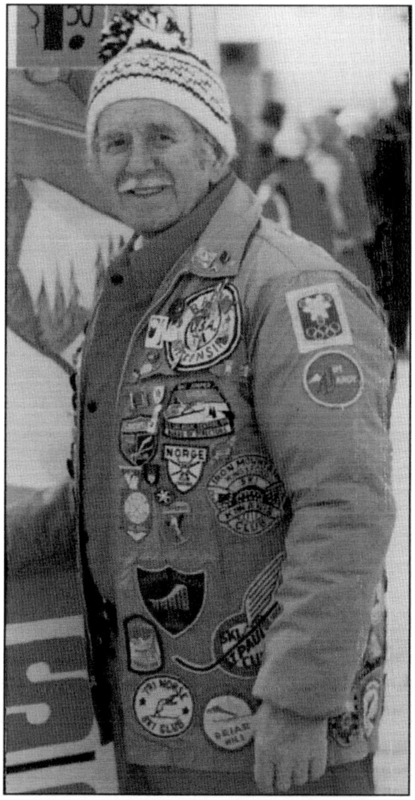

Art Knudsen is from Racine, Wisconsin, and is an honorary lifetime member of the Racine Ski Club, whose colorful work in support of the nation's ski teams has been recognized divisionally, nationally, and internationally. Much of Knudsen's adult life has been devoted to promotion of skisport, first as a competitor, then as a club and divisional officer and as a volunteer ski-team-pins-sales fund-raiser. Art served the Olympic movement twice in Squaw Valley, California, first during tryouts at the Olympic facilities at the North American Championships of 1959, and again in 1960 for actual competition.

He was elected to the U.S. National Ski Hall of Fame in 1973.

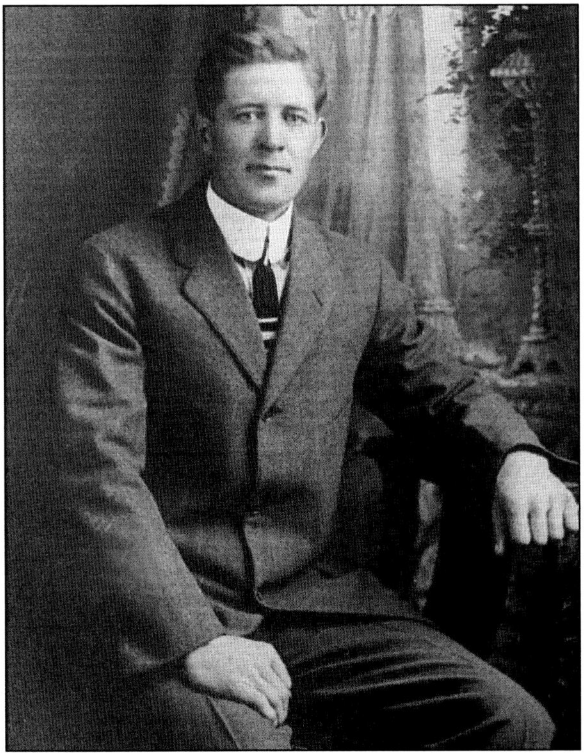

Anders Haugen (left) was born in Norway in 1889, and his brother Lars was born two years later in 1891. Both were on skis almost before they could walk, and developed into championship caliber skiers in their teens. The brothers emigrated to the United States in 1909 to join three siblings who had emigrated a few years earlier. Anders settled in Milwaukee, Wisconsin, where he joined the Milwaukee Ski Club and helped the club design and build a jumping hill.

He was elected to the US National Ski Hall of Fame in 1963.

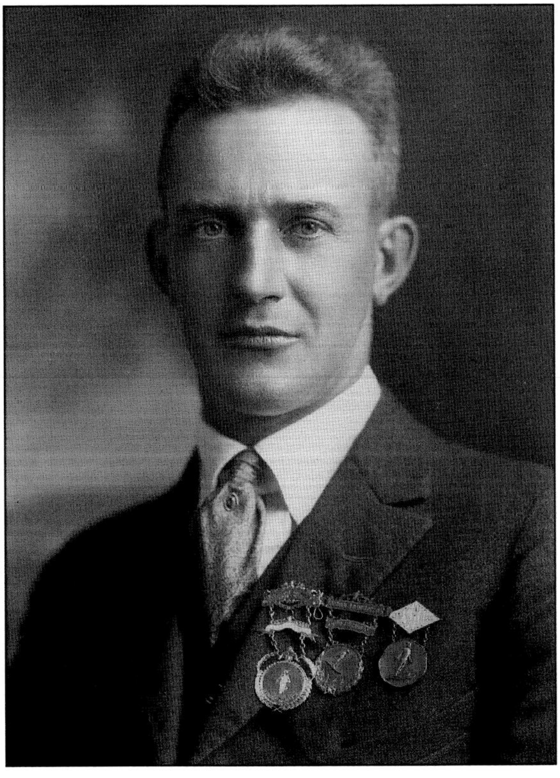

Lars Haugen (right) first settled in Red Wing, Minnesota, and later in Chippewa Falls, Wisconsin. He skied the meets in the Upper Midwest for several years, winning six United States National Championships between 1912 and 1928. He then decided to go west to the mountains of California. Lars was afforded the opportunity to join the US Olympic Team in Chamonix, France, but declined after turning professional. Upon Lars's recommendation, Anders was chosen as his replacement on the team. See related story on page 53.

He was elected to the US National Ski Hall of Fame in 1963.

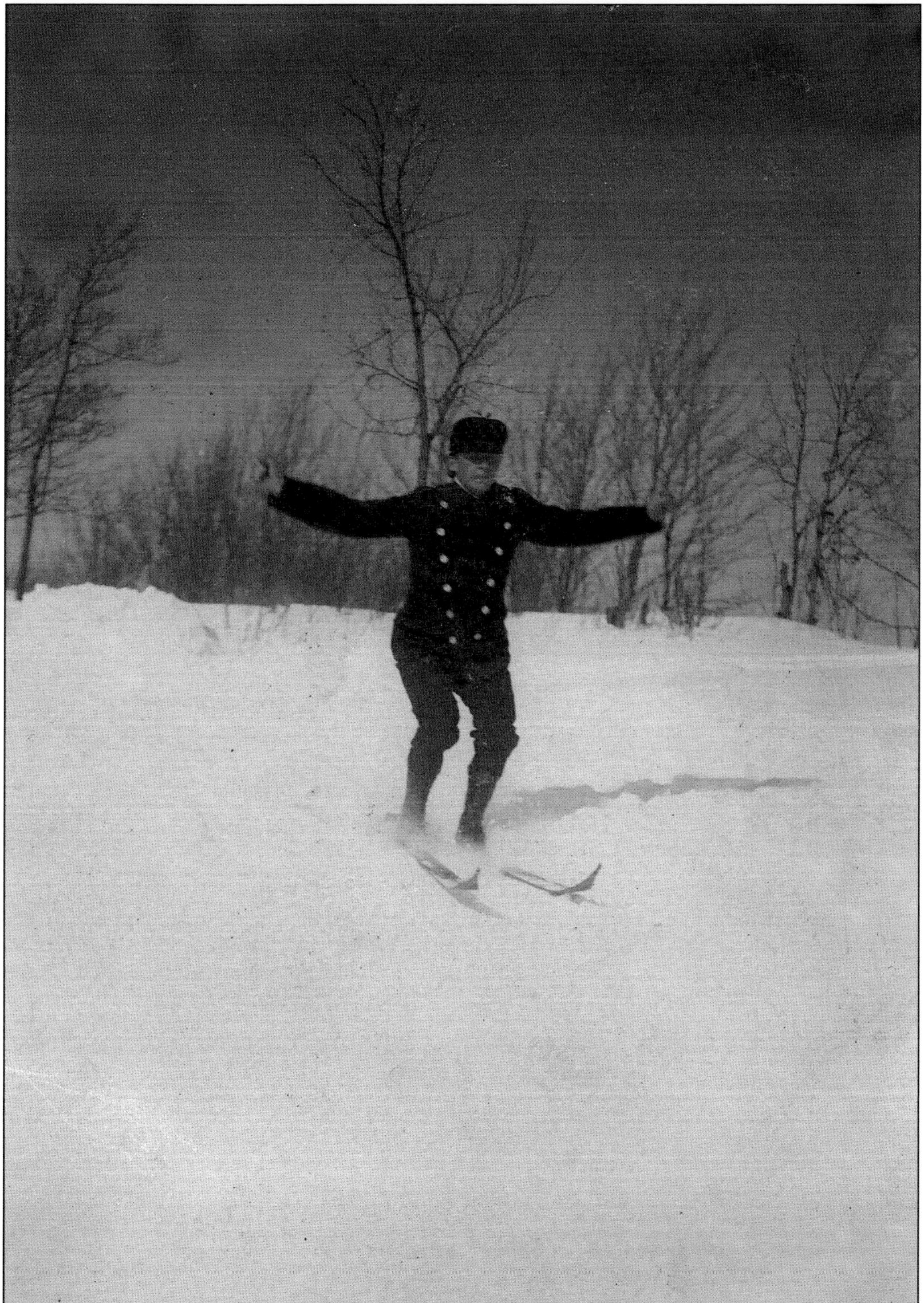

Conrad Thompson, first National Ski Jumping Champion in 1904 is pictured here. He was from Ishpeming, Michigan, and was elected to the US National Ski Hall of Fame in 1966.

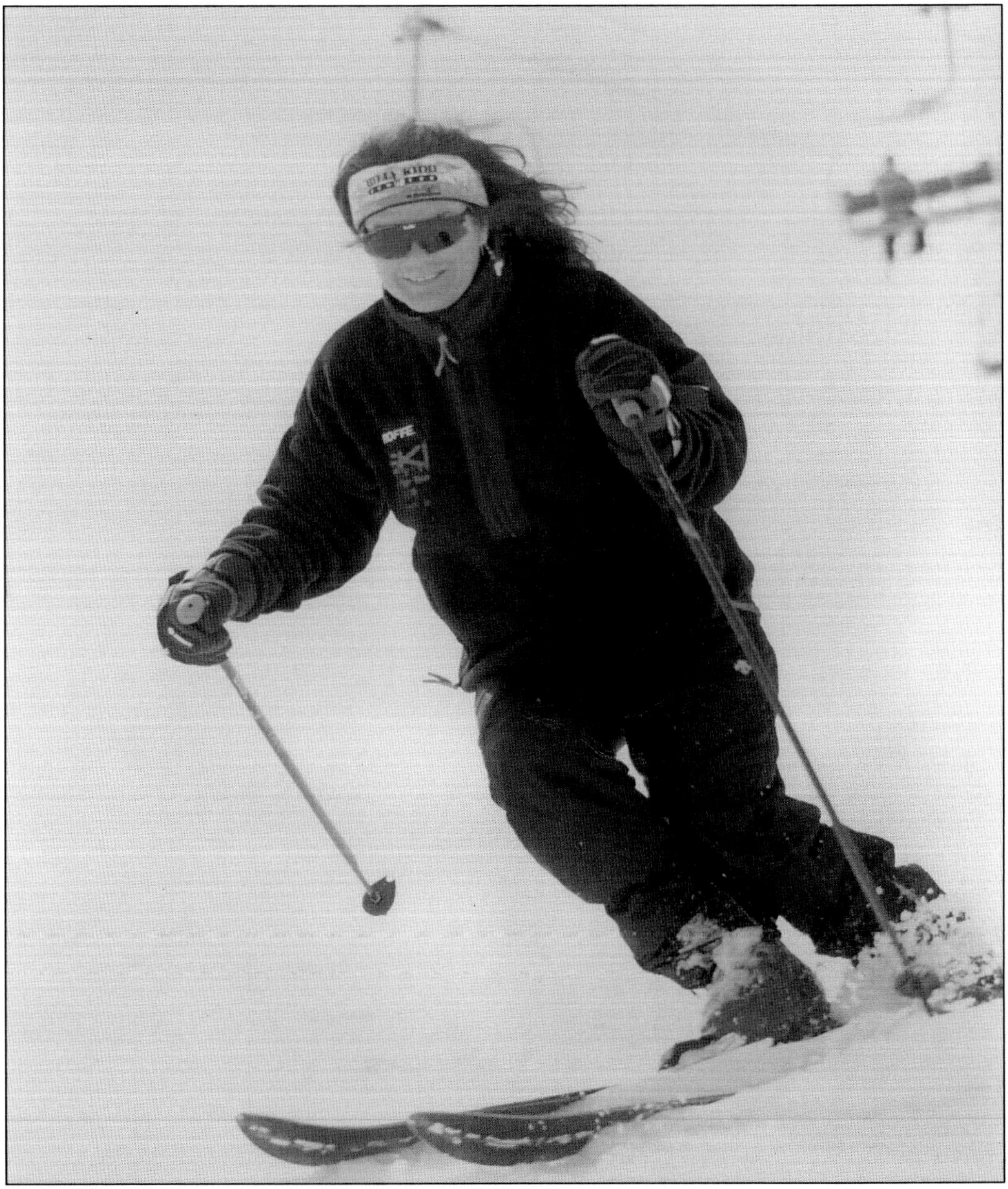

Jeannie Thoren was born in Marquette, Michigan, in 1946. She earned a spot on the Junior National Alpine Team while a junior in high school, and she often trained with the Northern Michigan University men's alpine team, as there was no women's team at that time. After graduation, Jeannie continued to ski and began to discover that the ski equipment she and other women were using wasn't designed with women in mind. Using herself as a "guinea pig," Jeannie has been working on a system of equipment modification, including placing heel lifts in boots and mounting bindings ahead of the manufacturer-recommended position, to move a woman's center of mass forward over her skis, thus enhancing turn initiation.

Jeannie Thoren has a mission: TO HELP WOMEN SKI BETTER BY MAKING THEIR EQUIPMENT BETTER. For this, she was honored by *Skiing Magazine* as one of the first four women to be included in the magazine's 1995 Women's Ski Hall of Fame.

Ten

Recreational Skiing

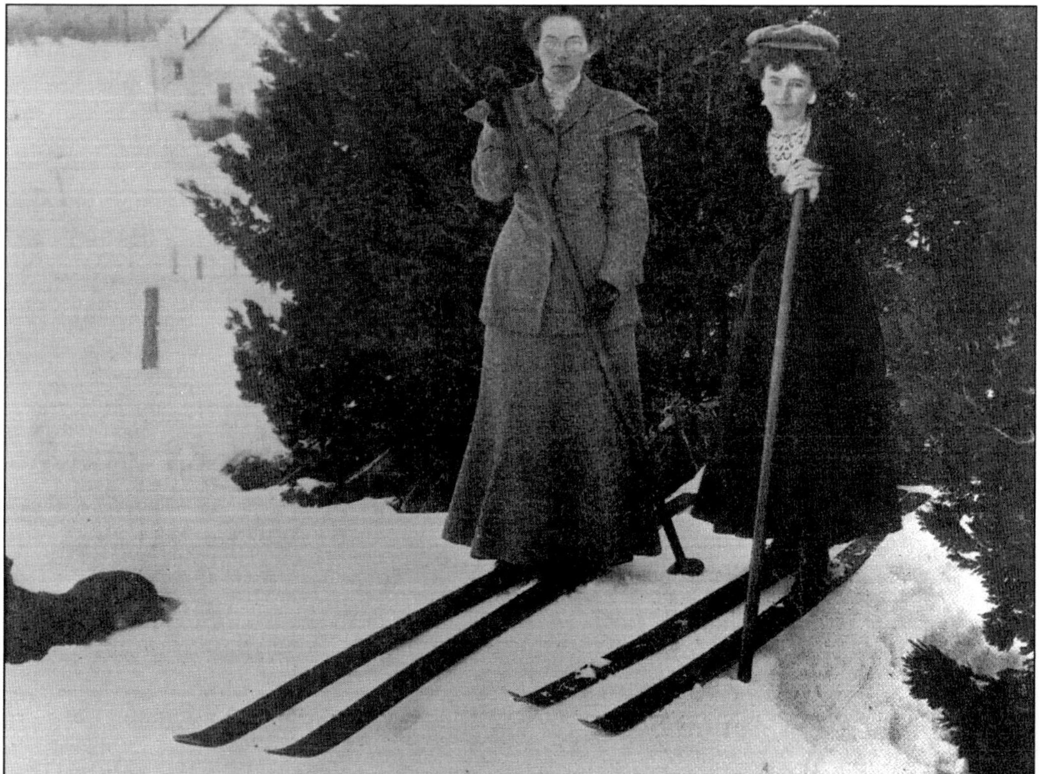

Local ladies are pictured above, out for a ski tour.

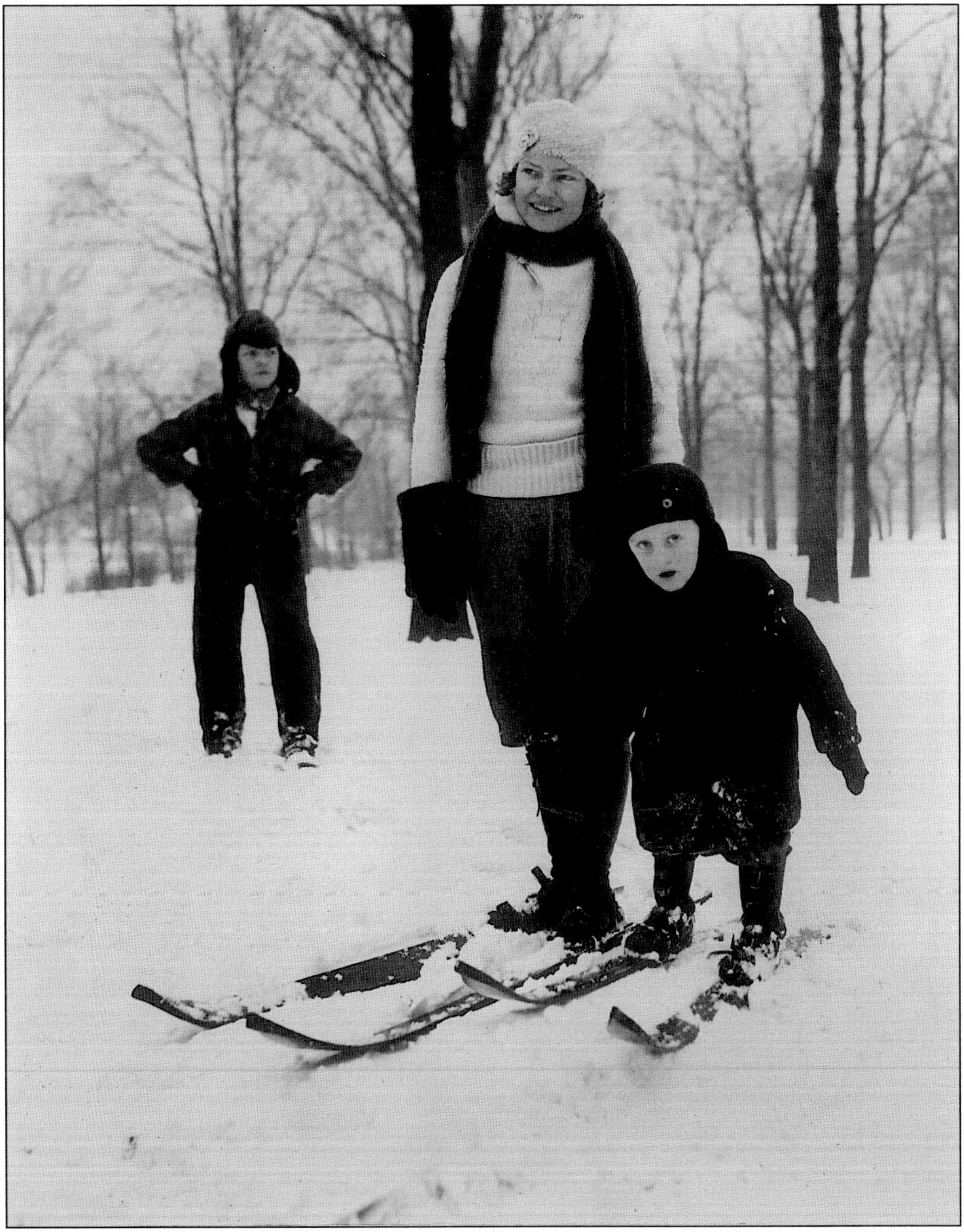

Agnes Barth and son Joe are getting an early start.

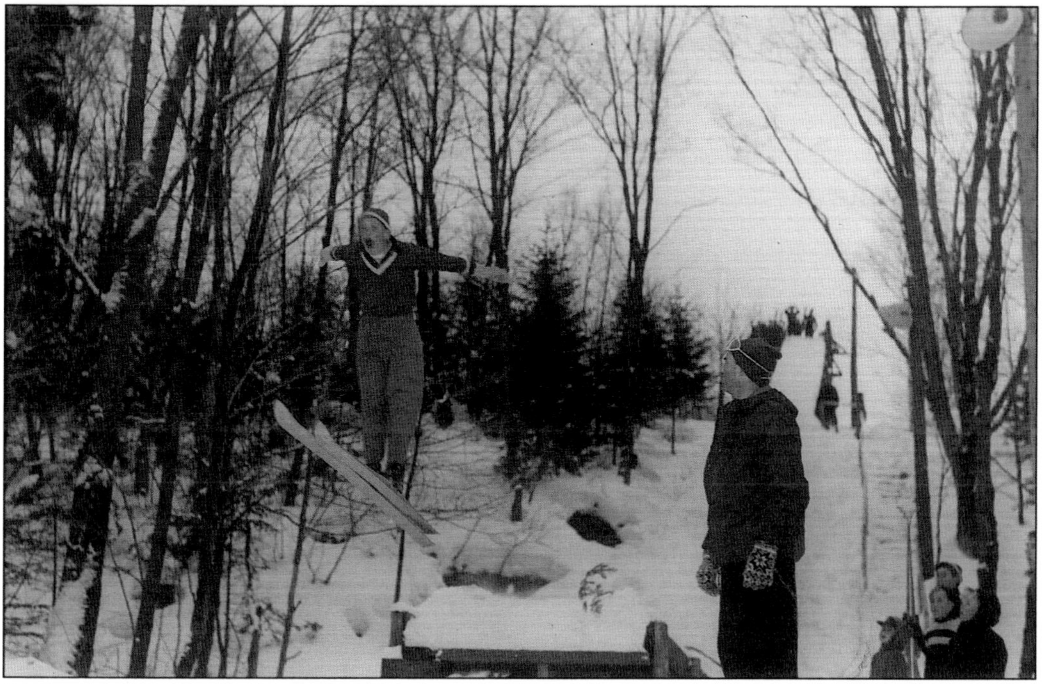

Pictured above is Ralph Bietila at Teal Lake, standing by the take-off. Teal Lake was a favorite beginning ski jumping hill, located at the Al Quaal recreation area in Ishpeming.

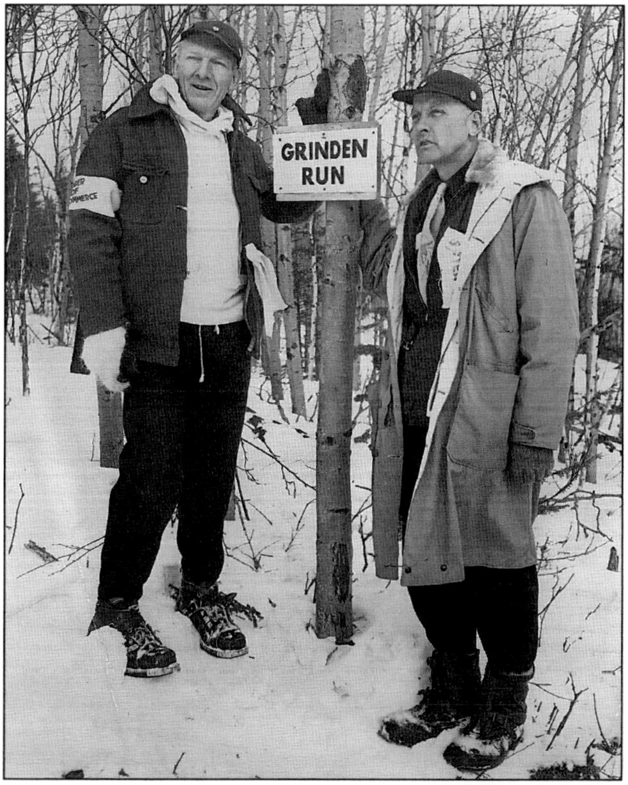

The photo at right shows Grinden Run, Grand Marais, Minnesota.

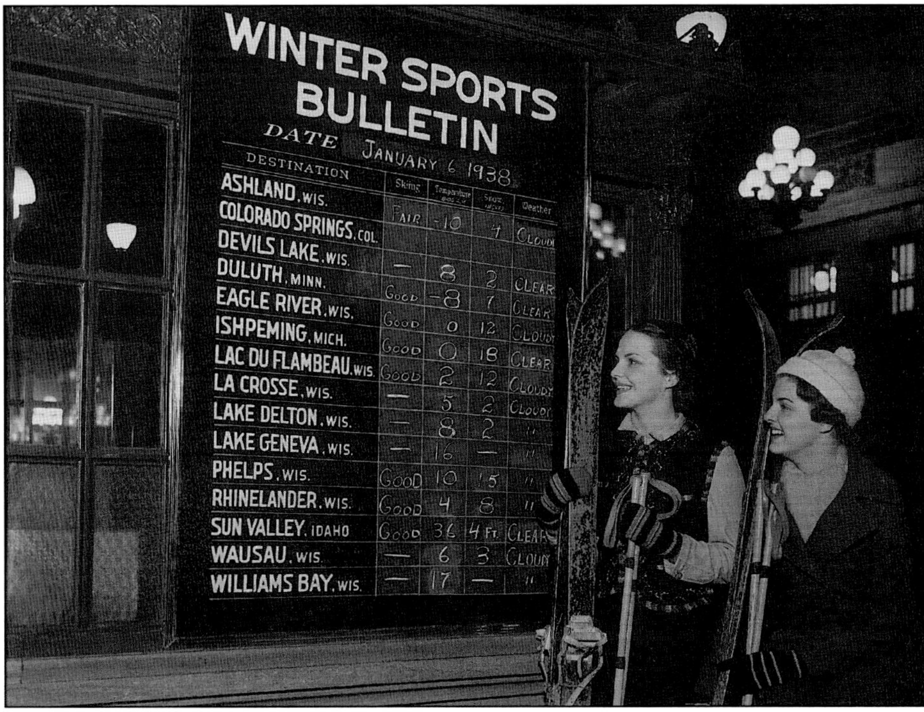

Patterned after the ski trains that left New York and Boston for the hills of Vermont and New Hampshire, the Chicago and Northwestern Railroad's "400," and Wisconsin Central Railroad ran ski trains, bringing recreational skiers from the Chicago and Milwaukee areas to the Upper Peninsula of Michigan for ski weekends. Ishpeming and Iron Mountain were two of the primary destination stops.

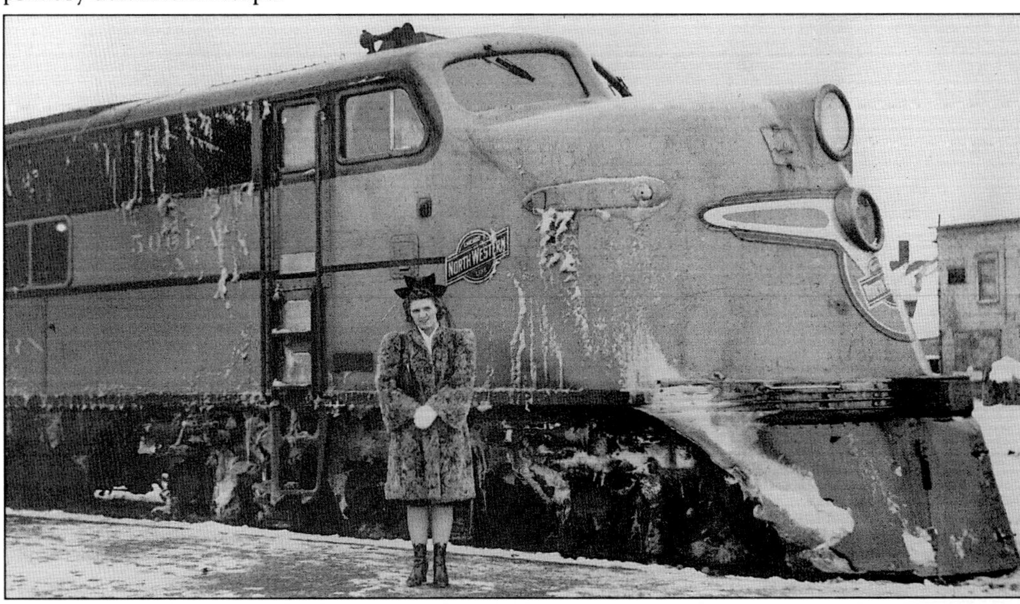

Mildred Sundblad is pictured above meeting the "400." This was the skiers' train, the streamliner from Chicago to Ishpeming. The Ishpeming Winter Sports Club was a destination ski area for many skiers from the Chicago and Milwaukee areas in the 1940s.

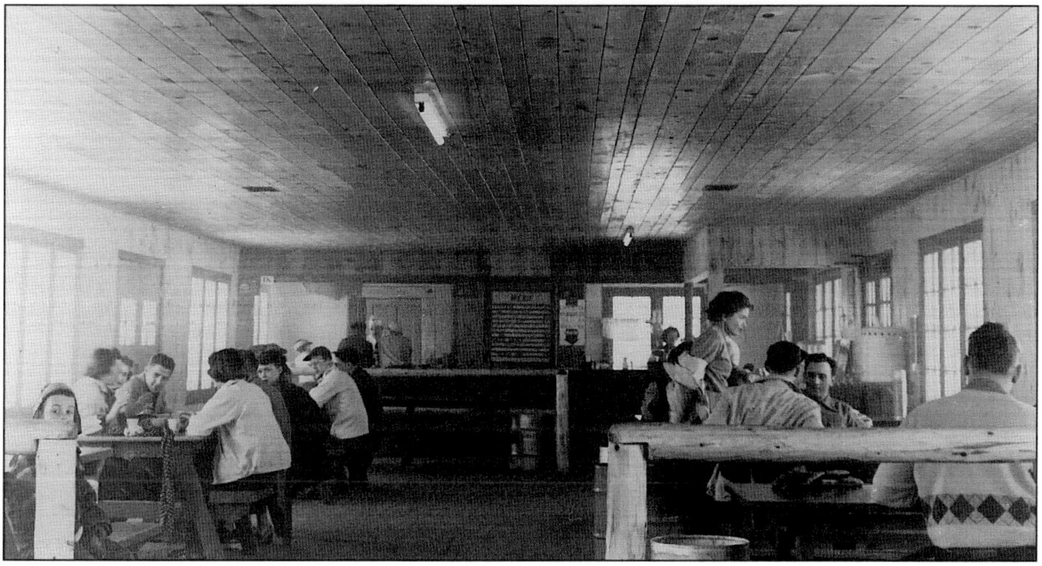

The large lodge at Caberfae, near Cadillac, Michigan, was the place to meet and rest during a day of winter play at Caberfae. Shown here in a photo from the 1950s, is the cafeteria portion of the lodge where meals were served throughout the four-month ski season. (*Cadillac Evening News*, Cadillac, Michigan.)

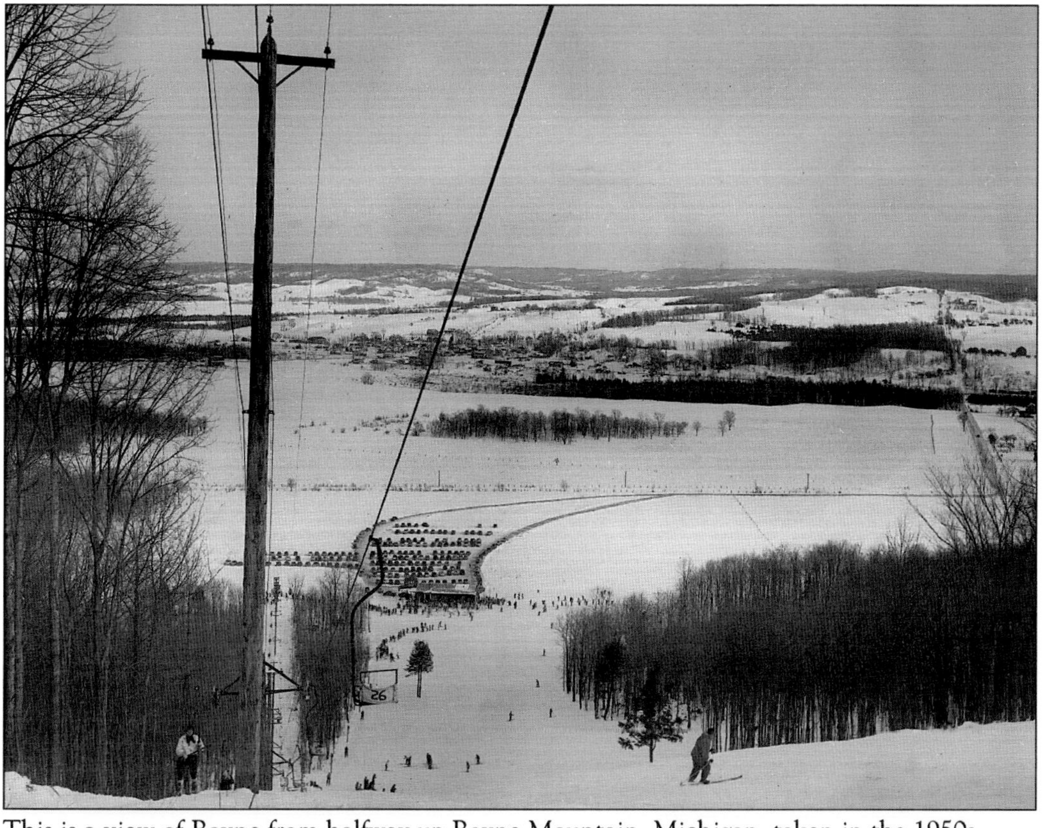

This is a view of Boyne from halfway up Boyne Mountain, Michigan, taken in the 1950s.

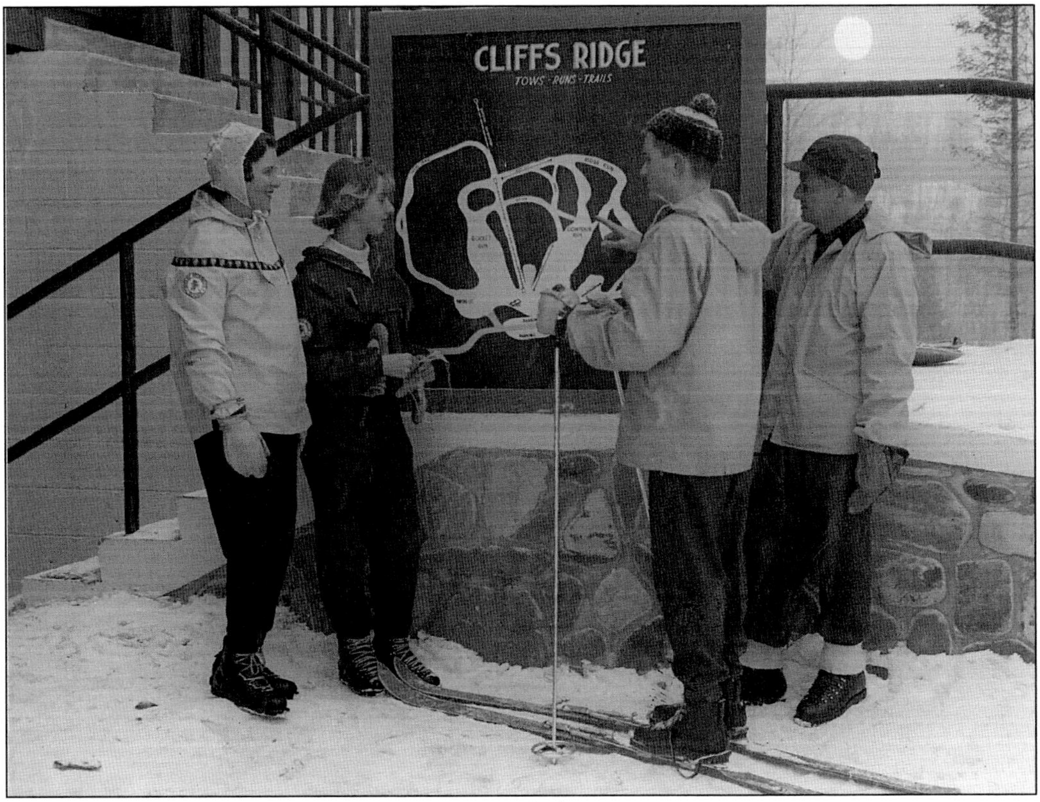

Cliffs Ridge, in Marquette, Michigan, is now called Marquette Mountain.

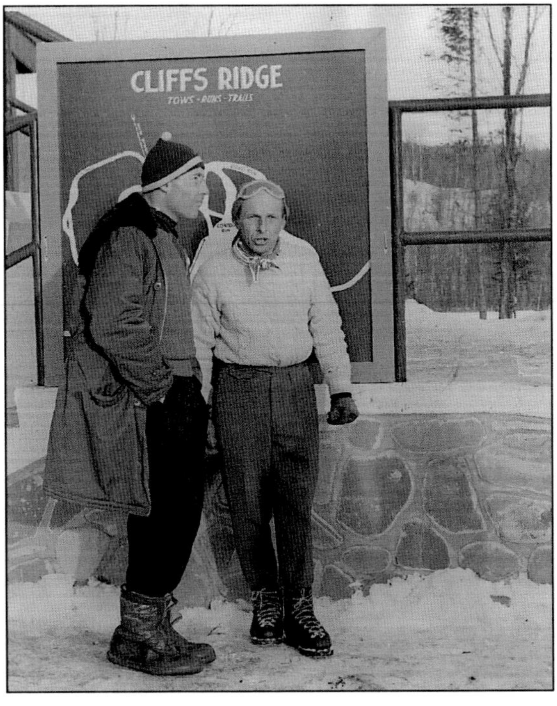

Note the fifties clothing styles for skiing, with an Austrian flavor. Sepp Hoedlmoser, ski instructor, is pictured discussing a race course with an alpine ski official.

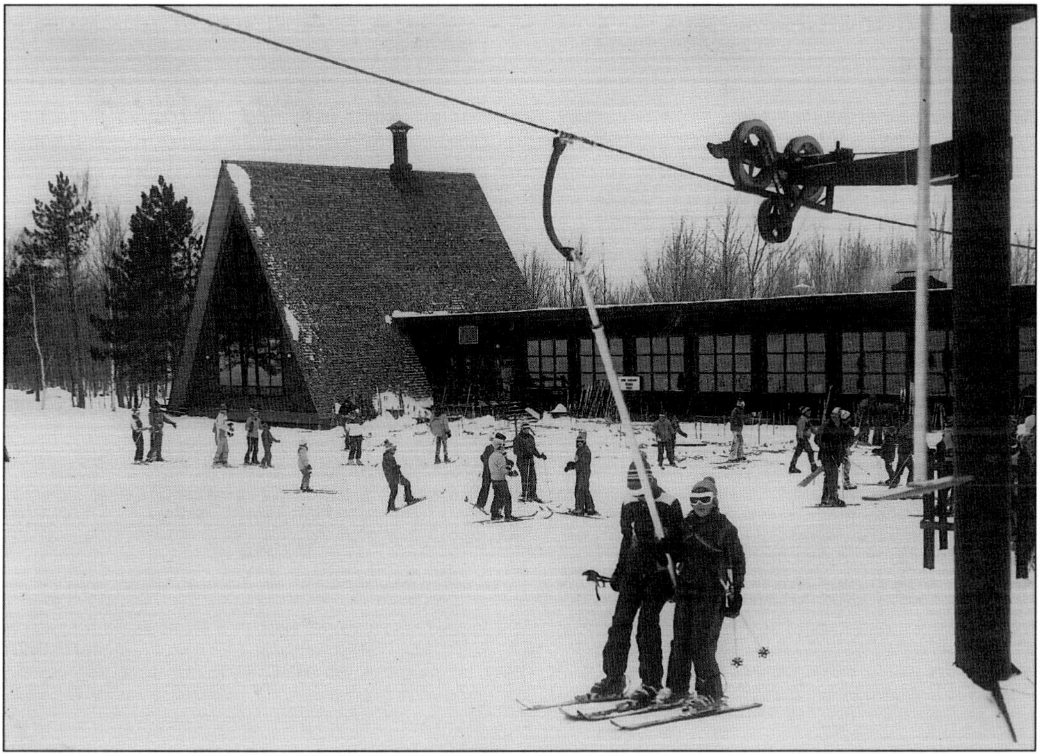

Pictured above and below is the Porcupine Ski Area, in the 1950s.

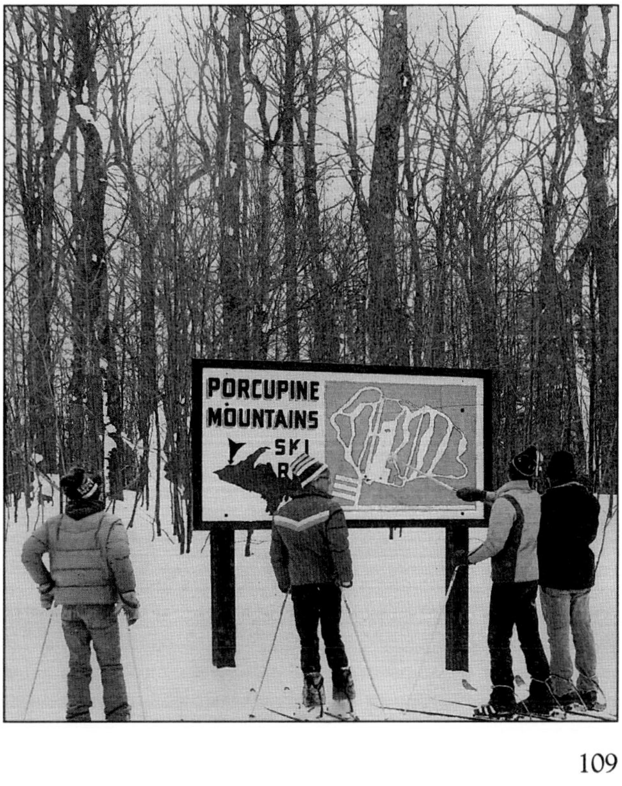

The Porcupine Ski Area is state owned and operated. It is located on the south shore of Lake Superior in the western Upper Peninsula of Michigan.

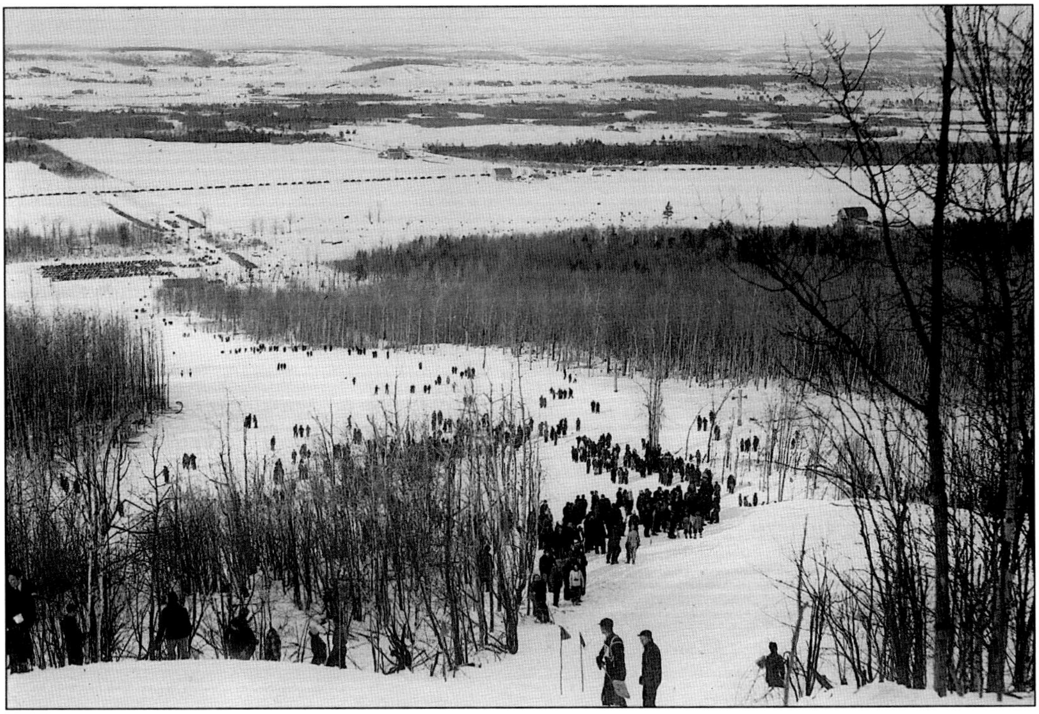

An alpine ski race in progress is pictured above at Rib Mountain at Wausau, Wisconsin.

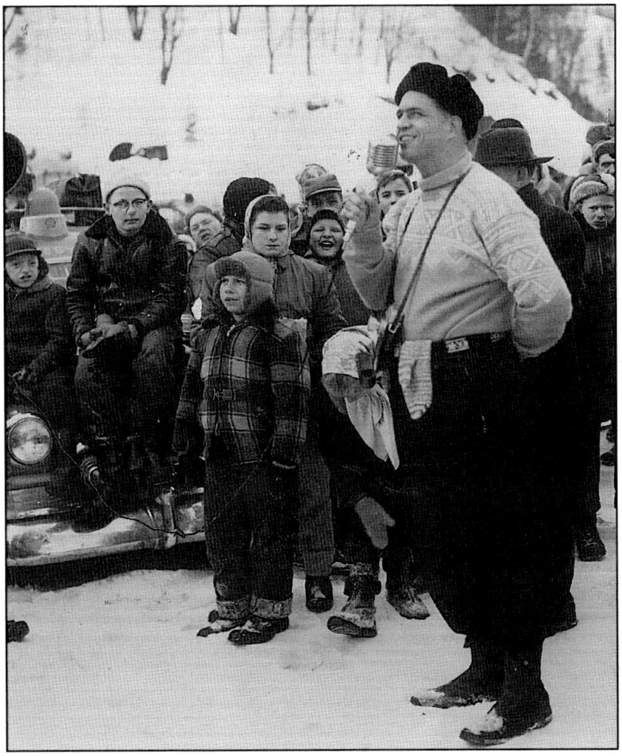

In February of 1957, Michigan Governor G. Mennen Williams, a ski enthusiast, took a weekend off from his duties in Lansing to attend the Paul Bietila Memorial Tournament and the 69th Annual Ishpeming Ski Club Classic in Ishpeming. The sportily attired governor is shown at left addressing the huge throng over the sound system of a Miller Brewing Company courtesy car, which was pressed into service when the club's public address facilities failed.

Eleven

BARNSTORMERS AND CIRCUS ACTS

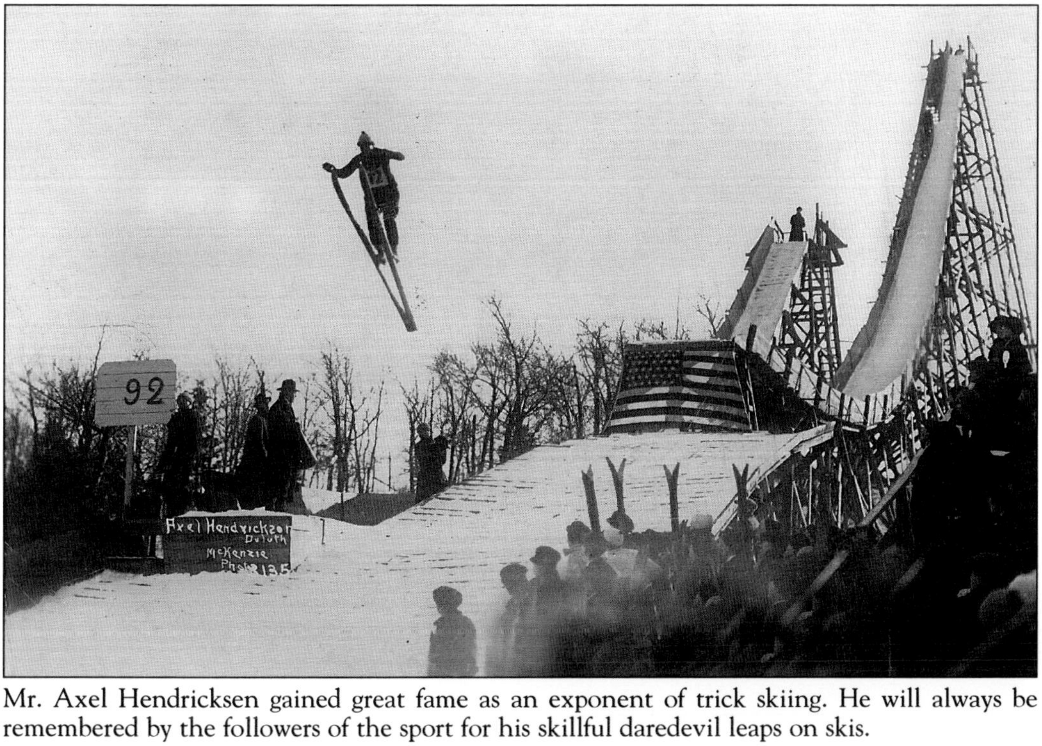

Mr. Axel Hendricksen gained great fame as an exponent of trick skiing. He will always be remembered by the followers of the sport for his skillful daredevil leaps on skis.

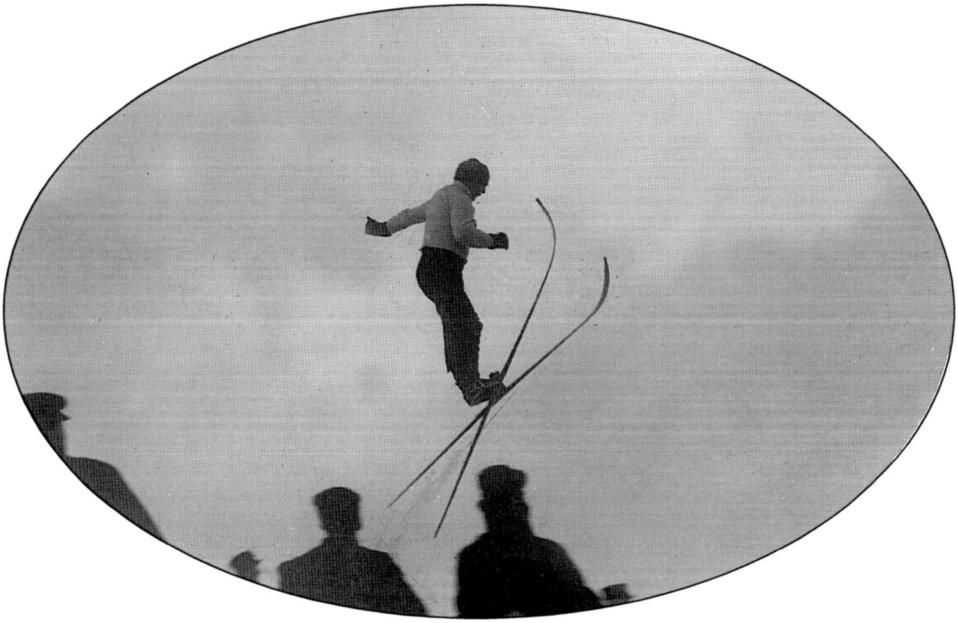

Pictured above is a ski jumper entertaining spectators in the early 1900s.

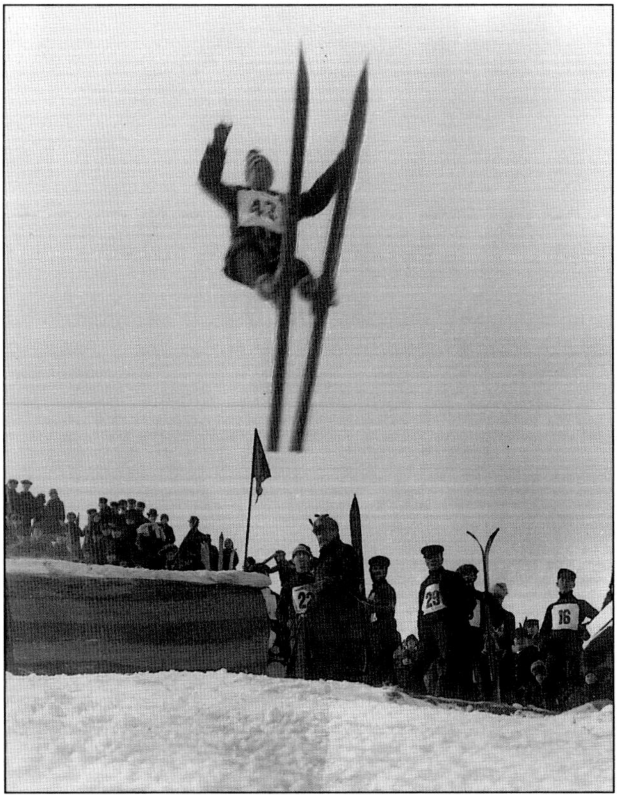

This ski jumper is in for a rough landing.

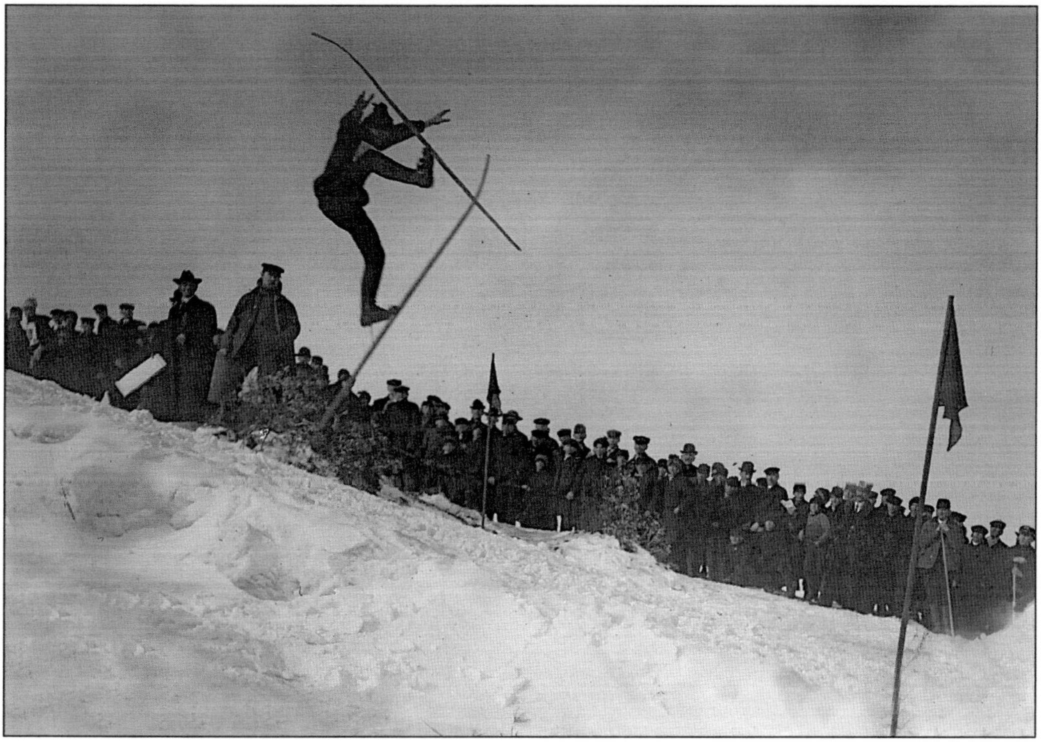

Not all jumpers were experts!

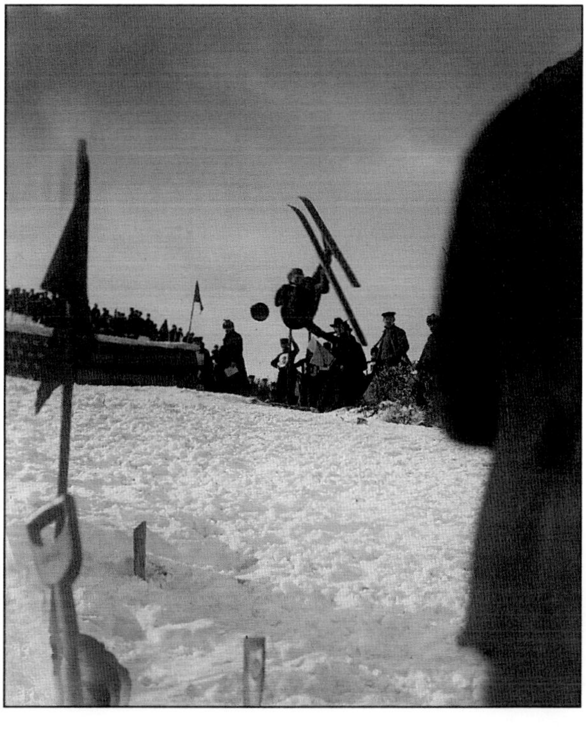

In the late 1800s and early 1900s, good form was not even considered. Getting as far down the landing as possible was the name of the game. Such efforts sometimes resulted in bizarre spills. Less-than-successful jumpers were probably embarrassed, but after the good-natured jeering of their "buddies" subsided, jumpers went up and tried again. As life threatening as the efforts appeared, very rarely were any of the jumpers seriously injured.

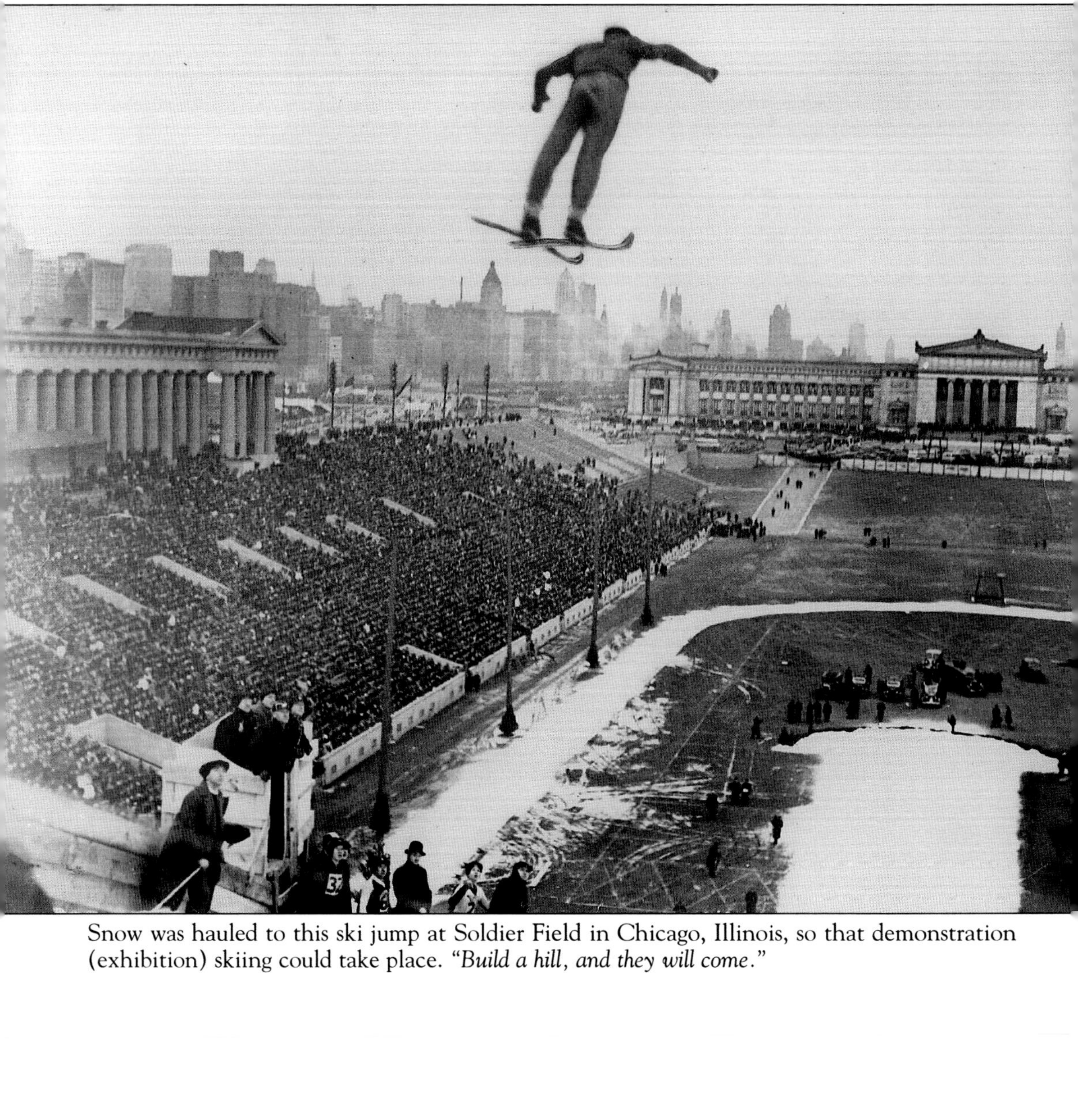

Snow was hauled to this ski jump at Soldier Field in Chicago, Illinois, so that demonstration (exhibition) skiing could take place. *"Build a hill, and they will come."*

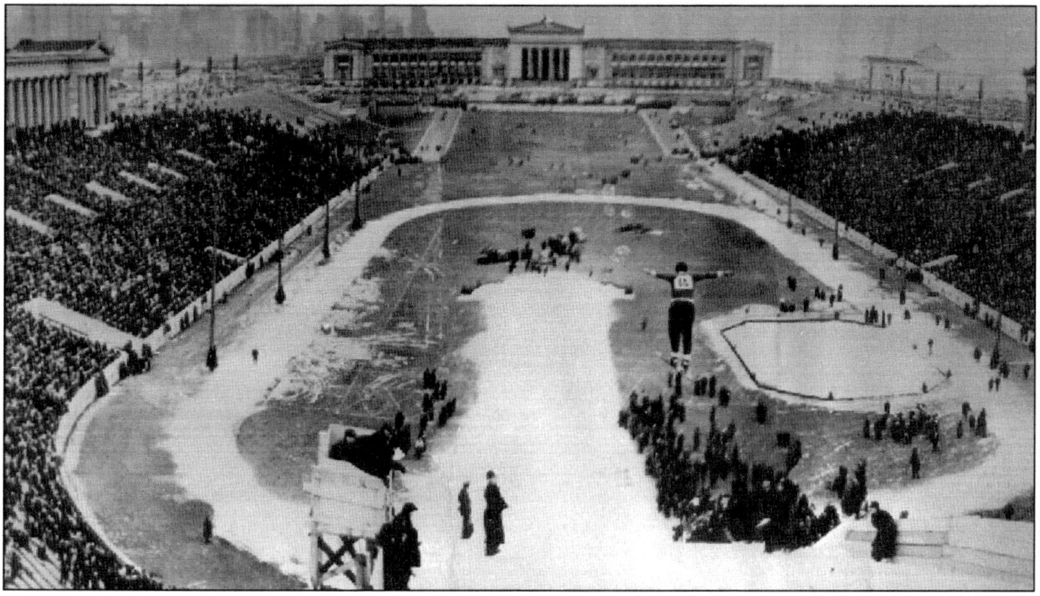

This photo shows the ski jumping exhibition area at Soldier Field in Chicago.

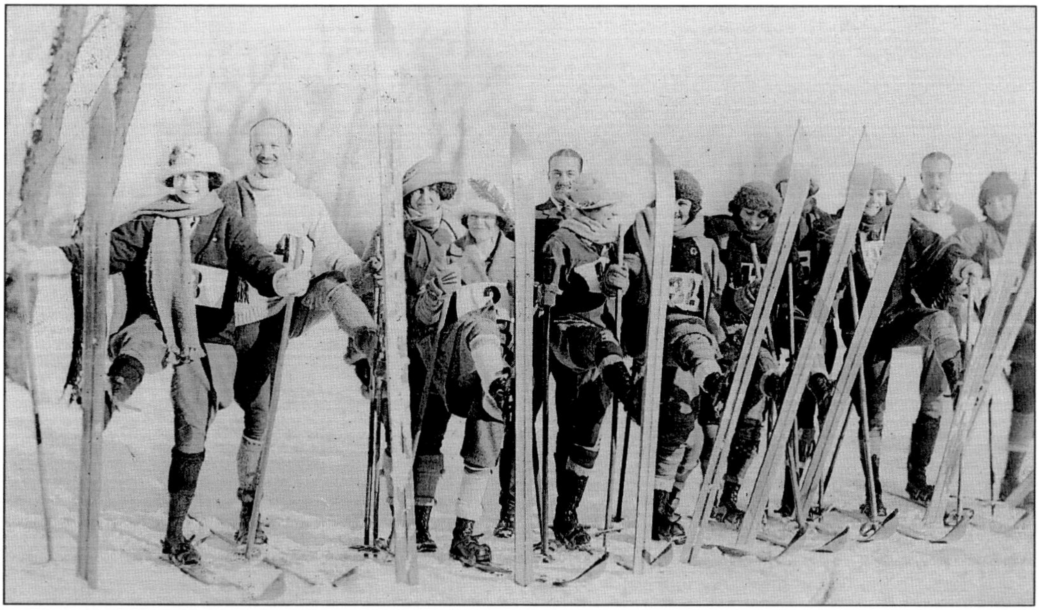

"Everyone...skis up!"

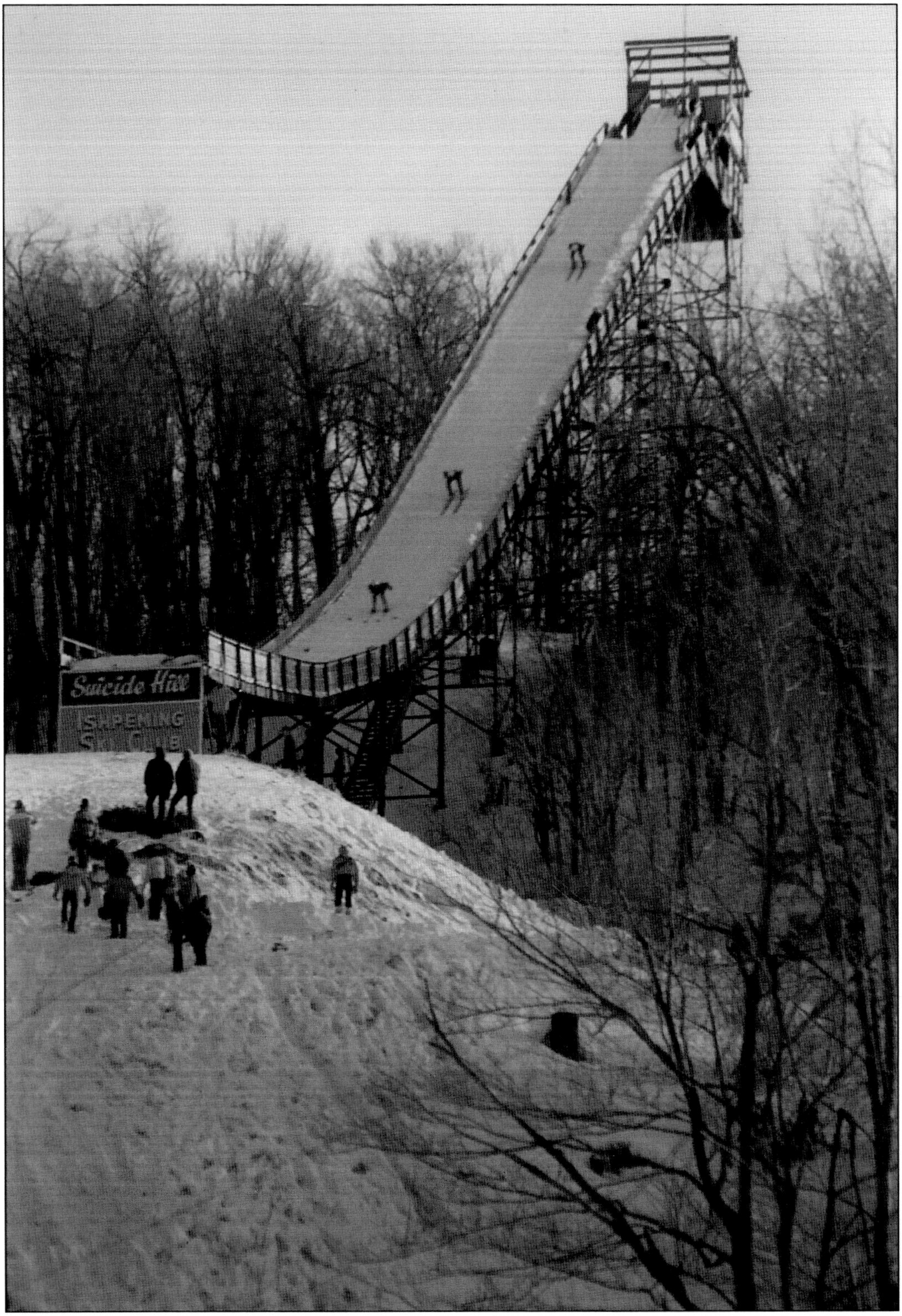

Pictured above is a triple jump on Suicide Hill at Ishpeming, Michigan, about 1965.

Twelve

CARVING A NEW TURN

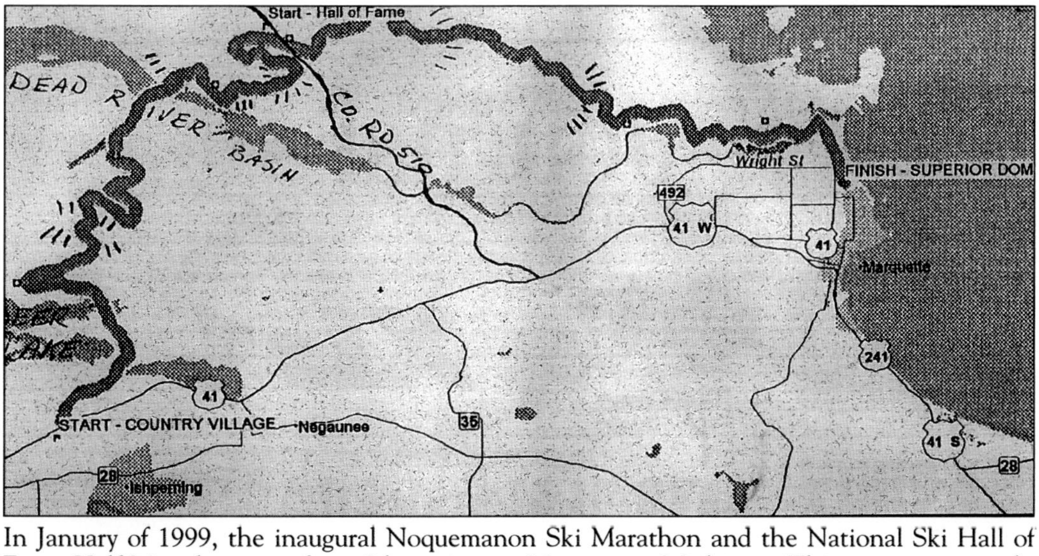

In January of 1999, the inaugural Noquemanon Ski Marathon and the National Ski Hall of Fame Half-Marathon ran from Ishpeming to Marquette, Michigan. This cross-country ski race is predicted to become the premier ski race in North America, according to those who participated in the first competition. This map traces the scenic route of the race.

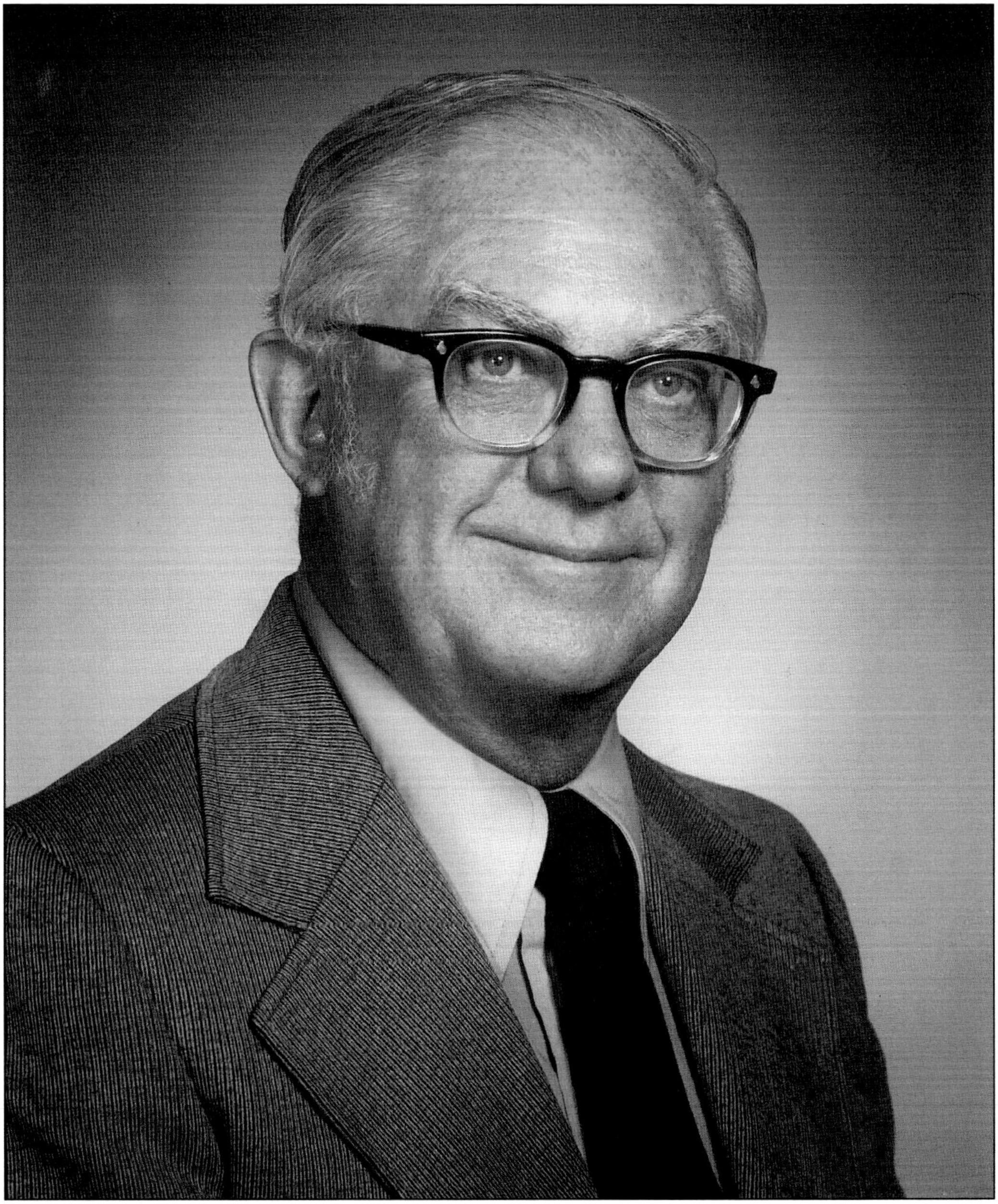

Burton H. Boyum, of Ishpeming, Michigan, is probably the most influential and positive personality involved in the founding of the US National Ski Hall of Fame and Museum, Inc. The concept and detailed plan for the Hall of Fame was presented and adopted at the 1948 Central Ski Association meeting in Chicago, Illinois, where Mr. Boyum chaired the committee presenting the plan. The new facility was dedicated in Ishpeming in 1954, and he was named its first curator. During his lifetime, Burt has presided over local ski clubs, the Central Division Ski Association, and was twice a delegate to the International Ski Federation (FIS). He managed the US Ski Team in 1962, and was a member of the 1964 Olympic Ski Games Committee. He has served as chairman of the U.S. Ski Hall of Fame board of directors and is still a member. He became an enshrined member in 1965.

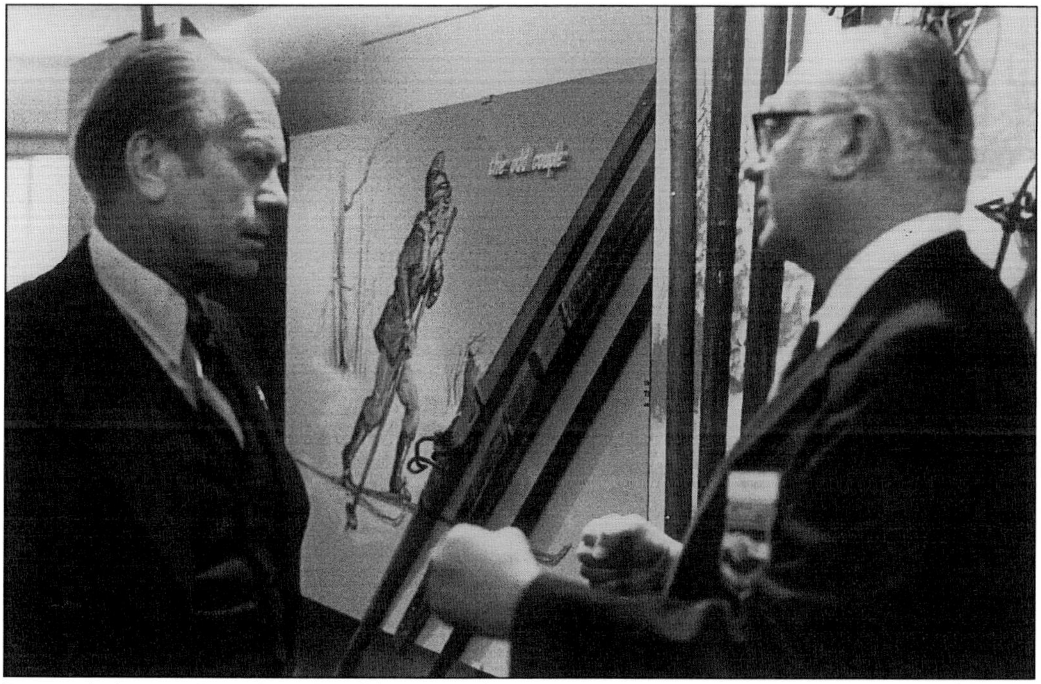

Pictured above is President Gerald Ford with Burton H. Boyum, president of the US National Ski Hall of Fame. Mr. Boyum is explaining the use of the single ski pole, and the kick and slide of the "Odd Couple" ski exhibit.

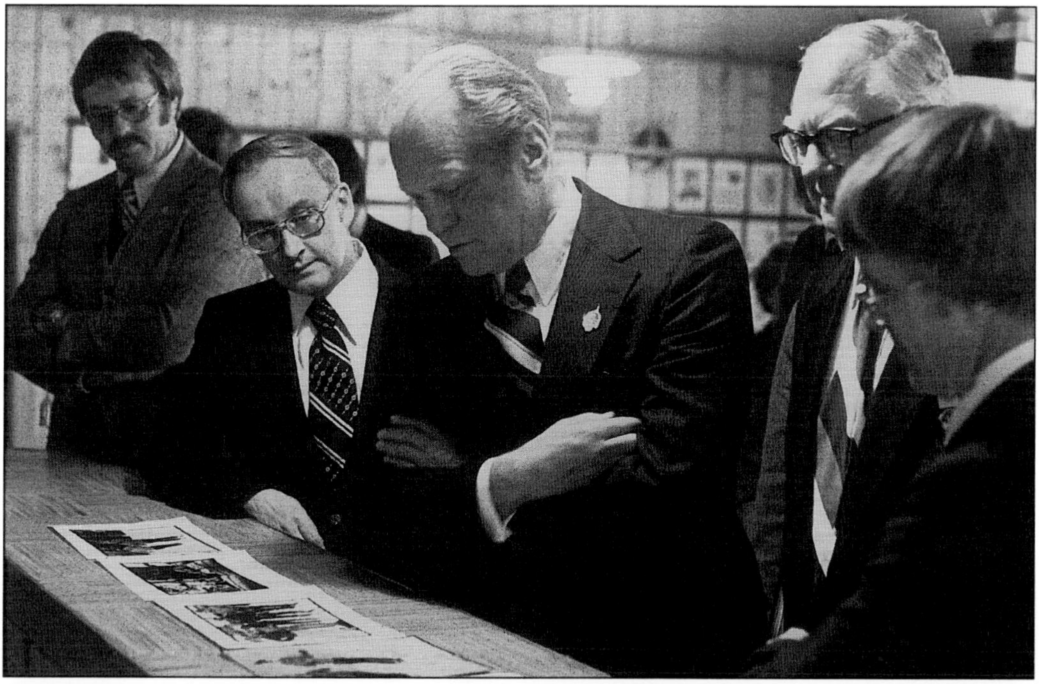

Shown here examining some of the exhibits at the original US National Ski Museum in Ishpeming, Michigan, are, from left to right: unidentified, Ray Leverton (curator/manager), President Gerald Ford, Burton Boyum, and Dr. Don Hurst.

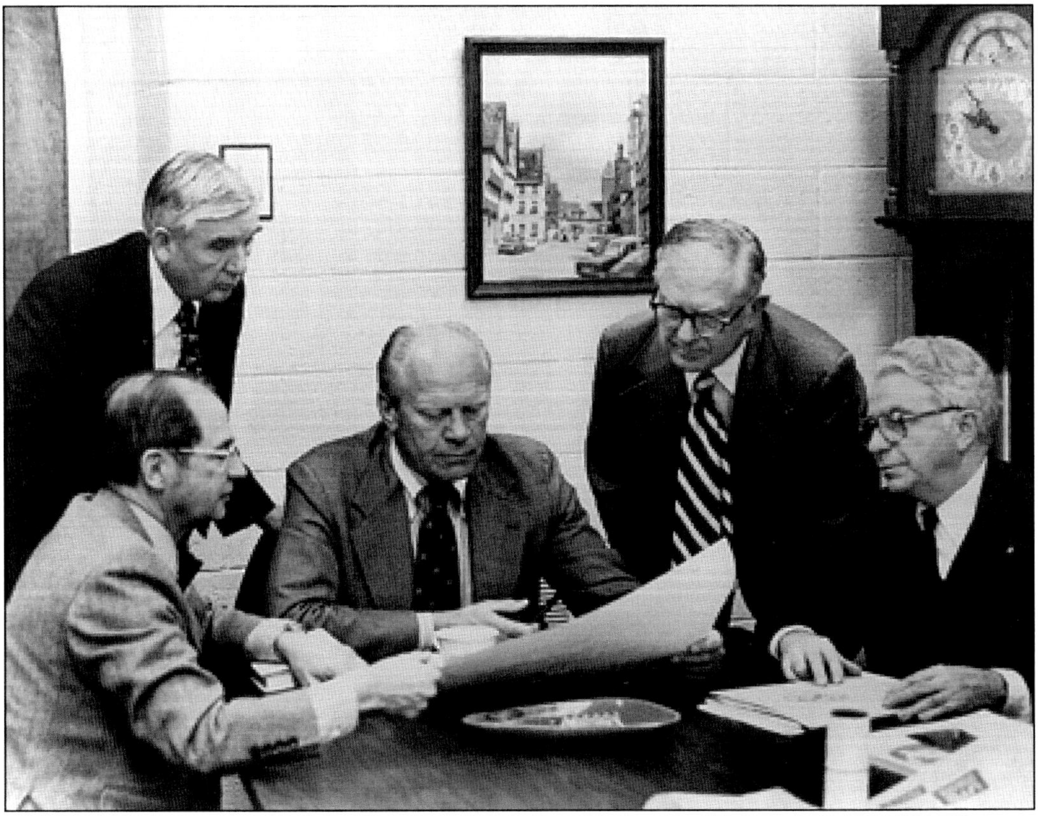

President Gerald R. Ford endorsed Northern Michigan University's proposal to the US Olympic Committee for designation as a Midwest training site. Pictured above is a March 31, 1978, meeting in Dearborn, Michigan, in which the NMU bid was discussed. Attending were, from left to right: NMU President John X. Jamrich, John McGoff (standing), Ford, Burton Boyum (standing), and Dr. Roy Heath (dean of graduate studies). Boyum was head of a citizens' committee supporting the project. McGoff was president of Panax Corporation and arranged the meeting.

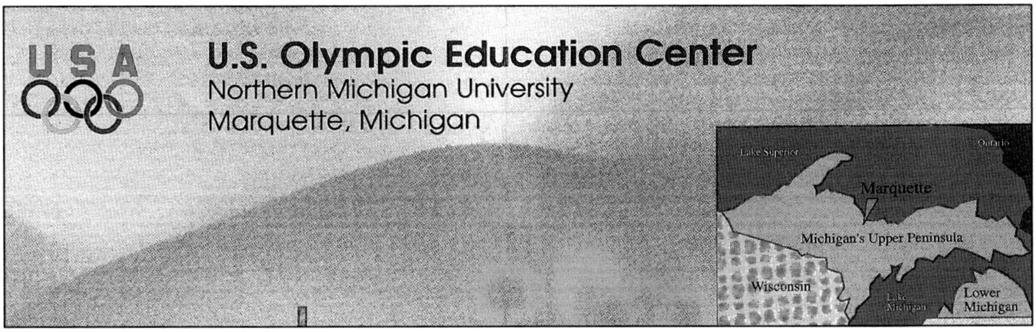

The US Olympic Education Center, (formerly the US Olympic Training Center), is located on the campus of Northern Michigan University in Marquette, Michigan. It is a unique, multi-sport facility, including skiing. It is the only facility in the country that is recognized by the US Olympic Committee, and is the only facility that accepts athletes of high school and college age, giving them the opportunity to train seriously while completing a program for a high school diploma or a college degree.

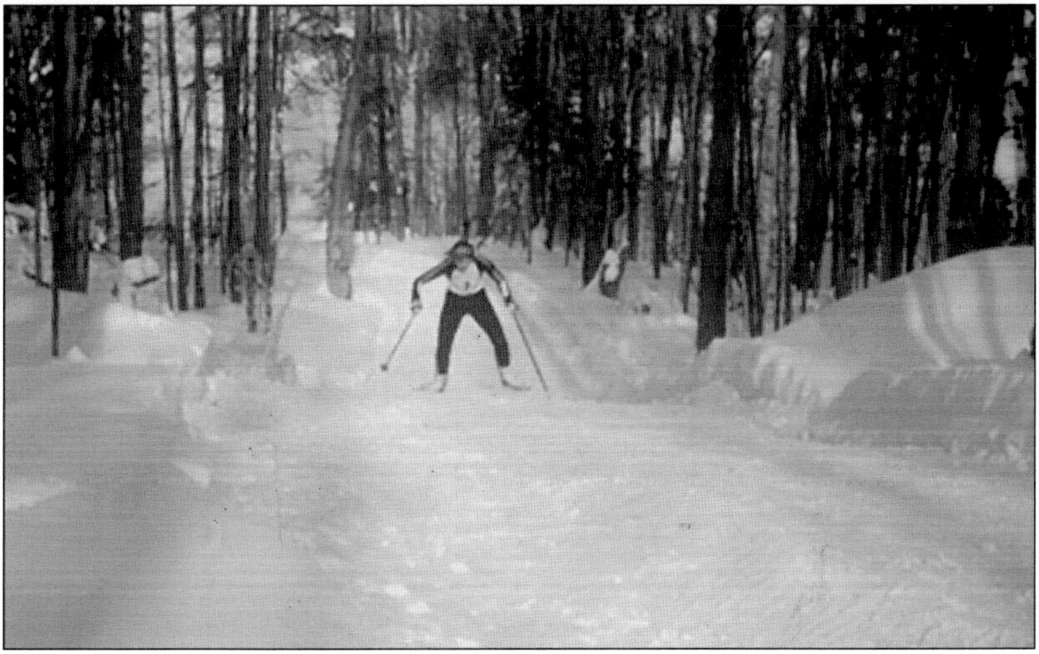

The cross-country ski competitor must be as adept at climbing hills on skis as he/she is at going downhill and skiing on a level track. Strength and endurance are key ingredients.

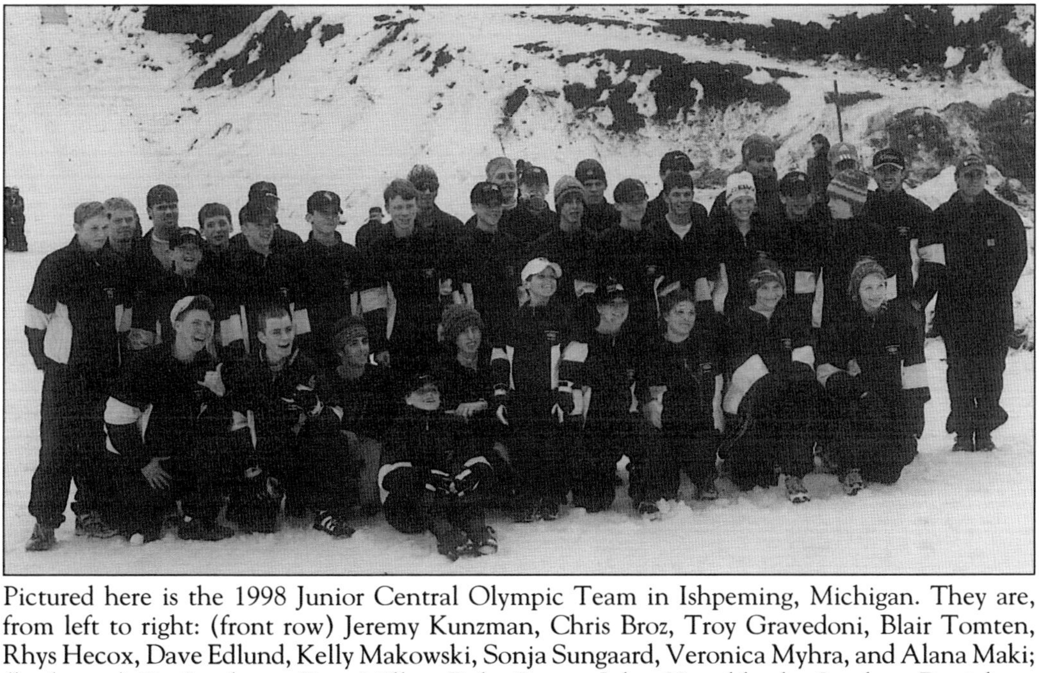

Pictured here is the 1998 Junior Central Olympic Team in Ishpeming, Michigan. They are, from left to right: (front row) Jeremy Kunzman, Chris Broz, Troy Gravedoni, Blair Tomten, Rhys Hecox, Dave Edlund, Kelly Makowski, Sonja Sungaard, Veronica Myhra, and Alana Maki; (back row) Ty Jacobson, Dan Miller, Dale Guyer, John Herschbach, Stephen Danielson, Brian Nelson, Ray Hocking, Adam Dimich, Ben Erlandson, Steve Krausert, Tom Brisson, Jim Denney, D. A. Carter, Kyle Buros (hidden), Tim Martin, Anthony Myhra, Berit Tomten, Coach Eric Hiatt, Jake Wolf, Karl Evanstad, and Coaches Jarrett Moe, Kurt Stein, Martin Bayer, and Mark Johnson.

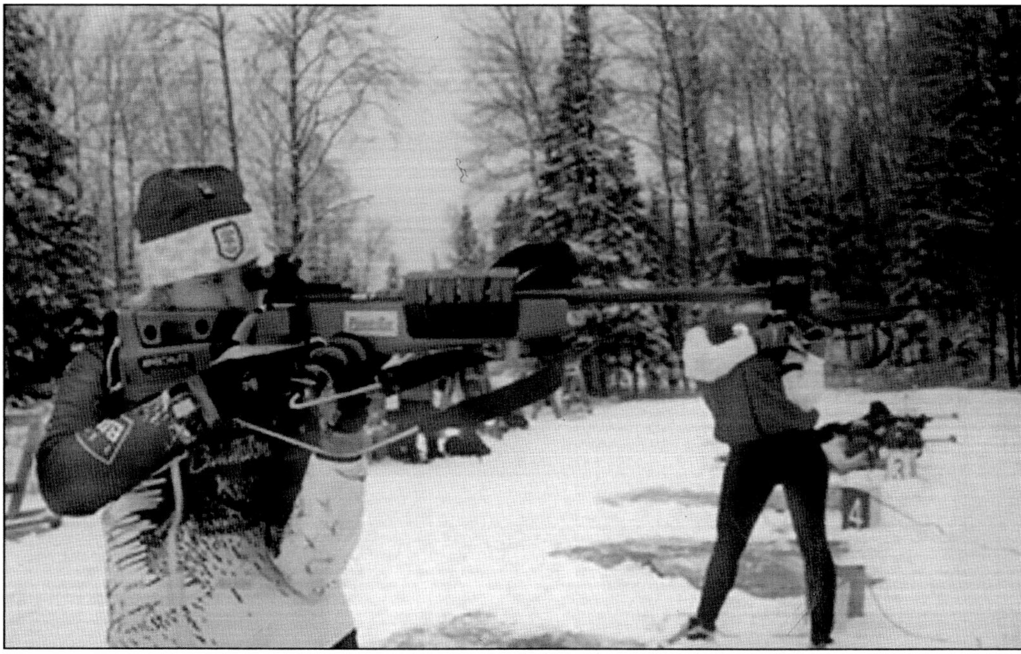

Shown above is one of the spin-offs of military winter training in the Nordic event called the biathlon. This event is a combination of skiing and rifle shooting, and was added to the Olympic winter games in 1960. Time and accuracy combine for scoring.

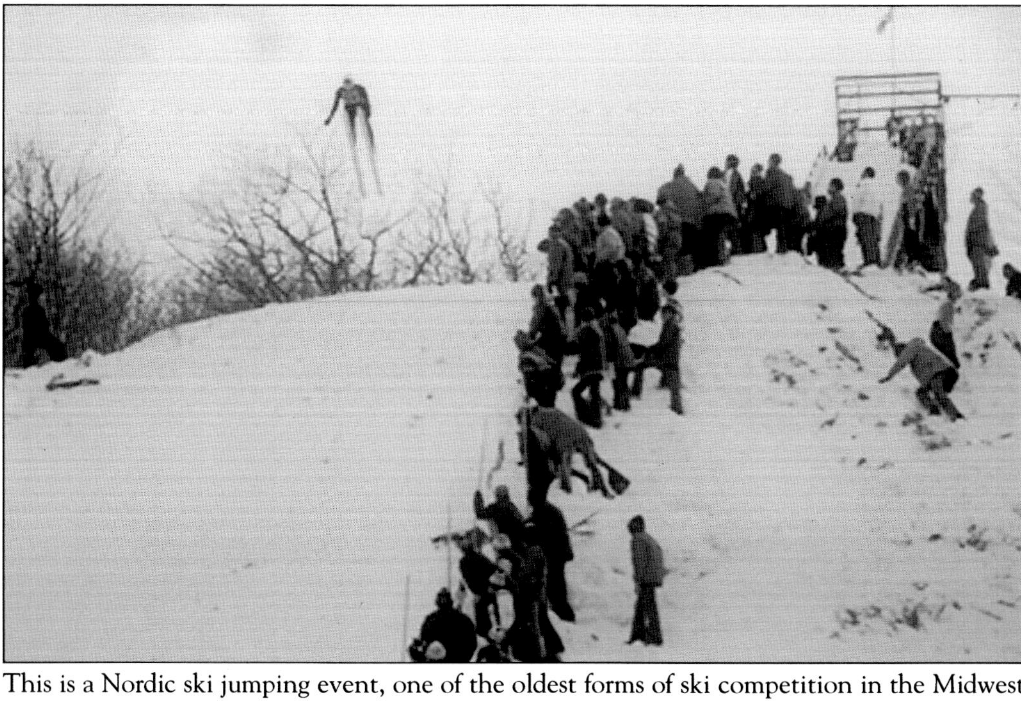

This is a Nordic ski jumping event, one of the oldest forms of ski competition in the Midwest.

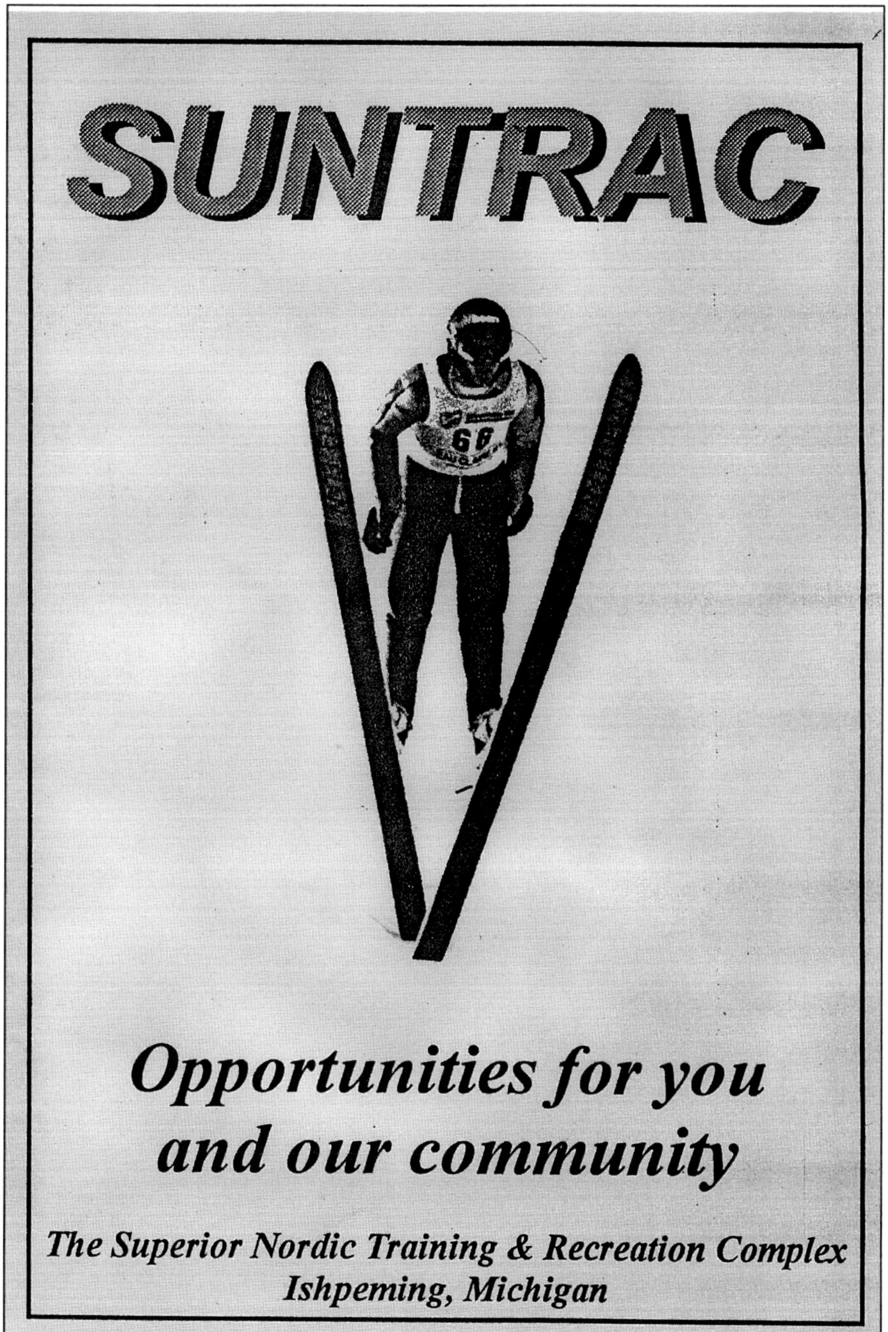

SUNTRAC, a Nordic training and recreation complex, is located in Ishpeming, Michigan. Home of the famous Suicide Bowl, SUNTRAC is the planned site for the development of one of the top Nordic training facilities in the country. Current SUNTRAC structures include five ski jumps, approximately 25 kilometers of cross-country ski trails, and a secured biathlon shooting range. With the acquisition of a groomer and proposed development of a chair lift and trail lighting, SUNTRAC's goal is to become one of the nation's premier training sites.

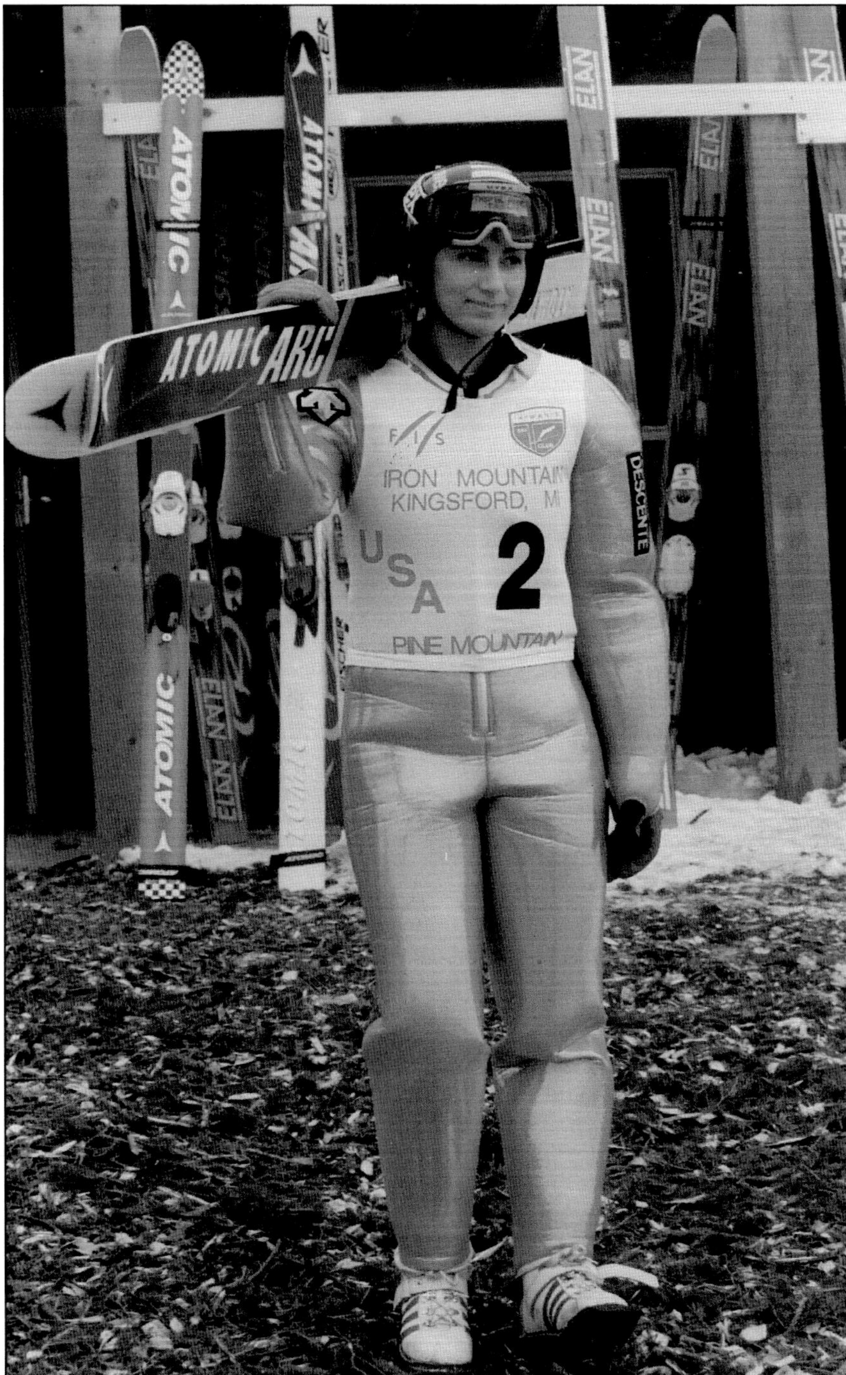

Karla Keck of Oconomowoc, Wisconsin, and her family are leading proponents of the establishment of women's ski jumping as an Olympic winter sporting event. She is an outstanding US woman ski jumping competitor, and is one of the pioneers in the advancement of women's international ski jumping.

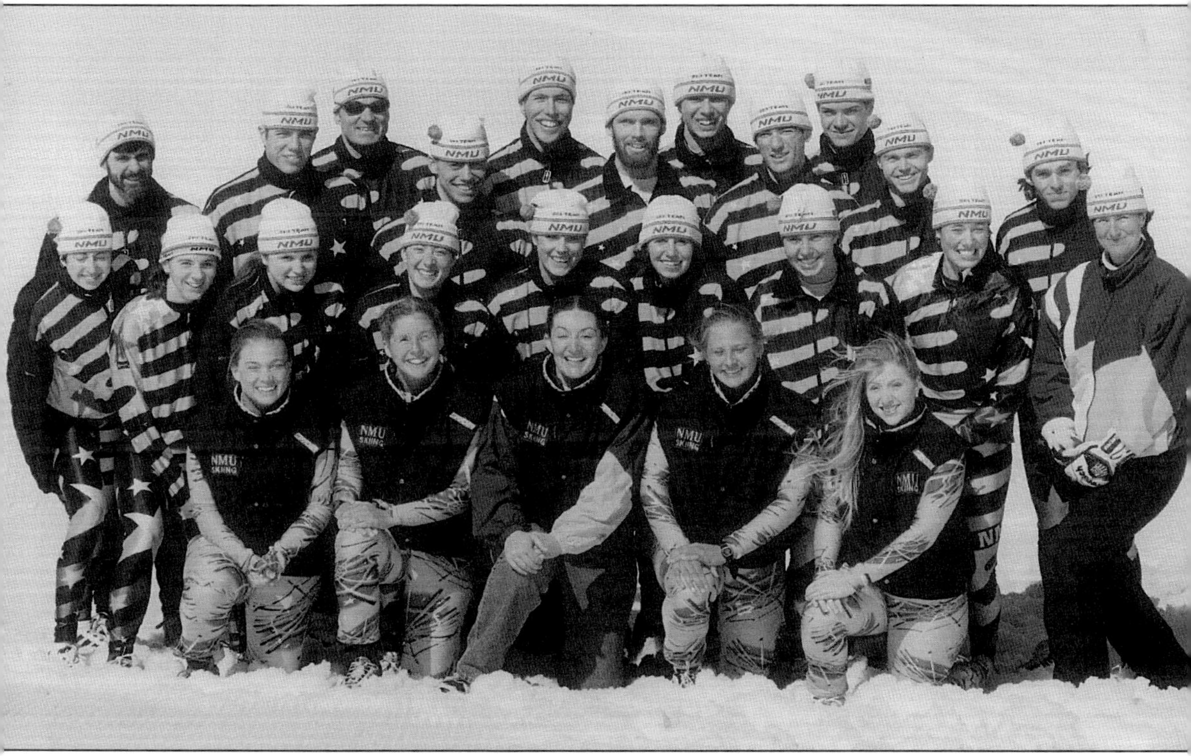

Northern Michigan University in Marquette, Michigan, still fields ski teams in the disciplines of men's and women's cross country and women's alpine. They compete in NCAA ski events around the United States. Many of the team members grew up in the Midwest states. Pictured above is a group photo of the 1998–99 Northern Michigan Alpine and Nordic Team. The coaches were Jill Rogers (alpine women) and Sten Fjeldheim (cross-country).

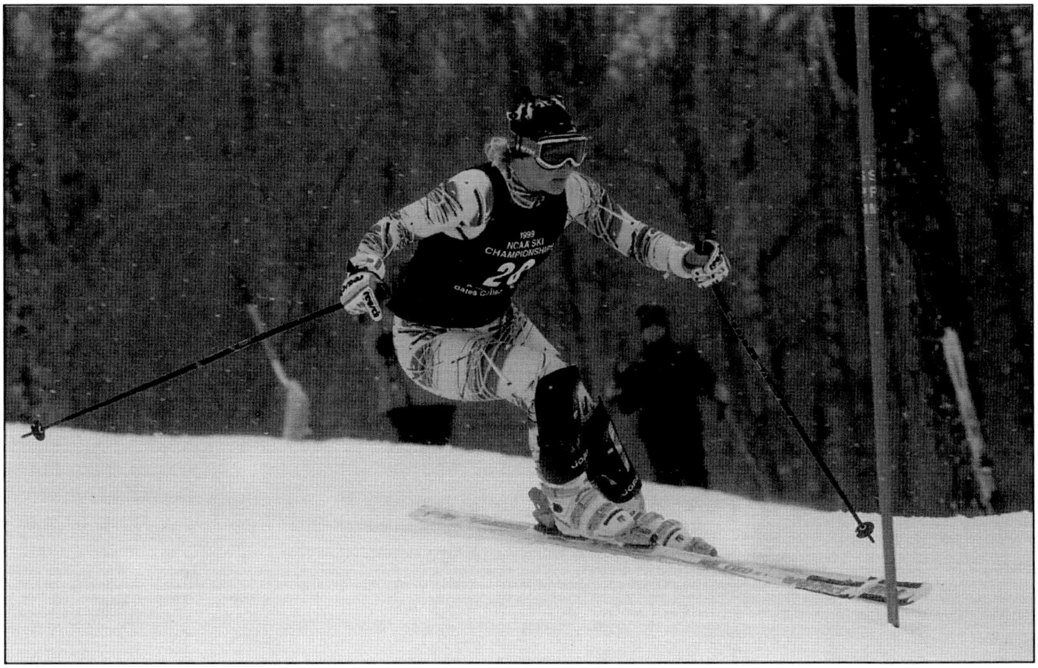

Pictured above is Christy Salonen, an outstanding Northern Michigan University student and athlete from Iron River, Michigan, racing in the NCAA National Alpine Ski Competition in 1999.

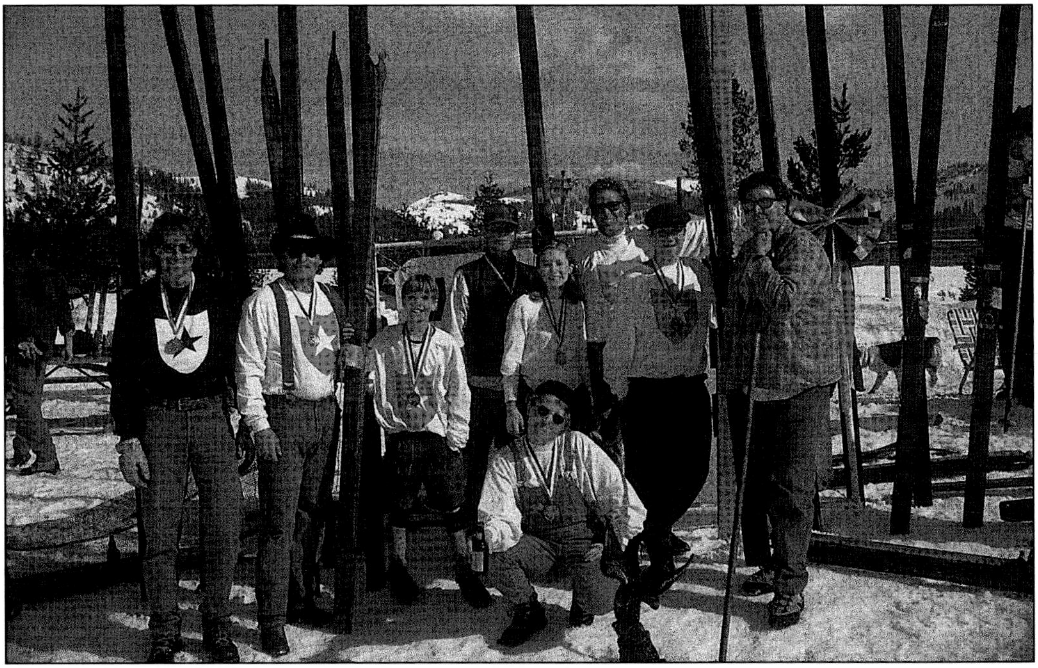

Pictured above are winners of the 1998 Long Board Races. This is a traditional race still carried on at the historic Soda Springs Ski Area of California.

EPILOGUE

Dedicated to Ken Luostari
(April 13, 1934 – December 15, 1999)

I am very sad to report the passing of my friend and co-author, Ken Luostari, on December 15, 1999, shortly before ***Midwest Skiing*** went to press. Ken has been a director and wonderful support to the US National Ski Hall of Fame and Museum since 1968. He will be greatly missed by all those who take pride in, and labor for, this institution devoted to the sport of snow. This book is dedicated to you, Ken.

John Pontti

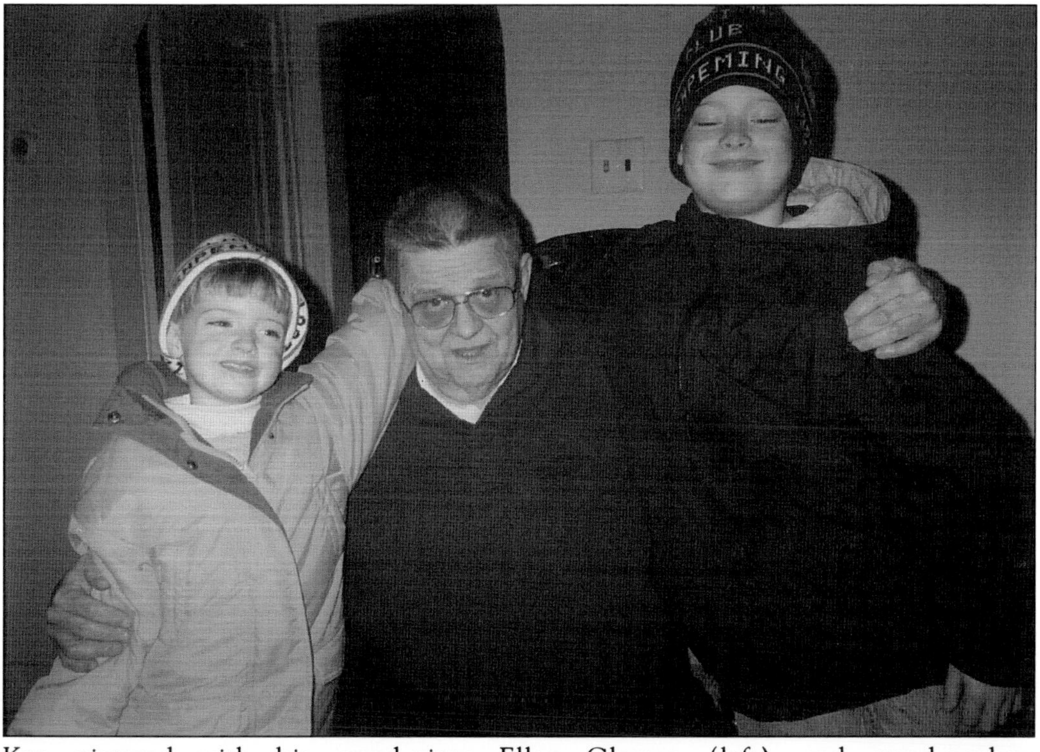

Ken pictured with his grand-niece Ellen Gleason (left), and grand-nephew Patrick Gleason (right).

Sources

Adamski-Peek, Lori, US National Ski Hall of Fame and Museum Archives Photographs: 58 top, 58 bottom.
Bays, Ted, *Nine Thousand Years of Skis: Norwegian Wood to French Plastic* (1980): 11 top.
Berg, Gosta, *Finds of Skis from Prehistoric Time in Swedish Bogs and Marshes* (1950): 9, 10 bottom, 11 bottom.
Bielicki, Jerry, US National Ski Hall of Fame and Museum Archives Photographs: 18 top, 19 top.
Bietila, Ralph: 54 bottom.
Blackhawk Ski Club – Campaign '97 (1995): 31.
Chapman Wentworth, US National Ski Hall of Fame and Museum Archives Photograph: 79 bottom.
Dehlin, Jim: 86.
Ferris, Dick, US National Ski Hall of Fame and Museum Archives Photograph: 65 top.
Gleason, Christopher: 127.
Halverson, Jim, US National Ski Hall of Fame and Museum Archives Photograph: 79 top.
Holter, Aksel, *The Skisport Seventh Annual Report: National Ski Association of America* (1910-1911): 20.
Johnson, Alice: 15.
LaCerte, W.I., US National Ski Hall of Fame and Museum Archives Photograph: 106 top.
Keck, Robert: 124.
Marquette Mountain Ski Patrol: 77.
Northern Michigan University: 125, 126.
Sør, Østlandet, *Norske Skiløpere* (1956): 10 top.
Sundblad, Lloyd: 102 bottom.
Toné Maguire Productions: 126.
Any image not identified comes from the US National Ski Hall of Fame and Museum Archives.

Select Bibliography

Allen E. John B. *From Skisport to Skiing: One Hundred Years of an American Sport, 1840-1940*. Amherst: The University of Massachusetts Press, 1993, 188.

Bays, Ted. *Nine Thousand Years of Skis: Norwegian Wood to French Plastic*. Ishpeming, Michigan: National Ski Hall of Fame Press, 1980.

Berg, Gosta. *Finds of Skis From Prehistoric Time in Swedish Bogs and Marshes*. Stockholm: Generalstabens Litografiska Anstalts Förlag, 1950.

Bulger, William T. *The Michigan Historical Review* 16 (1). Detroit: Wayne State University Press, Spring 1990.

Cohen, Stan. *A Pictorial History of Downhill Skiing*. Missoula: Pictorial Histories Publishing Co., 1985.